Tennessee Statesman

HARRY T. BURN

Tennessee Statesman

HARRY T. BURN

Woman Suffrage, Free Elections & a Life of Service

TYLER L. BOYD

Foreword by Beth Harwell,
Former Speaker of the Tennessee House of Representatives

THE
History
PRESS

*A principled and accomplished man, Harry T. Burn's vote to ratify the Nineteenth Amendment was far from his only action that changed the course of our state and nation's history. Tyler L. Boyd's research on Burn, his great-granduncle, sheds a new light on a great man....Burn lived the life of a public servant. He led the fight against the adoption of a state income tax and fought for home rule, which gave local governments the ability to govern themselves without burdensome oversight from the state....*Tennessee Statesman Harry T. Burn: Woman Suffrage, Free Elections and a Life of Service *makes me even more proud to walk in Burn's footsteps, having held the same seats as him in the Tennessee House of Representatives and the Tennessee Senate. Boyd's work tells the story of a remarkable American and Tennessean who changed the course of history for good.*

—State Senator Mike Bell (R-9ᵗʰ District)

As we approach the 100th anniversary of the ratification of the Nineteenth Amendment next year, Americans are discovering the history of the woman suffrage movement and the stories of the Americans who led it to victory. These stories are a vast part of our nation's history but they are not often discussed. It would be a tragedy if the stories of these trailblazers were forgotten by future generations. Works like this will keep their memory alive.

—U.S. Senator Marsha Blackburn (R-Tennessee)

Tyler L. Boyd deserves enormous credit for his research on Harry T. Burn, an important Tennessee public servant. In addition to Burn's deciding vote in 1920 to enfranchise women, he also voted to remove the onerous poll tax, authored bills to protect against election fraud and for permanent voter registration, and to lower the voting age to 18. What a great legacy!

—Paula F. Casey, cofounder, Tennessee Woman Suffrage Heritage Trail

I encourage others to take time out and read this book and realize how a mother's love and persuasion moved her son to do what was right, even though unpopular at the time, and turned hysteria into history.

—former congressman Bob Clement (D-Tennessee)

The most remarkable aspect of Harry T. Burn's illustrious public service was his consistent and profound connection to our nation's founding principles. As the representative who currently holds Burn's seat, this book made me keenly aware I stand upon the shoulders of one of the greatest statesmen in our history.

—State Representative Mark Cochran (R-23rd District)

As a woman in an elected position, I take pride in the 19th Amendment. As a Tennessean, I take pride in the role Tennessee had in its pilotable ratification. And as a person who feels immense pride in their family legacy, I recognize the passion and detail Tyler L. Boyd put into this book on his ancestor and the voice that led to the 19th Amendment, Harry T. Burn.

—State Senator Becky Duncan Massey (R-6th District)

This book by a proud descendant lets the rest of us know more intimately the man who seized the opportunity "to free 17,000,000 women from political slavery." The story of what happened before and after Burn's fateful vote has been told often but often told wrong. Tennessee Statesman Harry T. Burn: Woman Suffrage, Free Elections and a Life of Service *by Tyler L. Boyd gives us the real story, one well worth remembering as we commemorate the ratification of the Nineteenth Amendment in August 1920, courtesy of the Volunteer State.*

—Marjorie J. Spruill, author of Divided We Stand; New Women of the New South; One Woman, One Vote; *and* Votes for Women: The Woman Suffrage Movement in Tennessee, the South, and the Nation

Harry T. Burn is known as the young Tennessee legislator who listened to his mother, taking her advice to support ratification of the 19th Amendment in 1920. Burn secured the right to vote for American women, but his life and character have remained unexplored. Now, in this deeply researched biography, Tyler L. Boyd finally brings us the full man, putting into context Burn's singular act of conscience, helping us to understand how one person can make a difference.

—*Elaine Weiss, author of* The Woman's Hour:
The Great Fight to Win the Vote

Tennessee Statesman Harry T. Burn: Woman Suffrage, Free Elections and a Life of Service *is the best work on Burn to date. Detailed and informative, this important biography reads well. It is a must read for history lovers as we approach the 100th anniversary of Burn's historic tie breaking vote.*

—*State Senator Ken Yager (R-12th District)*

Published by The History Press
Charleston, SC
www.historypress.com

Copyright © 2019 by Tyler L. Boyd
All rights reserved

Cover images: Images of Harry Burn and Febb Burn courtesy of the Burn family; image of Tennessee State Capitol courtesy of the Tennessee State Library and Archives; image of the envelope courtesy of the Calvin M. McClung Historical Collection.

First published 2019

ISBN 9781540240156

Library of Congress Control Number: 2019939743

Notice: The information in this book is true and complete to the best of our knowledge. It is offered without guarantee on the part of the author or The History Press. The author and The History Press disclaim all liability in connection with the use of this book.

For James Lane Edwin Burn and Rebecca Brooke Winslett.

CONTENTS

FOREWORD

I have a newspaper clipping from August 1995 that details the seventy-fifth anniversary of the ratification of the Nineteenth Amendment in the Tennessee House of Representatives. I have treasured this clipping over the years because of our personal family connection to it: as a state representative at the time, I invited my husband's great-aunt, Margaret Wyatt, to sit on the floor with me. She was there to witness a reenactment of the very thing she'd seen in person seventy-five years earlier. Sensing history might be made that day way back in 1920, her mother had allowed her to skip school. They watched from the House gallery as the Tennessee House of Representatives voted to extend them—and women all across our country—the right to vote. Detailed in this book, Harry T. Burn gave an interview in 1974 in which he described the atmosphere that day: "The gallery of the Capitol was packed as it has never been since."

I first met Tyler L. Boyd when I was traveling the state, something I did frequently as Speaker of the Tennessee House of Representatives. He mentioned that he was writing a book about Harry Burn, known for casting the deciding vote ratifying the Nineteenth Amendment, and I was interested in hearing more. As the state's first female Speaker, I feel a connection to that moment, not only because of our family history but also because these are the very events that led to a woman being elected Speaker. He stayed in touch over the course of the next few months and traveled to the capitol to observe and photograph the settings detailed in the book. We were happy to accommodate him, because this is a story that deserves to be told. When he asked me to write the foreword, I was truly honored.

This book details the rich history of Harry T. Burn and his extended family, a family that impacted their community in countless positive ways. The book details the Harry Burn beyond the famous vote that put him in the history books—we often distill people who do something extraordinary down to only that achievement, but author Tyler L. Boyd manages here to show you a full picture of the man who is credited with giving women in the United States the right to vote. Boyd, a relative of Burn, weaves a loving tale of a close family that put down roots in Niota and throughout East Tennessee, taking an interest in improving and modernizing their community. We learn more about Burn's mother, Febb, who wrote the legendary note to him asking him to vote for suffrage. But we also learn that Febb was a strong woman who insisted on a good education for her children, who taught her children to learn more about the world around them and who valued taking a stand for what you believe is right.

This book debunks myths, repeated many times over the years, about Burn and that hot August day. It is a valuable addition to history, to have this story told, and by a family member who researched the topic meticulously.

As the author notes in the introduction, the tireless efforts of suffragists around the country made his vote possible. Similarly, I stood on the shoulders of the women who came before me, paving the way to make my speakership possible.

There is much Tennessee has to celebrate—the music, the mountains of East Tennessee, the plains and bluffs of West Tennessee and the numerous people who have left their distinctive and indelible mark on history and this country. With this book, Harry T. Burn rightfully takes his place among these giants.

The Honorable Beth Harwell
Speaker of the Tennessee House of Representatives, 2011–18
Nashville, Tennessee

PREFACE

I first heard the story about Harry Thomas Burn and the Nineteenth Amendment in junior high school from my mother. Teachers always called on me in class during the lesson. For our family, it is an honored connection to American history. Along with the Battle of Athens in 1946, it is the most nationally recognized historical event connected to McMinn County, Tennessee.

While working on my eighth-grade family history project, I became interested in genealogy. My great-uncle, James Lane Edwin Burn, had already researched much of the Burn family history. I researched the Boyd genealogy and rekindled my interest during college.

My late cousin, Harry Thomas Burn Jr., was a great cousin. We all miss visiting with him. After my grandfather Burn passed away, we made it a tradition to visit Cousin Harry, the last Burn of his generation, every Christmas Eve after our evening church service. We enjoyed his informative discussions. Occasionally, we got in a comment or two!

I am grateful for the many family stories Cousin Harry shared with us. He did not discuss his renowned father often, but he was an exemplary steward of his father's legacy. He shared helpful resources with me that I use when teaching about the Nineteenth Amendment, including one of his father's campaign posters. He and our cousin Tyler Forrest helped researchers with their many questions about Harry T. Burn and his deciding vote for the Nineteenth Amendment. Those questions still persist. So do the myths and apocryphal stories. During college, Cousin Harry sent an e-mail informing me that his late father's papers were at the Calvin M. McClung Historical Collection in Knoxville. I bookmarked that fact in my mind and planned to look at the papers one day. Almost ten years later, I finally did.

Over the years, interested readers have found Harry T. Burn referenced in various works of history: local history books, woman suffrage books, encyclopedias, newspaper clippings and online articles. I eventually realized that the information about him has always been limited and brief. Other aspects of his life are listed in various sources as mere fragments. Nothing comprehensive has ever been written about him. I also began to notice inaccuracies, especially about his deciding vote for the Nineteenth Amendment and the aftermath.

With the passing of Harry T. Burn Jr. in 2016, the door to another generation of the Burn family slammed shut forever. Shortly afterward, I went to a festival in Niota. The Suffrage Coalition had a booth in the historic Niota Depot raising funds for the Burn Memorial. I had not heard of the project until that day. I signed their petition to make August 18 "Febb Burn Day" in Tennessee (which became state law in 2018). I toured Hathburn (the Burn family home) for the first time. Cousin Harry had sold the property in 2003. I will never forget when I first walked through the home that once belonged to Jim and Febb Burn, my great-great-grandparents.

The following spring, our cousin Tyler Forrest looked through Cousin Harry's things in his Athens home. I thought to myself that there must be so much history in that home that he had hardly spoken of. Tyler generously gave Febb Burn's "fainting couch" to my mother and my aunts. They placed it in the lobby of the now majority female-owned family hosiery business. Harry T. Burn's place in American history began to dominate my thoughts again.

I began to think of the apocryphal stories I had read about Harry T. Burn and the Nineteenth Amendment. Cousins Harry and Tyler spent many years debunking them. As a history teacher myself, I wished for the record to be set straight. But the complete, true story of his role in the ratification of the Nineteenth Amendment would only be appropriate in an essay. I wanted something bigger. Every time I teach about him, I always find myself wanting to tell the students more about him. But there is never sufficient time. I did some light research about his life and career after 1920. I visited the local libraries and accessed a few online resources. I stumbled upon even more details of his life I never knew about.

I started joking to myself that I should write a book about him, but I thought that such a task was foolish due to the lack of material. I kept thinking about it and I researched further. I asked friends and family if they believed that such a project was plausible. Eventually, I decided that it was. I discovered resources I never knew existed. With these resources near at hand, I set my goal: to write a comprehensive biography of Harry T. Burn, my great-granduncle.

As I conducted my research, I was amazed to discover what he accomplished. He did so much more than just cast the deciding vote to ratify the Nineteenth Amendment. Although it was his most impactful action, it birthed a lifetime of civic service. I knew I wanted to share his life story with people in a single source.

The Burn and Ensminger family histories, his childhood, his campaign for governor, his State Senate career, his legal and banking career and more found their way into the book. It was a privilege to interview people who knew him. They told fascinating stories. I proudly share details and stories about his wife and son, to whom he was so devoted. I also had another major source of inspiration: timing. The centennial celebrations of the Nineteenth Amendment's ratification will be in 2020. I knew that it was the perfect time to complete this project.

In 1962, after a national television appearance, Burn told a friend that the history department at the University of Tennessee had spent a few years "insisting" that he write a book about his role in the Nineteenth Amendment's ratification. They suggested the title "The Day the Women Got the Vote."[1] Ever so busy, he never got around to it. I am thankful to have been able to write this book in time for the centennial of the Nineteenth Amendment.

ACKNOWLEDGEMENTS

When I began working on this book, I never could have imagined the gracious and enthusiastic support I have received from nearly everyone I approached for help. My parents, Michael and Sandra Boyd, have been supportive in so many ways and deserve my first expression of gratitude. I am also grateful for the encouragement of my sisters, Blair and Betty Catherine, and my brother-in-law Daniel Thomason. My cousin Tyler Forrest has relentlessly encouraged this project from the very day I told him about my idea. This book would not have been possible without the information and leads he generously provided for me. I greatly appreciate the support and encouragement of the Burn family. I also thank my Boyd cousins for their support and encouragement. June Boyd Price, author of many recent books, has been a longtime source of inspiration to me. I would also like to thank my friends and colleagues for their support.

I want to thank Fred Underdown, Mary Ellen Nolletti and the McMinn County Historical Society for their assistance and encouragement. I am grateful to Robert Bailey of the Roane County Heritage Commission for his assistance during my research. The leads he provided helped me secure interviews with many friendly Roane Countians who knew Harry T. Burn. Jo Stakley at the Monroe Archives was very helpful.

The staff at the libraries of Niota, E.G. Fisher (Athens), Sweetwater, Rockwood, Cleveland–Bradley County (History Branch) and Chattanooga (Downtown Branch) assisted me in many ways. I also received helpful assistance at the John C. Hodges Library and the Joel A. Katz Law Library at the University of Tennessee. The Tennessee State Library and Archives provided invaluable assistance. Rae Sauer at the S.A.R. Library shared helpful information with me. I cannot thank Steve Cotham and the staff at the Calvin M. McClung Historical Collection enough for granting me complete access to the Harry T. Burn Papers. I also appreciate the staff at the University of Tennessee Library Special Collections for permitting me to access the Harry T. Burn Scrapbook.

I appreciate the enthusiasm and assistance of Patsy Duckworth, Ann Scott Davis, Gail Rogers, Rebecca Aarts, Catherine Bush, William Howard Moore, Eddie Bilbree and Richard Bourne. I am thankful for the support of many families, including the Willson, Snyder, Clark, Powers, Reagan, Michael and Scandlyn families. By allowing me to tour the home and grounds of Hathburn (now the Rutledge estate), Richard Rutledge provided me a great source of inspiration. I am also grateful to Wanda Sobieski and the Suffrage Coalition for the inspiration their work provided me.

I am indebted to everyone who shared their memories of Harry T. Burn and the Burn family through interviews and correspondence. I wish I could list all of you here, but I must thank J. Polk Cooley, Gerald Largen, Geraldine Wallick and Bill McFarland for their time spent sharing a wealth of information from their detailed memories of Harry T. Burn. Sadly, J. Polk Cooley passed away shortly before this book went to the presses. Thankfully, he was able to read the manuscript during the winter, and he wrote me a thoughtful letter telling me how much he enjoyed it. I extend my gratitude to the many people and organizations who provided images for this book. They have helped to enhance the way I tell this life story.

I am thankful that The History Press appreciated this story enough to agree to take on publication of the project. The team at The History Press did a great job preparing this book for publication. I am humbled and overwhelmed by the many people who agreed to read this book in advance and write a blurb. My proofreaders provided invaluable feedback.

Lastly, I thank my love Sarah for her support and encouragement from day one. I could not have done this without her.

INTRODUCTION

W orking on the farm on a humid August day in the sleepy, tiny city of Niota, Tennessee, Febb Ensminger Burn would not have it any other way. She grew up on a farm. The middle-aged widow was the matriarch of a family of four. Her little girl, Otho, attended school. Her son Jack ran the farm across the railroad tracks. Her eldest son, Harry, followed in his father's footsteps working for the railroad. But Harry had to leave his post to represent McMinn County in the state legislature in Nashville. A special session had been called to consider action on the Susan B. Anthony Amendment. After seven decades of grueling work, national woman suffrage needed only one more state to become part of the U.S. Constitution.

McMinn County was divided on the issue of suffrage. Febb Burn did not engage in political activism, but she knew most of the principal suffrage leaders and was cognizant of the struggle to ratify the Nineteenth Amendment. She subscribed to three daily newspapers.[1] Before leaving to attend the special session, she told Harry that she wanted him to vote for suffrage.

On the fifth day of the special session, the State Senate voted in a landslide to ratify the amendment. Although pleased to learn of the Senate's ratification, the comments of her own county's senator disappointed her. State Senator Herschel M. Candler cast one of only four votes against the amendment. Blasting the idea of woman suffrage in his "bitter" speech, he warned of "petticoat government" should the amendment be ratified.

After reading the papers, Febb Burn sat down in her little chair on the front porch of Hathburn and wrote a "folksy" seven-page letter to her son. She included a message not of admonishment, but of motherly advice: "Hurrah and vote for suffrage." Her other son, Jack, took the letter to the Niota Post Office and addressed it in ink to "Hon. H.T. Burn" in Nashville.

Harry T. Burn received the letter on the morning of August 18, 1920, the day of the fateful vote. Like her son, Febb Burn had a remarkable sense of timing. The young representative read the letter before the legislature convened that morning. The time had come for the Tennessee House of Representatives to take a vote. Would they concur with the State Senate's action? The House took two votes to "table" the resolution. Burn, torn between his support for suffrage and his desire to punt the issue to the next regular legislative session, voted to table both times.

Hoping to kill the amendment for good, the House Speaker called for a vote on the "merits" of the resolution. If the resolution failed to receive a majority this time, it was dead in Tennessee, maybe even in the country. Remembering his mother's words and following his conscience, Harry T. Burn cast the vote that changed the United States of America forever.

This vote further ensured the promise of the American Revolution. This vote was in the spirit of self-government. This vote supported legal equality. This vote permanently solidified the right for all women in the United States of America to be able to vote. No longer could suffrage rights be denied to a person based on their gender. For the previous seventy-two years, millions of women all across the country had worked hard fighting for their right to vote. The tireless efforts of these women made Burn's famous vote possible. He also had a little help from his mother. The twenty-four-year-old freshman representative gained nationwide accolades and vicious condemnation after his vote. In the face of fierce criticism and slander on a national scale, he never wavered in his decision. He took pride in casting that vote to his grave.

Most people best remember Harry T. Burn for his deciding vote to ratify the Nineteenth Amendment. But few people know that there is so much more to his life story. For the next half century, he served in state government in various capacities. He voted to amend the U.S. Constitution not once but on three separate occasions. He also played a role in amending the Tennessee Constitution at four conventions. He served in the State Senate and ran for governor.

In his long public service career, he worked to achieve universal suffrage in Tennessee. He advocated for laws and reforms to increase political equality. He had remarkable foresight. Unlike most politicians, endless ambition did not drive him. He never stayed in public office for long. He worked in many ventures outside of politics. Active in his communities, he worked on ways to improve them. He was opinionated, headstrong and relentless. He encountered, and even caused, more controversies throughout his life. Equipped with quick wit, near-perfect timing and uncompromising principles, he shaped and affected federal, state and local government simply by his actions as an engaged citizen. This is his story.

Chapter 1

BURN AND ENSMINGER FAMILY HISTORIES

BURN FAMILY

The farthest back that records have proven to go begin with William Burn, born circa 1758. His place of birth was most likely Maryland (or possibly Scotland). He married Mary Wilson, a descendant of Thomas Claggett, a former lord mayor of Canterbury. Wilson also descended from Charlemagne. William and Mary Burn had several children, including a son named Adam in 1794. William Burn moved his family from Baltimore County, Maryland, to the Boyd's Creek area of Sevier County, Tennessee, in 1814.

William Burn purchased the Buckingham House, possibly the first brick house built in Tennessee. William also built a still house. He and his sons took to drinking heavily. Adam Burn married Mahala Blair in 1819. Mahala later said she remembered her father-in-law bringing slaves to Tennessee. Mahala Blair Burn was a daughter of Samuel Blair, a Revolutionary War veteran. Blair fought with John Sevier at the Battle of Kings Mountain.

On a "cold Friday," February 5, 1836, Adam and Mahala Burn and their eight children arrived in McMinn County. They settled on a farm in the Mount Harmony community near Eastanallee Creek. Mahala was expecting. They named their new home the Mountain View Farm and built a log cabin shortly after the birth of their son Harrison Blair Burn, their ninth child

Southeast-facing view from the "Mountain View Farm" in McMinn County's Mount Harmony community. *Photo by Caitlynn Beddingfield Smith.*

and the first Burn born in McMinn County. The southeast-facing farm has breathtaking views of the Unicoi Mountains of Appalachia.

The family lived among a "nest" of slaveholders in the Mountain View Community.[1] Thanks to Mahala Burn's convictions, her children began a new lineage of Burn descendants who did not own slaves. Adam Burn, an alcoholic, died in 1855. Mahala influenced her children to not be drunkards like their father.

Once the Civil War broke out, two of the children, Hugh and George, slipped off with their mother's blessing "under the cover of darkness" to join the Union army.[2] Both died in the conflict fighting to end slavery and preserve the Union. Although already fighting with Union forces, the Confederate army reported Hugh and George Burn in the *Athens Post* as failing to report for duty. The Confederate army also tried, unsuccessfully, to conscript Harrison, Otho and Samuel Burn.[3] McMinn County's allegiance was split during the war, providing twelve Union regiments and ten Confederate regiments. A small majority of McMinn Countians voted to remain with the Union in June 1861.[4]

Mahala Burn "went about in fear for her safety throughout the war."[5] The ardent Unionist widow worried that the Confederate army would

James Lafayette "Jim" Burn. *Burn family.*

confiscate her horses. Soldiers had left one horse, and she knew they would be back for it. She smeared the horse with raw eggs and stood him in the sun tethered in a distant field. When the soldiers returned for it, she told them to take the mangy old thing as it was of no use to her. Of course, the soldiers left empty-handed.[6] Eventually, all of her property was ordered confiscated by the Confederates, but the war ended before the order could be carried out.[7]

Mahala Burn is not buried with her husband, Adam. She passed away in 1879. The Burn matriarch refused to be buried in the same cemetery as "slavers and rebels." She and her children are all buried at the Mountain View Cemetery. "Mahala Burn has always been held up in the family as having set a great example of courageous fidelity to conviction," Harry T. Burn Jr. later wrote.[8]

Harrison Blair Burn's innovative and enterprising efforts brought him remarkable success. Nicknamed "Hi," he was a potato farmer and made hosiery for the Union army during the Civil War. In September 1865, he married Margaret Elizabeth Barnett. The couple had eight children. Their oldest child was James Lafayette (Jim) Burn, born in 1866.

Jim Burn attended Parsons College, a small school near Niota. He began working for the East Tennessee, Virginia and Georgia Railroad in 1888. A few years later, it became the Southern Railway Company. Harry T. Burn Jr. described his grandfather's style:

> *James Lafayette always wore a uniform suit with a white shirt and tie to the depot, except in summer, when he "dressed down" to a crisp white linen suit that was changed every day or two! These suits soiled easily around the side pockets and thus were unsuitable for extended wear. His dress always was immaculate.*[9]

Jim Burn had seven younger siblings. One of his sisters, Julia, passed away at age eight. Two of his sisters, Mayme and Anne, married two brothers, John Isbell and James Benjamin Forrest, respectively, both of Niota. The other three sisters married and remained close by. His baby brother Walter was sixteen years his junior. Many of Jim's siblings have living descendants in and near McMinn County.

ENSMINGER FAMILY

The Ensminger family has traced lineage back to Europe. Febb Ensminger researched much of the Ensminger genealogy. She even wrote a small family history.[10] The Ensminger family once lived in Lorraine and Friesland (in the southwest corner of Germany, near the Netherlands).

"The Ensmingers were of the Lutheran faith," Febb wrote. "They spoke high German and read the Lutheran Bible that was printed in high German." She described the family as one of the many German families "braving the rough Atlantic" seeking new homes to "be free from religious persecution.... All the history that has been found of the Ensminger family shows they were brave, God-fearing, liberty-loving people."[11] Peter Ensminger, born in 1694, lived in Rotterdam, Holland. On August 17, 1733, Peter and his wife, Cathrina, sailed from London bound for the New World. The couple had five children. They initially settled in the colony established by William Penn. "No wonder we proclaim 'America, the land of the free and the home of the brave'—when we think of the 4,000 or more miles of stormy seas these Pilgrim fathers traveled, to be free from religious oppression and tyranny of kings," Febb wrote of her ancestors.[12]

Peter and Cathrina settled in Manheim, Lancaster County, Pennsylvania. Their eldest son, Hendrick, had eight children, including a son named Henry. Henry Ensminger's neighbor was the Baron Henry Stiegel in Manheim, Lancaster County, Pennsylvania. The Baron Stiegel was a friend of George Washington and sometimes entertained Washington in his home.

Henry Ensminger served in the Revolutionary War, enlisting in the Second New Jersey Regiment in 1778 (Second Battalion of the Lancaster County Militia). A musket ball in the left leg and a bayonet in the left thigh wounded him in the Battle of Monmouth. After suffering for six months as a prisoner of war, he was released in an exchange. He returned to service fighting at the Battles of Tioga Point and Yorktown. Febb Ensminger shared a verse that the family believed applicable to Henry: "We bring the man who helped steel the line at Trenton, Monmouth and Valley Forge, who helped give strength that would not yield on these fields. We bring the man who helped make us free, with Yorktown's guns and victory."[13]

Henry Ensminger and Eve Wilson had several children. The family moved to Virginia. One of the sons, Jonathon, married Sarah Garber. Jonathon and Sarah's youngest son was Elijah King Ensminger, born in 1809.

Febb Ensminger was close with her grandfather Elijah Ensminger. "He was possessed with striking personality, was a great reader, and a scholarly man, well educated for his time."[14] He married Nancy Cook in 1832. They had several children in Roanoke County, Virginia, and worked in the tobacco business. "But on hearing that the state of Tennessee offered a more profitable field for the growing of the weed, he decided to move to Tennessee," Febb wrote of her grandfather.[15] The family arrived in East Tennessee in 1846, bringing their slaves with them.

At the outbreak of the Civil War, Elijah strongly supported the Confederacy. "He was southern in sympathy," Febb Ensminger wrote.[16] His eldest son to reach adulthood, Jonathon Thomas "Tom" Ensminger, born in 1839, enlisted to fight for the Confederate army.

Tom Ensminger fought with the Old Nineteenth Tennessee Cavalry, serving as a sergeant under Captain Lowry. The group's actions at the Battle of Shiloh earned the group the moniker "Bloody Nineteenth." Tom was one of the sixty who lived to spike the Federal batteries at Shiloh.[17]

After fighting in several battles, including at Chickamauga, Tom was wounded in the jaw by a Minié ball (which passed through to his back) at the Battle of Missionary Ridge in Chattanooga. Left for dead on the battlefield, Silas Riggins, a fellow soldier, discovered Tom was alive. The ball was removed from between his shoulders. He was transported by train to Marietta, Georgia, where he remained on his back for sixteen weeks at a Catholic nursing home. He then went to recuperate in White Sulpher Springs, Virginia. He was semi-invalid for the rest of his life. With only six weeks of schooling, he learned to read and write, but his prospects for making a comfortable living were bleak.

Tom's father, Elijah, brought his son back to East Tennessee after the war. Tom's son later wrote, "He stayed a while, but conditions were so rotten in McMinn County that they were calling rebel soldiers to their doors and shooting them down."[18] Elijah and Tom

Jonathon Thomas "Tom" Ensminger. *Burn family.*

moved to Jefferson, Texas, remaining there for three years. Febb Ensminger described her father:

> *He was a man of keen intellect. He saw the beauty in common things—and impressed his family thus. My father was a poet. It was he who pointed out the beautiful to me; the loveliness of blossoms, and of trees; the billows of golden waving grain...to see eternal kindness in it all. My father never penned a verse in rhyme; yet wrote appreciation for all time upon my heart. And gave me eyes to see in all these common things divinity.*[19]

Tom returned to East Tennessee and married Sarah "Sallie" Snyder in 1871. They lived an impoverished life but managed to buy a farm in the Mount Verd area of McMinn County, where they raised three children. Their second child was Febb King Ensminger, born on November 23, 1873.

Febb Ensminger's given first name at birth has never been verified; speculation continues among the family. Her daughter believed she was named for Miss Feriba Ann "Phoebe" King, Sallie Ensminger's close friend. As a child, Febb was called "Feebie" or "Febbie," and her schoolmates continued to call her "Feebie" in later years. She experimented with the names "Pharibe" and "Faribe," and she registered in 1891 at Grant Memorial University (now Tennessee Wesleyan University) as "Faribe" Ensminger.[20] She often went by Febb K. Burn after marrying Jim Burn, but Febb E. Burn is on her tombstone. She is sometimes referred to as Phoebe, but the family has been unable to confirm if that was her given name.

Febb Ensminger moved to Mouse Creek (now Niota) with her family in 1889. She studied for one year at Mrs. McAdoo's classes in Knoxville before completing the preparatory school program at U.S. Grant Memorial University in Athens in 1892.[21] She taught at a school near present-day Long Mill Road (just outside Athens) after completing her education. She later farmed for a living. Although never active in any political organization, she had strong beliefs of her own.[22]

According to Harry T. Burn Jr., his grandmother "was an impoverished gentlewoman....She had beauty, intelligence, and the social graces, but no money."[23] His clearest boyhood recollection of her was their visits to the pool at Springbrook, a country club in Niota. "She remained a voracious reader all her life—a habit she passed along to my father," Harry T. Burn Jr. later wrote.[24] She enjoyed the classics and popular novels. She was of the Methodist faith. One newspaper described her as having "coal black hair,"[25] while another described her as a "small, spare built woman with pale blue-

Febb King Ensminger in 1892.
Burn family.

grey eyes that twinkle."[26] She was above average in height, especially for her time. Based on photographic evidence, the Burn family believes that Febb Ensminger stood five feet, eight inches tall as a young woman.

Febb Ensminger's younger brother, William "Bill" Ensminger, became the family breadwinner at a young age. In 1895, Tom and Sallie Ensminger moved to Ogden (in Rhea County) after a Mouse Creek physician suggested that the mountain air would be good for Tom. After working as a railroad telegrapher, Bill began working for the First National Bank of Rockwood in 1906. He remained with the bank through good times and bad. Bill influenced Harry T. Burn's eventual move to the city. Febb's older sister, Martha "Mattie" Ensminger, married Beriah F. Sykes in Rhea County. They had no children.

Chapter 2

BIRTH AND CHILDHOOD IN NIOTA

Febb Ensminger recalled meeting James Lafayette "Jim" Burn: "He courted me when I was a young lady, and after seven years of kindly attention he asked me to marry him."[1] The young man from a Republican family would unite in marriage with the young lady from a family of "unreconstructed Democrats."[2] Jim Burn, the nephew of fallen Union soldiers, and Febb Ensminger, the daughter of a disabled Confederate veteran, became husband and wife on December 26, 1894. The couple lived in Mouse Creek.

Mouse Creek, a small East Tennessee town of fewer than five hundred residents, changed its name to avoid confusion with the Mossy Creek train depot in Jefferson City, Tennessee. Several gallons of ice cream were mistakenly delivered to Mossy Creek's depot. After sitting on the platform for several hours, the ice cream melted—Mouse Creek had to change its name. Jim Burn recommended the name "Movilla." The town postmaster, John Boggess, recommended the name "Neeotah," supposedly the name of a Native American chief in a dime novel he had read.[3] Mouse Creek became Niota (pronounced "nye-oh-tah") in 1897. Jim Burn wrote "Neeotah" as "Niota."

Niota is located in northeastern McMinn County. The earliest known records of the first property registered in Niota dates to the 1820s.[4] Nestled just west of a small ridge in the Sweetwater Valley, two small creeks run through the community. The creeks converge south of the city to form the stream called Mouse Creek. Over the ridge a few miles to the east is the unincorporated community of Mount Harmony, the home of Adam and Mahala Burn. Beautiful views of the sunset can be seen from atop the ridge. On a clear day, the steam from the Watts Bar Nuclear Power Plant on the Tennessee River is also visible from atop the ridge.

Main Street in Niota is one block east of U.S. Highway 11. Many businesses and community buildings that front or have fronted Main Street include the home where Burn was born, the post office and the first bank in Niota. Also fronting Main Street is the Niota Depot, the historic heart of the city.

In 1854, the East Tennessee and Georgia Railroad built the train depot in Mouse Creek. Still standing, it is the oldest standing train depot in Tennessee, currently serving as Niota City Hall. The railway proved a boon for the development of Niota. McMinn County was the site of the first railroad to be developed in Tennessee. State Senator James Hayes Reagan played a major role in securing state funding to help finance the project. The depot in Reagan, an unincorporated community a few miles northeast of Niota, was named for State Senator Reagan. Developers wanted a railway to connect Dalton, Georgia, to Knoxville, Tennessee. The Tennessee Valley, located between the Cumberland Plateau and the Appalachian Mountains, provides a perfect natural route for travelers moving north and south. Realizing the geographic advantages of their county, McMinn Countians committed to raising the necessary funds to build the railway.[5]

Jim and Febb Burn's first child, Harry Thomas Burn, was born on November 12, 1895, in Mouse Creek. The middle-class family lived in a Victorian frame house near the corner of modern-day Main Street and Burn Road. The home no longer stands, and the site is now the fellowship hall of the First Baptist Church of Niota. The family worshiped at the First Baptist Church, where their son was baptized Harrison Thomas Burn. With the exception of his high school diploma, "Harry Thomas Burn" appears on every other known document. He was never referred to as Harrison.

Harry T. Burn attended school in Niota. Mrs. McCorkle ran a play school out of the Schultz Mansion (now Fountain Hill) on Farrell Street. He later attended elementary school in Niota. Febb Burn made sure that her children never went to bed until after she had gone over each lesson with them. She blamed the mother if a child grew up in ignorance.[6]

When Burn was a little boy, a mountain lion had been spotted lurking about the region. Local newspapers reported on the sightings. One day, he was walking down the railroad tracks to see his father at the depot. He heard the roar of the mountain lion. When recalling the incident in a conversation with his great-nephew many years later, he said he thought the noise was a

Harry T. Burn at eighteen months. *Burn family.*

person. He investigated the noise. Fortunately, for his family, his son yet to be born and millions of future women voters across the country, he never encountered the animal![7]

Febb Burn described her son's study habits. "He subscribed to thirty-five or more magazines and would stay up late at night reading."[8] She once told her son that he had the intelligence to be a Philadelphia lawyer.[9] He always wanted to be a public man and kept himself informed of public affairs both local and national. Full of aspiration, his schoolmates nicknamed him "President." He took great pride in his little hometown and never stopped thinking of ways to improve it. "When he was a small boy," Febb said, "he used to lay and dream of the future for Niota, of the buildings he would like to see take place of the old ones."[10]

Febb Burn taught her son the importance of taking a stand. Throughout most of his career, he never kept people guessing and was always straightforward. She taught him the value of standing up for what you believe in, regardless of the consequences. She instilled in him the value of treating others with kindness and fairness. She also admonished her children to always mind their manners. A sensitive subject, she instructed her children to never mention the Civil War.

Thanks to his father's teachings, Burn learned telegraphy and Morse code as a teenager.[11] He played basketball at Niota High School and was among the first graduating class of the school in 1911, the same year the city was first incorporated. He finished the three-year program, graduating after completing the eleventh grade.[12] He graduated with five other students. He never attended college.

Jim Burn taught his son the value of voluntary cooperation and collaboration with members of the community to make it a better place to live. Burn watched as his father worked with fellow citizens to develop Niota into an industrialized, modern city. Jim Burn, Harrison Burn, Otho Burn, Amanda Burn and several other leaders from prominent Niota families, including the Forrest family and Willson family, established a hosiery mill. These entrepreneurs combined to invest $12,500 and founded Crescent Hosiery Mills in September 1902. Jim served as the first vice-president. Burn later described his father as the "guiding light" in the early development of the mill.[13] At the time of this writing, a fourth generation of the Burn family continues to own and operate the mill, now called Crescent Sock Company.

Jim Burn also served as the first president of the Bank of Niota. At age sixteen, Harry T. Burn made the first deposit at the new bank.[14] Jim served on the board of directors of Niota Water, Light and Power Company. He served as the treasurer of the local lodge of the Junior Order of the United American Mechanics and was also a member of the Order of Railway Telegraphers.

Burn had the enterprising spirit of his father. As a young boy, he would load tomatoes on his little red wagon and sell them in the village. By watching his father collaborate to establish a hosiery mill to kick-start the city's industrial base, develop utilities for the area and organize the city's first bank to provide financial services, Burn learned the power of free enterprise and the prosperity it brings.

Burn had three younger siblings: James Lane "Jack" Burn (born in 1897), Sara Margaret Burn (born in 1903) and Otho Virginia Burn (born in 1906). Otho was named after her great-uncle, Otho Sevier Burn. Otho pronounced her name "Otha." Febb Burn said that Sara had a natural talent for music.[15] Otho also loved music.

The Burn siblings were very close. One Halloween night, Harry and Jack snuck out and turned over a privy. They were horrified when they learned that it was occupied! The next day, Febb Burn said her sons couldn't have been involved, as they were at home in bed.[16]

Burn had a close relationship with his grandfathers. Tom Ensminger passed away in 1909. "He lived to almost seventy years, lacking twelve days, after being shot to pieces like he was," Bill Ensminger later wrote.[17] One evening when Burn was a boy, he spent the night with his Grandfather Burn up on the ridge. Something at the house spooked him so terribly he burst out of the house in the middle of the night and ran all the way down the ridge back home! Harrison Burn passed away in 1910.

Burn's paternal grandmother, Margaret Burn, passed away before he was born. His maternal grandmother, Sallie Ensminger, lived a long life, long enough to see his deciding vote for woman suffrage. Burn later described his relationship with his Uncle Bill Ensminger as "the closest I think it would be possible to be."[18] He spent summers with his uncle in nearby Rockwood.

A meritorious employee, Jim Burn eventually became the stationmaster at the Niota Depot. In 1915, the president of the Southern Railway Company awarded him a gold medal for his long and efficient service to the company. He never received a demerit at any time during his almost three-decade employment with the railroad. In fact, he received a four-dollar-per-month raise (from thirty-six dollars to forty) as a token of appreciation after he came in for work and displayed good conduct during a railroad strike in 1900.[19] His thrift, savings and sound investments provided a good living for his family.[20]

While finishing high school, Burn began helping at the railroad by caring for switch lamps for $2.50 per month. He began his full-time career with the Southern Railway Company on May 13, 1913.[21] By this time, he had mastered Morse telegraphy. He worked all over the Southern Railway's line in East Tennessee. His first jobs were in East Chattanooga, Ooltewah and Calhoun. First hired as a relief agent, he learned fast and was soon operating telegraph machines, selling tickets and checking baggage.[22]

The railroad helped Burn secure a deferred classification for service in the Great War, or World War I. As a member of the telegrapher's union, his skills at the keyboard also kept him home during the war. "He is the only man on the road who can fill all jobs," railroad officials said of Burn.[23]

Burn was what was known in his time as a "joiner." If there were a civic organization to join, he would join it. As a young man, he became a Mason and a Shriner and joined the Junior Order of United American Mechanics and the Woodmen of the World.

The Niota Depot in 1902. *Left to right:* Harrison B. Burn, James L. (Jack) Burn, Walter A. Burn, James L. (Jim) Burn, James R. Lewis and John I. Forrest. *McMinn County Historical Society.*

Burn's sister Sara accidentally injured her spine and later contracted an illness. Her parents took her to New York City for treatment. Febb Burn had never been so far away from home in her entire life. After the doctors told the family that there was nothing they could do for Sara, they had a studio portrait of her made in New York. The family of six also stood for a photograph taken in front of their home.

Sara Burn passed away in Niota on March 28, 1914. She was only eleven years old. Her illness is believed to have been a spinal infection, possibly caused by the injury. She was laid to rest at the Niota Cemetery. "Prior to her death, the family had enjoyed a charmed life….Her death that year was an earth-shattering experience," Harry T. Burn Jr. later wrote.[24]

After Sara Burn passed away, the Burn family moved out of their Victorian frame house on Main Street, the home having become a "place of sadness."[25] With the help of a $6,000 loan, Jim Burn purchased an eleven-room colonial-style home at a public auction. The family had intended for its move to the northern Niota home to be temporary. The home fronts East Farrell Street but formerly had a driveway accessible from U.S. Highway

Above: The Burn family in front of
their Main Street home in 1914.
Burn family.

Left: Sara Margaret Burn. *Burn family.*

11. The home is situated on a property that includes a 120-acre farm. Jonathon Franklin Shearman oversaw the building of the home from 1846 to 1849. Slaves fired the bricks used for the home in the front yard. The *Nashville Tennessean* later wrote that the home had "the atmosphere of Mount Vernon," the northern Virginia home of George Washington.[26]

"Hathburn" was the name Febb Burn later gave the home as a combination of her eldest son's first, middle and last names (**Ha**rry **Th**omas **Burn**). The Tennessee Department of Agriculture registered the property as Hathburn through an act of the General Assembly in 1926. Members of the Burn family occupied the home for the next nine decades. The family disliked the term *mansion* when referring to the home, and it was rarely referred to as such in their presence.[27]

J. Polk Cooley recalled Burn's many stories about Hathburn. Burn showed him a nick in the doorframe over the back staircase left by a Union soldier during the Civil War. "Harry loved that story," Cooley said.[28] J. Reed Dixon enjoyed the Hathburn parties. "He called Hathburn his ancestral home even though his ancestors never lived there," Dixon laughingly recalled.[29] Bill Snyder remembered riding with Burn in a red convertible with suicide doors. Burn took the middle school–aged Snyder to the home shortly before World War II. "When I walked through the doorway of Hathburn I pinched my finger in the door," recalled Snyder.[30]

Two years after the family moved into their new home, Jim Burn passed away unexpectedly after contracting typhoid fever. His death came on June 30, 1916, in Niota, one week after his fifieth birthday. The *Niotan* memorialized him in an obituary:

> *Death has cast the shadow of his dreadful presence over this community and taken from our midst one of its most respected citizens. He was a faithful, devoted husband and father and an exemplary Christian. His long and useful life was spent in making his family happy and comfortable and in assisting those less fortunate than himself….He was one of the pioneers in the upbringing of our town and was always ready to lend his assistance and means in any undertaking that was for the betterment of the community.*[31]

Hathburn was now a home of four: Febb, Harry, Jack and Otho. Harry and Jack were coming of age and venturing forward without their father. Otho was still in school. The family grew even closer.

The Burn family moved into this home in 1914. Febb Burn later named it Hathburn.
Burn family.

Burn took over many of his late father's positions in the community. Febb Burn took the life insurance money from her late husband's policy and paid off the notes on the home and farm. "After Grandfather Burn died, my grandmother managed the farm and managed it very successfully," Harry T. Burn Jr. later wrote.[32] Burn was one week too young to be able to vote in the 1916 election. But by 1918, not only was he voting, he was also a candidate for public office.

Chapter 3

ELECTION TO STATE HOUSE OF REPRESENTATIVES AND FIRST TERM

B urn's political career began at the age of twenty-two. McMinn County's seat in the Tennessee House of Representatives was vacant. The previous representative was Herschel M. Candler, who was running for the State Senate seat representing McMinn, Bradley, Roane and Anderson Counties.

Many citizens encouraged Burn to run for the open seat. Being well known and respected throughout the community, he decided to enter the race. He faced W.W. Lowry in the Republican primary. Lowry lived in Riceville, an unincorporated community in southern McMinn County. A former Union soldier, Lowry was elderly. Burn won the primary against the Civil War veteran on August 1, 1918, by a vote of 933 to 432.[1]

Burn went on to face Colonel D.B. Todd in the general election. Todd was a middle-aged Democrat from Etowah, a railroad boomtown in southeastern McMinn County. Burn ran an ad in the local paper: "Your vote and influence will be appreciated, and I pledge you that I shall always conduct myself so that anyone voting for me shall never have cause to regret having done so."[2]

One week before his twenty-third birthday, Burn defeated Todd by more than seven hundred votes on November 5, 1918.[3] Thus began Burn's political career. The electorate rarely favored candidates as young as he in the past. But his family had been recognized as solid Republicans since the Civil War. "Burn's popularity was attained by his unwavering integrity, ambition and attention to business. He is a very ambitious young

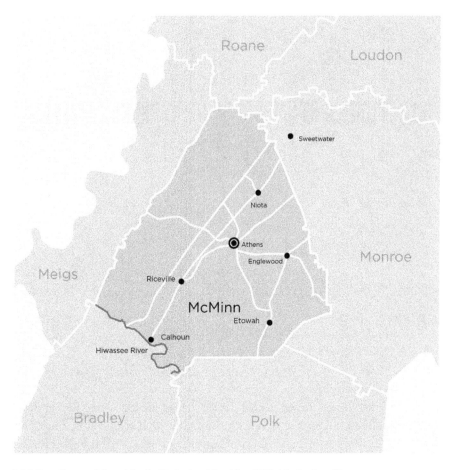

McMinn County Map. *Map by Navigation Advertising, LLC, Murfreesboro, Tennessee.*

man who appreciates the honor he has been given but also recognizes the responsibility that goes with the same. His record as a member of the next General Assembly will be watched with great interest," wrote the *Tri-Weekly Post*.[4] Herschel Candler, who played a "large part" in electing Burn, won election to the State Senate.[5]

At the time of Burn's first election to office, McMinn County was one of the largest counties in East Tennessee, with a population of almost twenty-five thousand. The arrowhead-shaped county has several creeks, low ridges and fertile soil ideal for agriculture.[6] The Hiwassee Purchase led to the establishment of McMinn County in 1819 on land previously owned by the Cherokee. The county seat and largest city is Athens. Situated in the heart of the county, Athens is a few miles southwest of Niota.

Burn's term was for two years, which is the term of office for Tennessee state representatives. The Tennessee General Assembly, similar to that of many states, meets on a part-time basis. Burn had a busy schedule during the first four months of 1919. At this time, the legislature met only during odd-numbered years, convening the first week in January and usually adjourning in April.

Burn entered the Tennessee General Assembly as a Republican in a Democratic-controlled state, not an uncommon circumstance for an East Tennessee politician during the era of the Solid South. The region opposed secession from the Union before the Civil War, but West and Middle Tennessee voted the state into the Confederacy. After the Civil War, East Tennessee became a Republican stronghold with little power compared to the capital city of Nashville and the largest city, Memphis. The state had elected only two Republican governors between the end of Reconstruction and Burn's election to the legislature. Ben Hooper, one of the two Republican governors, was from northeastern Tennessee. Democrats had controlled the state legislature since 1869. After Reconstruction, Republican presidential candidates failed to win Tennessee's electoral votes. With one brief exception, both of Tennessee's senators had been in Democratic control since the end of Reconstruction. Tennessee's First and Second Congressional Districts have been Republican strongholds since the Civil War.

While Burn was away in Nashville, he wrote home often. On December 31, after arriving at the Hotel Tulane, he wrote that it would "probably be his permanent home" while in Nashville and that he had "already succeeded in becoming the 'joke' of the lobbyists on account of my age."[7] When a crowd of men asked Candler what kind of representative McMinn had, Burn wrote, "I actually believed he looked embarrassed. Ha! Ha!" Burn wrote that he had an audience with Governor Albert Roberts the next day.[8]

Governor Roberts quickly gave the freshman legislator a nickname: "Baby Burn." Burn was barely one year older than the minimum age for a state representative, which is twenty-one. In fact, one of the oldest men in the legislature, sixty-six-year-old Wesley S. Tucker from Erwin, occupied the desk to the right of Burn.[9]

On Monday, January 6, 1919, Burn began his first session in the 61st General Assembly as the "County Representative" for McMinn. He introduced his first bill, House Bill No. 27. Unfriendly to the idea of universal suffrage, it intended to create a delinquent poll tax collector for McMinn County.[10] The bill failed to pass. But his beliefs on the poll tax would later change.

Representative Harry T. Burn in 1919. *Tennessee State Library and Archives.*

In another letter to his family, Burn wrote, "Only three sessions but being a member of the legislature is getting so that it seems old to me! Ha! Ha!" He wrote that he was "decidedly the youngest member of the House" and that it was helping in a great many ways.[11] He wrote of his habits of working after dinner at the hotel until bedtime and not going out often. "Love to everybody, Harry T. Burn. The Mountaineer Boy Statesman! Ha! Ha! No, am not smoking or drinking coffee."[12]

Burn and Candler were elected to positions in the Republican Caucus. Senator Candler was chosen as chairman of the joint committees of the House and Senate, while Burn was chosen as secretary of the House caucus and joint caucuses. In fact, the Democrats selected Burn as the only legislator in the General Assembly to serve as a secretary on three different committees.[13]

Unbeknownst to many, Burn voted to amend the U.S. Constitution not once, but three times. His first opportunity to amend the document was not his 1920 vote to ratify the Nineteenth Amendment. In January 1919, the General Assembly voted on the Eighteenth Amendment (Prohibition). The twenty-three-year-old freshman legislator with only a three-year high school education was preparing to cast a vote to amend the supreme law of the land.

Article V of the U.S. Constitution provides the process for amending the document. An amendment can be proposed one of two ways: 1) by a two-thirds vote in the U.S. Congress or 2) by a two-thirds vote of the state legislatures to call a convention to propose amendments. An amendment can be ratified one of two ways: 1) by a three-fourths vote of the state legislatures or 2) a three-fourths vote of the state conventions. The Founding Fathers intended that the several states play a major role in amending the document. Given that the several states gathered in Philadelphia in 1787 to create the federal Constitution, this process for amending the document has proven appropriate.

The U.S. Congress plays a limited role in the amendment process, if it plays a role at all, while the executive branch and the judicial branch play no role. The safeguards that the Founding Generation put in place to prevent the federal government from playing a substantial role in amending its own power demonstrate their wisdom. State and local governments play a role in checking the power of the federal government, just as the federal government plays a role in checking the power of state and local governments. It is proper that all levels of government play a role in major changes to our system of government.

Burn understood that state and local governments are just as important to individual rights and daily life as the federal government. His public service never extended beyond state government. He arguably did as much to influence our system of government during his career as anyone in the federal government have in their careers.

The temperance movement in the United States had been growing in power throughout most of the nineteenth century. Established in 1895, the year of Burn's birth, the Anti-Saloon League led efforts to ban the sale of alcohol through a federal amendment. Automobile accidents, domestic violence, barroom brawls, disorderly conduct and poverty were all blamed on alcohol. Women and children often fell victims to abusers of alcohol. Many were beaten, neglected and even widowed as a result of the drunkenness of the men around them. Carrie Nation, a militant prohibitionist, gained notoriety for her acts of violence against illegal manufacturers and sellers of alcohol. Several religious leaders, Protestants in particular, waged a crusade against alcohol.

Tennessee banned the sale of liquor near churches as early as 1824. Despite a series of laws to ban the sale of liquor near schools, the liquor business continued to thrive, especially in the major cities. In 1890, Harriman became "the only city founded on the principles of industry and prohibition."[14] Located in Roane County, Burn's future home, Harriman failed to live up to its promise. The city never became the industrial powerhouse people had hoped, and it was never a dry community.

In an attempt to eradicate the sale of liquor statewide in both rural and urban areas, a 1909 law banned liquor sales within four miles of any school. Some of Tennessee's major cities continued to defy the liquor laws. In 1917, Governor Thomas Rye signed into law a "bone dry" bill. In his farewell address to the General Assembly, Rye urged ratification of the Eighteenth Amendment. The receipt, possession and transportation of liquor in or out of the state were now illegal.[15] By the time Burn began his first term in 1919, prohibition was about to go national.

The U.S. Congress had proposed the Eighteenth Amendment to the states for ratification on December 18, 1917. Both chambers overwhelmingly approved the measure. A bipartisan issue, the resolution received a solid majority of votes from Democrats and Republicans. Section 1 of the Eighteenth Amendment is as follows:

> *After one year from the ratification of this article the manufacture, sale, or transportation of intoxicating liquors within, the importation thereof into, or the exportation thereof from the United States and all the territory subject to the jurisdiction thereof for beverage purposes is hereby prohibited.*

Mississippi became the first state to vote for ratification on January 7, 1918. One year later, Tennessee voted for ratification on January 13, 1919. Burn joined in a landslide vote as Tennessee became the twenty-third state to vote for ratification.

In an op-ed written two years later for the *New York Times*, Burn defended his vote for Prohibition. "My grandfather was for Prohibition and my father had the same opinion and I had the pleasure of voting for the Eighteenth Amendment."[16] Burn had grown up hearing stories about his alcoholic great-grandfather Adam Burn.

In his op-ed, Burn defended East Tennessee from what he perceived as slanderous stories portraying the region as a "hooch paradise." He urged readers not to paint with a broad brush by judging the people of an entire region based on the actions of a few. He pointed out that most moonshiners lived in the mountains twenty-five miles from the railroad in "primitive conditions." "A few days ago the enforcement officer for this district visited it without finding a drop," Burn said of McMinn County. He continued:

> *To say that the people in these little cities and villages and crossroad settlements are, in the majority, either in favor of violating the law in regard to moonshining or they are only passively opposed to such violation is an error in its worst form....I have worked in the small towns of East Tennessee and Western North Carolina and I know the maker of the statement is in error....In no section of the country is there a more universal sentiment for law enforcement. It appears that many articles are predicated on the unusual and the statements of extremists. Probably most villages have one or two men who drink moonshine liquor or traffic in it, but it would be just as reasonable to say that New York was in favor of murder or passively opposed because there are murders committed there.*[17]

East Tennessee has always been an ideal geographic location for moonshining. The vast hills and hollers of the Great Smoky Mountains provide a more than adequate natural refuge for such illegal activity. Moonshiners thrived in the mountains of East Tennessee throughout the Prohibition era and after.

A few days after Tennessee voted for ratification, the amendment finally gained enough support from northern, midwestern and western states. It was ratified on January 16, 1919, after the Nebraska legislature voted for ratification. In October, the U.S. Congress passed and overrode President Woodrow Wilson's veto of the Volstead Act. The act provided for the enforcement of the amendment, which went into effect on January 16, 1920. (The Twenty-First Amendment later repealed the Eighteenth Amendment in 1933.)

An examination of Burn's voting record demonstrates his low tolerance for vice. He would vote for increased restrictions on alcohol and tobacco throughout his career. In the 1919 session, he supported a failed bill attempting to prevent the sale of cigarettes and another bill "to promote mitigation and suppression of vice."[18]

Burn introduced two successful bills to incorporate two small cities in McMinn County. The first bill incorporated Englewood, an eastern McMinn town that, like Niota, was a hosiery manufacturing center.[19] The other bill re-incorporated Niota and changed it from a town to a city.[20]

Two bills in January stand out in particular. Burn voted aye on a bill to designate a day for Mother's Day.[21] He also supported a bill enabling the "kindred of deceased negroes to inherit property."[22]

In February, Burn thought of his late grandfather Tom Ensminger when he voted aye on a bill to provide relief for Confederate soldiers.[23] He also voted aye on a Senate bill to "provide no registration of voters in certain counties."[24] In March, he introduced a successful bill authorizing certain towns to improve streets in McMinn County.[25] This bill led to the construction of the first concrete section of the Lee Highway in East Tennessee, connecting Athens and Calhoun. Just a few years later, an average of one thousand cars passed through Athens daily.[26]

Burn introduced and supported various education bills for the benefit of McMinn County. His bill to restructure and consolidate the McMinn County school system abolished the previous elementary and high school boards of education to create a new county commission of education, splitting the county into five school districts.[27] The commissioners were to be elected by the people. The bill stipulated that at least

The Hotel Tulane. *Tennessee State Library and Archives.*

two commissioners must be "persons of skill and experience in the art of teaching."[28]

Burn supported a bill introduced in the State Senate by Herschel Candler to issue and sell bonds for the construction or acquisition of a building for a new county high school in Athens.[29] The bill also provided for the construction and improvements of the county's elementary schools in Calhoun, Etowah, Englewood, Niota and Riceville. The bill stipulated that the bonds would only be issued upon the approval of a majority of McMinn voters. Burn also introduced a bill to levy a tax for educational purposes. All of his education bills were signed into law. The new county high school operated from 1925 to 1981. Part of the building is now the McMinn County Living Heritage Museum.

In April, Burn supported a bill to "provide for display of flag by public schools."[30] He voted aye on a bill to "provide an oath of allegiance in pension cases."[31] His standout votes in April were two bills in the spirit of equality under the law for men and women. Burn voted aye on a bill to "make women eligible as deputy clerks"[32] and for a bill that granted suffrage to women in municipal and presidential elections.[33] The state constitution prevented the legislature from extending women voting rights in county and state elections. Known as the "limited suffrage" bill, its passage later gave suffragists hope that Tennessee might be a state to rely on for ratification of the Nineteenth Amendment.

Toward the end of the session, Burn voted aye on a bill to "provide for election of delegates to constitutional convention."[34] Tennessee failed to hold a convention for another three decades, but it was not for a lack of trying. He was eager for an opportunity to serve as a delegate to amend the state constitution and always voted for such opportunities. At the time of his first election, the Tennessee Constitution had not been amended for almost half a century. He had remarkable foresight, and he never stopped trying to improve the state constitution.

By the close of the 1919 Session, Governor Roberts had signed nine of Burn's thirteen bills into law. The 61st General Assembly adjourned in April 1919 and, under normal circumstances, would not have convened again until January 1921. But in August 1920, the legislature would be called to Nashville for an "extraordinary session." Burn had no idea just how extraordinary it would prove to be.

Chapter 4
"HURRAH AND VOTE FOR SUFFRAGE"

The concept of the right to vote (suffrage) originated in ancient Greece, where all property-owning males over age eighteen could vote.[1] For most of history, this pillar of self-government has been recognized for only a privileged few. The U.S. Constitution, as ratified in 1787, did not specify who could and could not vote. The new document granted to the several states the power to conduct elections and determine voter qualifications. This structure has advantages and disadvantages. While designating control of voting rights to the federal government can enfranchise all citizens, it can also disenfranchise certain groups nationwide through a single legislative act. It would have been devastating for the few women and minorities who gained the right to vote in their state legislatures to have been disenfranchised nationwide by a Congress hostile to equality under the law for all people.

At the beginning of the American republic, most state legislatures enfranchised only white, land-owning men. Tennessee's 1796 constitution permitted free blacks to vote. Unfortunately, the 1835 Tennessee Constitution abolished suffrage rights for free blacks. The poor, minorities and women had virtually no suffrage rights at the beginning of the American republic. Even worse, many black residents, particularly in the South, lived as slaves.

The U.S. Constitution did not reference the evil of slavery, and the few compromises on the issue did little to weaken it. The imperfect Founding Fathers crafted an imperfect document. Abigail Adams wrote to her husband, John Adams, while he served in the Continental Congress, "Remember the ladies."[2] Adams replied that he could not help but "laugh" at her suggestion.[3]

It was a white man's world. But Abigail Adams's letter to her husband would not be the last memorable correspondence relating to suffrage rights in American history.

Fortunately, the ideas and principles that the flawed but virtuous Founding Generation believed in have endured. The inconsistencies and contradictions of the Founding Generation were thankfully not permanent, nor were they intended to be. The Founders inserted into the U.S. Constitution a method by which to change the document. Article V has enabled the United States to improve and further realize its promise.

The U.S. Constitution established a democratic republic based on the ideas of individual rights and a limited government. The sovereign of the United States is not an autocrat or an oligarchy. Sovereignty rests in "We the People." But at the beginning of the republic, "We the People" failed to include all people regardless of gender, race, religion or class. Self-government is not possible without equality under the law and suffrage rights for all citizens. Every single citizen must be able to own their own life, have a voice, be able to vote for the person they wish to represent them in government, be able to hold public servants accountable and be able to participate in government. It is for these reasons why the right to vote is cherished.

More than 600,000 Americans perished in the Civil War, including two of Burn's great-uncles, Hugh and George Burn. The Union's victory secured the end of the institution of slavery in the United States. After the war, the states ratified three federal amendments. The Thirteenth Amendment in 1865 abolished slavery. In an attempt to guarantee equal protection of the laws to all people born in the United States, the Fourteenth Amendment was ratified. The Fifteenth Amendment prohibits denying suffrage rights based on race or ethnicity. Self-government and equality under the law gained in strength but were still far from complete.

State governments in the South severely limited civil rights, especially suffrage rights, after Reconstruction ended. Equal treatment under the law still eluded many people. This is a flaw in our imperfect system. Both the federal and state governments can deny an individual their rights. This demonstrates the wisdom of a structure that splits the government's power into not only branches but also levels. Government power must be shared, and the different branches and levels must be able to keep one another in check.

The woman suffrage movement in America began in Seneca Falls, New York, in 1848. Part of a protest convention, the delegates demanded "political, economic and social" equality for women.[4] Inspired by the

Declaration of Independence, a group of more than three hundred people, led by Elizabeth Cady Stanton and Lucretia Mott, attended the event. "All men and women are created equal," wrote the delegates in their Declaration of Sentiments.[5] These women were improving on the revolutionary but incomplete works of Thomas Jefferson.

Shortly after the Seneca Falls Convention, Stanton met Susan B. Anthony, a social reformer. The two became fast friends. Stanton and Anthony were like the Jefferson and Adams of their time. The pen of the movement, Stanton, was the leading thinker. The legs of the movement, Anthony, was the leading organizer. The two suffrage leaders also worked for the abolition of slavery. They devoted their life to equality for both genders and all races.

One year before Febb Ensminger was born, Susan B. Anthony voted illegally in the 1872 election. She was arrested and convicted but refused to pay the fine. In 1890, just a few years before Harry T. Burn was born, the territory of Wyoming joined the Union, becoming the first state to recognize the right of suffrage for women. Wyoming had given women the vote as a territory in 1869. By 1900, the territories of Colorado, Utah and Idaho had joined the Union with enfranchised women. These gains would have been extremely difficult had the Founding Generation given the new federal government exclusive powers to determine voter qualifications. The U.S. Congress did not propose the woman suffrage amendment until many decades later.

The two giant figures of the woman suffrage movement, Anthony and Stanton, lived into the twentieth century. Sadly, both would pass away before full suffrage was achieved nationwide. Carrie Chapman Catt, a protégé of Anthony's, took over the leadership of the National American Woman Suffrage Association (NAWSA) at the start of the new century. History professor Dr. Janann Sherman described supporters of woman suffrage in this period as "better organized and more politically sophisticated."[6] Under Catt's leadership, the movement narrowed its focus on securing the vote, setting aside the more radical goals of full gender equality.

Remarkable progress had been achieved, but it would require a constitutional amendment to guarantee full suffrage in all elections in every state. Alice Paul and the National Woman's Party (NWP) began the drive for an amendment to the federal Constitution. Several states only partially recognized suffrage rights for women.

The United States entered the Great War in April 1917. Catt, although opposed to war, knew that a massive war effort on the part of women would make a persuasive case for ratifying the woman suffrage amendment as recognition of their patriotic efforts. While Burn worked as a railroad telegrapher, NAWSA suspended its activism to focus on the war effort. Millions of women across the nation worked several different jobs, with many filling in for their husbands who were away at war. Victory would not have been possible without these women. Catt's reasoning for a strong support of the war effort paid off. Support for woman suffrage gained in strength.

Alice Paul led the "militant wing" of the woman suffrage movement. In contrast with Catt, she believed that the Great War was no excuse to suspend working toward securing woman suffrage. Paul and the NWP suffragists conducted demonstrations in front of the White House. Its most effective tactics included hunger strikes, protest marches and burning President Woodrow Wilson in effigy. Paul served time in prison during these protests. By 1918, they had finally convinced Wilson to announce his support for the woman suffrage amendment.

After failing to pass the U.S. Congress for several decades, the amendment gained the requisite support at last. Both chambers overwhelmingly voted for the amendment. On June 4, 1919, the Susan B. Anthony Amendment was officially proposed to the states for ratification. Section 1 of the Nineteenth Amendment reads as follows:

> *The right of citizens of the United States to vote shall not be denied or abridged by the United States or by any state on account of sex.*

Eleven state legislatures had ratified the amendment by July 4. Illinois, Michigan and Wisconsin led the way. The North and Midwest followed in the first wave. Texas became the first southern state to ratify. In the fall, many western states joined in ratification, while two southern states, Georgia and Alabama, had rejected it. Rhode Island became the twenty-third state to ratify in January 1920. Three more southern states—Mississippi, South Carolina and Virginia—rejected the amendment shortly afterward. The thirty-fifth state, Washington, ratified the amendment in March.

Ratification then stalled. Florida never acted on the amendment. The governors of Connecticut and Vermont still refused to call their legislatures into special session. Suffragists held out hope that Delaware, North Carolina or Tennessee would be the "Perfect 36th" state. Time was of the essence. Suffragists wanted to cast their ballot in the 1920 U.S. presidential election. Americans still had the efforts of millions of women during the war effort at home on their mind. Catt knew that such sentiments would not last and had to capitalize on them with haste.

"Antis," short for anti-ratificationists, opposed the amendment. The South proved to be the region most unfriendly to the amendment. "The South's paternalistic, hierarchal social structure which placed special value on the southern white woman" helps to explain the region's fierce opposition to woman suffrage, wrote history professor Marjorie Spruill.[7] In the minds of many people, men and women alike, women had no place in the political realm.

Antis in the state of Ohio began to circulate petitions to "recall" the legislature's earlier ratification of the amendment. If successful, this could have knocked the number of suffrage states back to thirty-four and influenced other states to recall. The idea of a state repealing an amendment previously ratified by their state through a recall election originated when many Ohioans wished to end prohibition in their state. Many people deemed this an unconstitutional move. Article V of the U.S. Constitution permits ratification only by state legislatures or conventions. No other method to ratify or recall an amendment is permitted.

The attempt at repeal in Ohio reached the U.S. Supreme Court. On June 2, the day Delaware rejected the amendment, the Supreme Court ruled against the recall efforts in Ohio. "The Federal Constitution, and not the Constitution of the several States, controls the method by which the U.S. Constitution may be amended," said the Court in *Hawke v. Smith*.[8]

Despite the fact that the Tennessee legislature had passed the "limited suffrage" bill, major opposition quickly arose. The Tennessee Constitution had been most recently amended in 1870, adding a provision in Article II, Section 32:

> *No convention or General Assembly of this state shall act upon any amendment of the Constitution of the United States proposed by Congress to the several states; unless such convention or General Assembly shall have been elected after such amendment is submitted.*

The recent Supreme Court decision did not pertain to this provision of the Tennessee Constitution, but the principle made an impact. Tennessee suffragist Catherine Kenny wrote a telegram to President Wilson requesting that he ask Tennessee's Democratic Governor Roberts to call a special session of the legislature. Tennessee's John L. Frierson worked for Wilson's attorney general. Issuing an opinion through the Justice Department, Frierson wrote, "If the people of their state through their Constitution can delay action on an amendment until after an election, there is no reason why they cannot delay it until after two elections or five elections...thus nullifying the article of the Federal Constitution providing for amendment."[9] While the opinions of the executive branch of the federal government have no force of law, their opposition to the provision in the Tennessee Constitution would make defending said provision difficult.

Throughout the summer of 1920, suffrage leaders lobbied Tennessee governor Roberts to call a special session of the legislature. Roberts refrained from taking any action, using the excuse of not violating the Tennessee Constitution. He worried about his reelection and had no guarantee that he would even be renominated by Tennessee Democrats in the primary. A recent tax increase he had signed into law did not help. A significant number of voters in both parties opposed suffrage, and many politicians attempted to please suffragists and antis. Tennessee's primary was scheduled for August 5. Burn later recalled the "terrific pressure" put on the governor to call a special session.[10] In late June, President Wilson sent a telegram to Governor Roberts telling him to keep in mind the recent Supreme Court decision and to call a special session of the legislature. Catherine Kenny's idea had worked. Governor Roberts was closer to caving in to the pressure.

Carrie Chapman Catt traversed the Volunteer State on a speaking tour. She endured the antis' arguments, especially the "oath of office" argument to not violate the state constitution. Catt always rebutted the argument by invoking Article VI, Section 3 of the U.S. Constitution, reminding them it was the supreme law of the land. With the recent decision in *Hawke v. Smith*, she also had the U.S. Supreme Court on her side. Burn later said that Catt and the suffragists were "beautifully organized."[11]

Concerned about keeping his oath, Burn looked to prominent and experienced figures for counsel, including the powerful Knoxville attorney James A. Fowler. A Republican who previously served as assistant U.S. attorney general for three presidents, Fowler assured Burn that he would not violate his oath by taking action on the amendment.[12] A. Mitchell Palmer, the U.S. attorney general, wrote to Burn urging "early, favorable action" on the amendment.[13]

In a July letter to Burn, Governor Roberts's secretary, Major Daughtry, wrote, "Let me know what the political situation is in your community. Although you are a Republican, you are pretty good, and a pretty fair judge of politics."[14]

Replying to Major Daughtry, Burn wrote, "As to the political situation in my home community, I believe the Governor is somewhat stronger than he was sixty days ago. He will receive sixty to seventy-five percent of the votes cast in the primary here." Referring to his own chances for re-nomination by the Republicans, Burn wrote, "I have opposition from within my party for re-nomination but am not fighting it very aggressively."[15]

Sue Shelton White, the only Tennessee suffragist ever imprisoned for her activism, worked with Alice Paul and the NWP to assign workers to collect pledges from legislators. They appointed Anita Pollitzer to collect pledges from East Tennessee legislators. During her travels, Pollitzer encountered several legislators who began to renege on their pledge to ratify by invoking the oath excuse. In late July, she stopped in Athens and met with the chairman of the McMinn County Republican Party. She knew that she had to attempt contact with the highly influential Republican state senator Herschel Candler.

A native of North Carolina, Herschel Candler was forty-one years old. He had served as a colonel in the Tennessee National Guard and was first elected to the General Assembly in 1904. Having once served as mayor, Candler had significant power and influence in McMinn County. But Candler had been defeated by twenty-seven votes in the 1919 election for mayor of Athens, an election in which forty-nine McMinn women voted for the first time thanks to the state's new limited suffrage bill.[16] Burn had become a protégé of Candler's, and the two were neighbors at the Hotel Tulane during legislative sessions.

McMinn's Republican Party leaders told Pollitzer that Candler could not be located. But the county's party chairman called Burn. After a brief conversation, he hung up the phone and told her that Burn would vote for the amendment.[17]

After her visit to Athens, Pollitzer wrote to Alice Paul to inform her of Candler and Burn's stance. She also reported on the importance of the railroad lobby, placing particular emphasis on Clem Jones, an Athens lobbyist for the L&N, and Milton H. Smith, president of the L&N in Louisville.[18] The Louisville and Nashville Railroad had significant power in McMinn County. At the turn of the twentieth century, the L&N Railroad laid down track in Etowah and built a depot along their line between Cincinnati and Atlanta.

Governor Roberts was not the only one unsure of his re-nomination in the August primary. One vote in particular caused a major controversy back home for Burn that almost cost him re-nomination. His support for a "road and dog law" resulted in just as much backlash as his vote for woman suffrage.[19]

The law stipulated that all dogs had to be kept on a leash or behind a fence. The sheep farm lobby pushed for the bill to protect their sheep from dogs running free. They convinced Burn to vote for it. He faced immediate backlash from virtually all other McMinn voters, especially farmers with no sheep. He quickly switched his position on the law and vowed to vote for a repeal bill if reelected. He later joked that he "ran as a reform candidate to succeed himself."[20]

The local paper interviewed Burn before the primary. Discussing the road law, he explained the bill he introduced specifically for McMinn County. The bill allowed the county court to order roadwork to be done. He said the law enabled the county court to adhere to the "wishes of the community."[21] He was assured that the roads in McMinn could not be any worse. He knew that he had to introduce a bill to address this problem. The newspaper reported that he was recognized as a leader in his party despite his youth. "Burn made a good record and deserves a second term."[22]

On August 5, 1920, McMinn County Republican voters re-nominated Burn to run for a second term in the Tennessee House of Representatives. No known records survive that reveal how many votes Burn won or who his opponent was. But in her famous letter, Febb Burn wrote to her son that his majority in the primary was about 140 votes. "Pretty good for a fellow that had made a road and dog law," she wrote.[23]

Tennessee Democratic voters re-nominated Governor Roberts. The governor finally took action and called the legislature into a special session, set to begin on August 9. Seventy-two-year-old Alfred A. Taylor, brother of former governor Robert Love Taylor, won the Republican nomination for governor. Despite not taking a stand on suffrage all summer, Governor Roberts began a strong push to ratify the amendment. He had a powerful ally in the legislature: House Speaker Seth Walker.

Pro-suffrage legislators expected Speaker Walker to be a major ally. Walker had even voted for the limited suffrage bill the previous year. "It would be a crime and a shame if women were not given this right," he had said. Walker would prove to be a turncoat. Burn later recalled, "But something happened. Other influences came into the picture and he became the floor leader of the opposition."[24]

Disappointed in Speaker Walker, the suffragists had less confidence in the House to ratify than the State Senate, where the amendment had strong support. The pledge count in the House was once as high as sixty-two but began to decline as the opening of the session drew closer. One suffragist leader explained that some legislators backed out of their pledges after they were "baited with whiskey, tempted with money and every other device which old hands at illicit politics could conceive or remember."[25]

Burn spoke with his mother before he left for the special session. Febb Burn told him that she wanted him to help give women the vote.[26] When Burn arrived in Nashville, he received phone calls from Republican presidential candidate Warren G. Harding and Democratic presidential candidate James Cox. "They were both supporting ratification," Burn said.[27] Congressman Will Hays, chairman of the Republican National Committee, wired Burn urging him to vote for ratification.[28]

Harding had been trying to placate both suffragists and antis. He never did explicitly endorse the amendment. In a letter to Judge George Tillman in Nashville, Harding expressed his beliefs on the amendment. He had recently been informed of the provision in the Tennessee Constitution prohibiting action on the amendment before the next election. "I quite agree with you that members of the general assembly cannot ignore the state constitution."[29] The calculating Harding very well might have believed in woman suffrage but would not make the leap to endorse. "I hope I make myself reasonably clear....I do not want you to have any doubt about my belief in the desirability of completing the ratification, but I am just as earnest in expressing myself in favor of fidelity to conscience in the performance of a public service," he said.[30]

Burn later recalled lobbyists from all over the country sieging Nashville "to agitate, one way or the other, or persuade."[31] He estimated that 100 to 150 lobbyists had arrived by the start of the session. The McMinn delegation stayed on the fourth floor of the Hotel Tulane. Burn later recalled, "I had the front room. Candler had the next two, and Clem Jones had the next two."[32]

The 61st General Assembly reconvened for the special session on Monday, August 9. A few of the legislators from the 1919 session had been replaced. Jacob Smith—floterial representative for Bradley, Polk and James Counties—had resigned due to an illness. One of his great-great-grandsons is Geoffery Suhmer Smith, my oldest and closest friend. Jacob Simpson, a great-granduncle of my friend Dennis Stewart, had been elected in Smith's place to represent Bradley and Polk Counties. (James County had been abolished in the interim after consolidation with Hamilton County.)

Governor Roberts reminded legislators that the national platform of both political parties included support for suffrage. He also told legislators that he and the state attorney general believed that the recent U.S. Supreme Court decision *Hawke v. Smith* made it appropriate for legislators to act on the amendment regardless of the Tennessee Constitution. Nevertheless, leading antis vowed to challenge ratification in court should it pass.

Shortly after the special session began, Senator Candler met with a caucus of seven prominent Republican leaders, including former governor Ben Hooper and Republican gubernatorial nominee Alfred Taylor. The group could not persuade Candler to support suffrage. He left the meeting still pledging to vote no.[33]

McMinn County was torn apart on the suffrage issue. Judge Samuel Brown recessed the court in McMinn County after the special session began. In his opinion, the legislature would be in violation of the Tennessee Constitution if they acted on the amendment.[34] He permitted use of the courtroom for a mass meeting. The citizens in attendance passed a resolution requesting that Burn vote no. "I already had a telegram from Judge Brown telling me that I couldn't please everybody; just to please myself," Burn later recalled. "I think that the agitation became so strong here [in McMinn County] that some of my political advisors and friends, especially around Athens, decided that there would almost be an uprising if woman suffrage was passed, and they probably got cold feet on the whole thing," he said.[35]

Tennessee suffragist Lizzie Crozier French had spoken to the Browning Circle, a prestigious women's club in McMinn County, in 1914. Her talk inspired some of the women in the club to establish the Athens Equal Suffrage League. The league became an affiliate of the Tennessee Equal Suffrage Association Inc. By 1918, mergers had led to the formation of the Tennessee Woman Suffrage Association. The Athens League reported at the 1918 TWSA state convention that it had conducted several suffrage columns in the newspapers of five counties in East Tennessee.[36] Local efforts such as those conducted by the Athens League "constantly kept the suffrage issue in the public eye" and "brought woman suffrage from being an object of ridicule in public…to the point of inevitability of its passage."[37]

On Wednesday, August 11, a resolution "relative to ascertaining will of the people" on the amendment came before the legislature for a vote. An anti delay tactic, it was hoped it would postpone action on the amendment until after county conventions were held to determine what the people of each county wanted. An attempt to table the resolution passed 50–37. Content to delay action on the amendment, Burn voted no.[38]

Burn quickly grew tired of the situation in Nashville. He eventually checked out of the Hotel Tulane. "I tell you, the only way that you got any rest…was to not let them know where you were," he later recalled. Major Daughtry invited Burn to stay in his home. "He knew I wasn't getting any rest at all," Burn remembered.[39]

On Friday, August 13, the State Senate voted on the resolution to ratify the amendment. "Our only hope of getting Candler is through Roberts persuading him it is legal," said Pollitzer of Candler.[40] But Candler's opposition ran deeper than the amendment's legality. For him, it was a moral issue. Candler stood up in front of his Senate colleagues and delivered what Febb Burn later referred to as the "bitter" speech.

Candler opened his speech, saying, "I am here representing the mothers who are at home rocking the cradle and not representing the low neck and high skirt variety."[41] He then warned that woman suffrage meant that "Negroes" would soon be elected to the legislature. Blasting his Senate colleagues, he said the Republican senators supporting the resolution were "Republicans for revenue only....I know men who a week ago were against this thing are for it today and I know why. Many of them have their names on the state payroll," he claimed.[42] He had absolutely no shame. "I know I am in the minority but I am proud to stand here and tell you that I am going to vote 'no.' I have wired Harding that I could not perjure myself in this fight just to support my party."[43]

Candler then directed his vitriol to NAWSA president Carrie Chapman Catt. He claimed that his colleagues were being dictated to by "an old woman down here at the Hermitage Hotel, whose name is Catt....I think her husband's name is Tom....Mrs. Catt is nothing more than an anarchist. I heard her say in an audience in New York that she would be glad to see the day when Negro men could marry white women without being socially ostracized. This is the kind of woman who is trying to dictate to us. They would drag the womanhood of Tennessee down to the level of the Negro woman."[44] Catt had never said such a thing, but she knew she had to make a public statement opposing interracial marriage. She could not allow the woman suffrage amendment to be associated with racial equality in a southern state.[45]

State Senator Herschel M. Candler. *Tennessee State Library and Archives.*

Onlookers in the gallery hissed Candler for his offensive remarks. It took Speaker Andrew Todd a full minute to restore order. Candler kept going, remarking that many childless women were among those working for ratification. "I don't like the class of women here lobbying for this bill. They are trying to put something over on the good women of Tennessee."[46] "These women know nothing of going down through the valley of the shadow of death," he said. "Motherhood does not appeal to them."[47]

Candler's next remark led to the eventual title of the speech. "If there is anything I despise, it is a man who is under petticoat government."[48] So the speech became known as the "Petticoat" speech. But to Febb Burn, it was bitter enough to be referenced in a letter to her son.

Candler concluded his speech remarking, "When I return home I want to look my people in the face and tell them I did what I believed to be my duty in voting against suffrage. I will vote no when my name is called."[49] According to the *Nashville Tennessean*, "Several speakers who followed Senator Candler characterized his speech as the 'most unfortunate one that has ever been made upon the floor of the Senate.'"[50] Speaker Todd condemned Candler's speech and welcomed the ladies there to do "their worst."[51]

Candler's racist, sexist speech failed to persuade his colleagues to oppose the resolution. "In spite of his efforts," Burn later recalled, "the Senate passed the resolution to ratify by a very strong majority."[52] The vote was 25–4. The *Knoxville Journal and Tribune* wrote that Candler's speech "will long be remembered by the women of Tennessee."[53]

Burn received numerous telegrams throughout the special session. Most came from McMinn County and other Tennessee counties, but some came from out of state. Dozens of telegrams came in from McMinn County, with a majority urging him to support suffrage.

Three of the telegrams from antis in McMinn were as follows:

> *Sentiment strong against ratification on grounds that it is not constitutional several ask me to wire you.*[54]

> *Strong opposition here to suffrage amendment we want it defeated.*[55]

> *Ninety percent of your friends and the people of McMinn County are expecting you to vote against ratification and not to violate your oath of office a vote for it will defeat you in spite of hell.*[56]

Burn later stated that he believed that a majority of his constituents opposed woman suffrage. A few of the telegrams from McMinn County supporting suffrage were as follows:

I want to urge that you use your influence and vote for woman suffrage I believe it will be a great help to you.[57]

Your friends at home expect you to vote for suffrage.[58]

Mr. and Mrs. John W. Bayless of Athens wired Burn on August 16:

Stand firm for the suffrage amendment it must not fail.[59]

National Republican Party leaders wired Burn:

Members of our Party Republican Leaders here consider it extraordinarily important that Republican members of TN legislature do not fail at this crisis.[60]

A common error in the story of Burn's role in the ratification of the Nineteenth Amendment that persists to this day is that he twice voted "no" on the resolution to ratify before his mother convinced him to change his mind with her letter. In reality, he voted twice to "table" the resolution. He did not intend to harm the resolution with his two votes to table. What follows is evidence from Burn's personal papers revealing his mindset before his tie-breaking vote for suffrage. In an interview for the notary public of Davidson County with Mrs. Margaret Ervin Ford, Mrs. John Blount heard (sworn statement) Burn make this statement before August 19:

The majority of my constituency demands that I vote against ratification, nothing can deter me but I prelude this decision by saying, if at the last moment it takes one more vote to turn the tide in favor of suffrage, in honor of my mother, I will change my vote of no against suffrage. I will arise and vote yes in favor of ratification. That is the only promise I can or will give.[61]

Soon after the legislature convened on August 9 I interviewed Mr. Harry T. Burn and he stated he had discussed the question of ratification with his mother before leaving home and that she wanted him to vote for ratification. After coming here he had received many letters and telegrams from his constituency some of which he later showed me and which telegrams claimed the majority of his constituency were against ratification and urged him to vote against it. He further stated he would vote against ratification but he said that he was personally in favor of woman suffrage and that if his vote was needed to turn the tide in favor of suffrage he would cast his vote for ratification....During the interim we had several conversations about ratification and I found him to be of the same mind.[62]

On the weekend before the fateful vote, Febb Burn sat down on the front porch of Hathburn in her "little chair"[63] and scribed a letter to her son Harry. Having run out of ink, she wrote in pencil. She wrote seven pages, but three passages refer to woman suffrage and politics. She wrote on page two, "Hurrah, and vote for suffrage and don't keep them in doubt. I noticed Chandler's [*sic*] speech, it was very bitter."[64] She wrote on page four, "But I do hope you are still in the notions of not making the race this fall. I hope you see enough of politicians to know it is not one of the greatest things to be one. What say ye??"[65] She referenced Candler's speech again on page six just before closing the letter: "Don't forget to be a good boy and help Mrs. 'Thomas Catt' with her '<u>rats</u>.' Is she the one that put rat in ratification? Ha! No more from Mama this time. With lots of love, Mama."[66]

Harry T. Burn Jr. later wrote of his grandmother, "I believe she thought that all adults regardless of station in life or any other characteristics had something to contribute to our political process....She was a very practical person."[67]

Febb Burn then placed the letter in an envelope and gave it to her other son, Jack. She wanted it addressed in ink. On Monday morning, Jack went into town, addressed the letter in ink and dropped it off at the Niota Post Office. "Mother was a very proud person, very much a stickler for etiquette," Burn later told his nephew. "When you see the envelope you will see your father's handwriting on it."[68] The letter then made its way from the foothills of Appalachia over the Cumberland Plateau to Nashville.

Around this time, suffragists from the NWP met with Burn. They had been meeting with legislators to update their polls to see where they stood in the vote count. "I cannot pledge myself, but I will do nothing to hurt you," Burn told them.[69]

Worried about Burn's lack of commitment to suffrage, Anita Pollitzer called the chairman of the McMinn County Republican Party. The next day, Burn received a letter from a prominent Tennessee politician urging him to vote no if he wanted to have a future in politics. Betty Gram of the NWP witnessed this particular letter. Burn asked the suffragists to trust him and requested that they not confront certain Tennessee political leaders who had broken their promise to support ratification and were pressuring him to vote against.[70]

Febb Burn wrote the letter to Harry in pencil but asked her other son, Jack, to address it in ink at the Niota Post Office. *Calvin M. McClung Historical Collection.*

An overlooked figure in the story of the ratification of the Nineteenth Amendment in Tennessee is Newell Sanders. He had briefly served as a U.S. senator for Tennessee, and Burn thought highly of him. He had sent Burn a telegram urging him to vote for the amendment.[71]

U.S. Senator Kenneth McKellar wrote:

> *Senator Sanders had gone back to Chattanooga before the final vote came; and he told me before leaving that if I found that one additional vote would result in favor of ratification, and would telephone him at Chattanooga, he would immediately call Burn, and we would receive that vote. On the final vote, Mr. Riddick told me that with Burn's vote the suffrage amendment would be ratified, and without his vote it would not be ratified. I immediately called Sanders…and he immediately called Burn.…This is exactly what Senator Sanders had to do with the ratification of the suffrage amendment. I am speaking from personal knowledge, not from hearsay.[72]*

The Nashville Post Office stamped Febb Burn's letter at 2:30 a.m. on Tuesday, August 17. That morning, the House of Representatives voted to push the vote on the amendment to the following day. Burn joined the majority and voted aye. The North Carolina legislature rejected the amendment that day.

Febb Burn's letter was sent out for delivery the morning of Wednesday, August 18. Burn did not receive the letter at the Hotel Tulane. Rather, a House page delivered it to him at the state capitol.[73] At 10:00 a.m., the House of Representatives convened with ninety-six members of the chamber in attendance. "The gallery of the Capitol was packed as it has never been since," Burn later recalled. Nothing as big or intense ever happened again in the Tennessee legislature, Burn said in a 1974 interview, "and I've been in state politics for about 55 years."[74]

As he walked onto the House floor, Burn had pinned to his jacket lapel a red rose representing his intent to vote against suffrage. A member of the NWP in the gallery noticed his red rose and said to Burn, "We really trusted you, Mr. Burn, when you said your vote would never hurt us." Burn replied, "I meant that. My vote will never hurt you."[75]

After the introduction of Senate Joint Resolution No. 1, Speaker Walker immediately moved to table it. Thanks to a vote against tabling the amendment from Banks Turner of Gibson County, the vote resulted in a 48–48 deadlock. Burn voted to table the amendment. But tabling an amendment does not kill it; tabling can only delay it. An aye/no vote to concur with the Senate's ratification of the amendment would eventually take place.

Explaining his vote to table, Burn said, "I had decided on the urging of my friends around Athens—the elderly statesman in the McMinn County Republican Party—that maybe we ought to let the matter go over to the regular session in January."[76] Burn remembered that Judge Brown had wired him that "there was enough antagonism to it" at the meeting in the courthouse to "put it off" for a while.[77]

Speaker Walker called for a second vote to table. The result was the same: a 48–48 tie. Turner voted against tabling, and Burn voted to table. The role of Banks Turner in the ratification struggle must not be overlooked. Previously unpledged, Turner's votes against tabling kept the resolution alive and Burn's opportunity to cast the deciding vote possible.

His mother's words "Don't keep them in doubt" stuck in Burn's mind. He had previously stated that he believed in suffrage. He had also previously stated that he wanted to delay action until the following legislative session in January (assuming he was reelected). He had told the suffragists that he would never hurt them and that he would vote for the amendment should it need his help to be ratified. No one knew what he was going to do before he cast his vote. Many suffragists doubted his reliability. But he had finally made a decision. He was about to remove their doubt with his impeding vote.

Believing the amendment would fail on a vote for the resolution itself, Speaker Walker called for a vote on the "merits" of the resolution. This was it. No more tabling or delaying tactics. If the amendment failed to pass on this vote, then it was dead in Tennessee. Suffrage leaders would have had to find another state to lobby to become the "Perfect 36th," a highly unlikely prospect in the imminent future.

The roll call began. Anderson and Bell voted aye. Bond, Boyd, Boyer and Bratton voted no. Next on the list was Harry T. Burn, sitting on the third row to the right of the rostrum.

An aye from Burn would put it over the top and enfranchise millions of American women. A no would kill the amendment, probably indefinitely. He had received several telegrams and letters for and against ratification. His district was split on the issue. His powerful mentor, State Senator Candler, vehemently opposed suffrage. Former U.S. Senator Newell Sanders had urged him to support suffrage. So had both presidential candidates. His mother had asked him to vote for ratification. Burn later said, "I had to make up my mind."[78]

Chapter 5

"AYE"

A ye," Burn said quickly. Some did not even hear his vote. He had answered in such haste that some thought he might have mistakenly voted to ratify. He then removed the red rose from the lapel of his jacket.[1] After the roll call, the total was 49–47. But the final tally turned out different. Speaker Walker then announced that he was changing his vote to aye. The final tally stood at 50–46. A constitutional majority had been achieved. The Tennessee General Assembly had just ratified the Nineteenth Amendment.

It was pandemonium. There is no better word to describe the House chamber after the vote. Like a room full of graduates tossing their caps into the air upon commencement, the suffragists in the gallery tossed their yellow roses into the air. They screamed, sang and danced in joy. The noises of celebration carried all the way down the hill at the Hermitage Hotel. Back in her hotel suite, Carrie Chapman Catt knew that victory had come at last!

Seven decades of hard work on the part of suffragists across the country had led to this moment. In 1848, Elizabeth Cady Stanton dared to state that all men and women are created equal at the Seneca Falls Convention. In 1873, Susan B. Anthony was convicted of voting illegally. In 1889, Lide Smith Meriwether founded the first woman suffrage organization in Tennessee. In 1914, Anne Dallas Dudley worked to bring the NAWSA convention to Nashville. In 1917, Alice Paul and Sue Shelton White suffered in prison simply for exercising their First Amendment rights by protesting in front of the White House. Carrie Chapman Catt spent years organizing hundreds of lobbying campaigns. Because of their efforts, Burn was able to vote to ratify the woman suffrage amendment in 1920.

Burn later recalled his deciding vote:

> *I hadn't anticipated that type of a situation. I had gone over there planning to vote for it....I figured at the time that I probably would be defeated... for reelection if I had voted for ratification. But, I decided that it was the better result—rather than to go ahead and vote against what I had planned to vote for all the time.*[2]

As it turned out, Speaker Walker's vote was needed to technically achieve a majority, even though 49 is a majority in a body of 96. However, three members of the legislature were absent. "Ordinarily a bill, by virtue of the provisions of the Constitution of Tennessee, doesn't become law until it has the majority of the 99 members of the House, and that's 50....I am not saying what would have happened if he had not changed. It was probable that it being a federal question, the U.S. Supreme Court might have said that 49 against 47 would have been a majority of those voting," Burn later explained.[3]

Of the 96 present members of the House of Representatives, Democrats voted for suffrage by a vote of 35–34, and Republicans voted for it by a vote of 15–12. The end result was similar to the start of the session: a near-even split in both parties. Now, American voters, this time with tens of millions of newly enfranchised voters, had to decide which party they wanted to support in the coming general election.

The most apocryphal accounts of Burn's role in the ratification of the Nineteenth Amendment entail what exactly happened in the moments just after he cast the deciding vote. He said in an interview in 1971 that the story of his role in the vote "sometimes gets garbled."[4] If he were alive today and had witnessed the stories printed in newspapers and books over the past few decades, he would consider "garbled" to be an understatement. The most egregious account claims that he was chased out of the capitol by an angry mob. Harry T. Burn Jr. spent several years politely dispelling the myths about his father's vote for woman suffrage.

False reports describing what happened after Burn's deciding vote began the next day. Although there is no mention of a mob chase, the August 19 edition of the *Chattanooga Daily Times* ran a complete crock of a story entitled "Rough Handling of Burn Witnessed by All":

But the youngster probably found his recompense. He was taken in tow by a number of good-looking women and escorted to The Hermitage. There he was rushed upstairs while emotional girls and women hugged him and openly declared him the big hero of the session. Then they gave him a big supper and showered him with attentions that probably have turned the heads of men much more mature in years....He declared his intention of staying with his newly-found love, and that he would vote on every ballot hereafter for suffrage, no matter in what form the test might come.[5]

The *Nashville Tennessean* magazine printed the article "The Women Had the Last Word" in 1948. Although mostly accurate in its description of the aftermath of Burn's deciding vote, it claimed that "sometimes angry anti-suffragist mobs threatened Harry Burn."[6] A 1965 article in the *Nashville Tennessean* noted that Burn "supposedly escaped an irate anti-suffrage crowd by climbing out on a hotel ledge and entering another room."[7] Burn did climb out of a window onto a ledge at the capitol, not at a hotel. Shortly after Burn died, an article in the *Tennessean* claimed he "barely escaped with his life," was chased out of a window and "had to cling to a ledge to make his escape."[8] A 1995 article titled "Suffrage Victory" in the *Knoxville News Sentinel* reported:

Harry got chased by thugs from the railroad and liquor lobby. He hid in the building and the only way out was to climb out a window. He jumped 18 feet to the ground, running down the street for his life because he could hear thugs and hooligans chasing him down the Main Street in Nashville.[9]

In a 2000 article, the *Philadelphia Inquirer* wrote that "outraged opponents chased Burn around the room" and that he climbed out of a window "to escape a mob."[10] As recently as 2012, a *Chattanooga Times Free Press* article wrote, "The angry 'antis' began chasing the young legislator around the gallery until he escaped through a 3rd-floor window to a ledge, which led to the Capitol's attic. There he hid until the furious crowd finally ended their pursuit."[11]

To quote Harry T. Burn Jr., "They are all amusing stories, but they never happened."[12] What follows are two separate testimonies from Harry T. Burn and Harry T. Burn Jr. clarifying exactly what happened after the tie-breaking vote. Harry T. Burn discussed it extensively in a 1968 interview, and Harry T. Burn Jr. discussed it briefly but clearly in a form letter that he sent to those who inquired.

Describing what happened just after the House voted to ratify the amendment, the elder Burn said, "When they were thinking that these men that had gone beyond the boundary of the state for the purpose of breaking a quorum and that they might want to slip back in a body; I don't know exactly their true motive, but the Speaker of the House and his sergeant at arms (several young fellows) were keeping a pretty close watch on those who were in attendance....Those that had been for ratification."[13] Harry T. Burn Jr. wrote:

> *My father was met by the chief sergeant-at-arms who told him that Governor Roberts had heard of threats made against him as a result of his vote and that he, the chief, had been instructed by the governor to see that my father remained on the House floor until state troopers could arrive to provide a bodyguard. Being under "house arrest" infuriated my father... especially as he thought the concerns for his safety were silly.[14]*

The younger Burn thoroughly debunked the apocryphal story about an angry mob chasing his father. The elder Burn continued reminiscing about his escape from the capitol:

> *One of these young fellows came to me and said that he had been told that he would lose his job if he let me get away from the Capitol. I said, "Well, I'll give you my word that I won't leave if you'll just quit hanging around me. (He was staying around close to me, trying to guard me). I won't run off. I have no reason to run off...pay no attention to me and I'll be here." He said, "No," he wasn't going to do it. He was going to stay around close to me....So I said, "Well, if you are going to be obnoxious that way your job is in grave danger. I am not going to have you hanging around me." So five or ten minutes after that I just went into a little room there on the right of the railing of the bar that we then had. We used to have a railing across the back. There was a row of offices on both sides, but this was on the right of the door as you enter the door facing the Speaker—there was a massive door with a thumb lock on it. I was about ten feet from the fellow, and I just stepped inside the door and slammed it and locked it. When I went in there I went over and looked out the window and there was a ledge. I imagine the center of gravity would not let me travel that ledge now as large as I am, but I was much more slender then. Of course, it was a foolhardy thing to have done—maybe. It must have been twelve or fifteen feet along the ledge to the portico. So, I just walked that ledge down to the portico and then went on across and went in what was then the State Library.[15]*

Above: To get away from the sergeant-at-arms, Burn went out this window to the right onto the ledge and over to the west portico. *Photo by Tyler L. Boyd.*

Left: Burn went across the west portico and snuck along this ledge to the northwest corner of the building into the old state library to hide in the attic. *Photo by Tyler L. Boyd.*

Mrs. John Trotwood (Mary) Moore, the state librarian, witnessed Burn hide in the library.[16] Burn described the situation:

> *The library had a spiral stairway...and this cast iron spiral stairway went to the attic and I went...up that stairway. It was in August and it was hot. I stayed up there fifteen or twenty minutes, maybe longer, and it just got so unbearably hot in an attic like that...no one was around. I had just disappeared...no one knew where I was, so far as I knew, so finally I came back down, and I went out the back end toward the back door of the House; it is on the Senate end of the Capitol Building through the big corridor. I went down the steps at the back and came around to the front down around to the Carmack Monument. I thought I was getting along beautifully. When I got around the Monument on the front, the people out on the balcony—somebody just motioned with their hand as a gesture to run...to get away. Two or three people did that and when I started moving on off, two or three of these young sergeants-at-arms were pretty close to me (10 or 15 feet); but I outran them. I ran to the Hermitage Hotel. It must have been six or eight hundred feet. Senator Candler said, "You certainly did a nice sprint there. Your coat tail stuck out so far behind you could have played checkers on it." That was his comment on my race. But, I knew that if I raced through the lobby of the Hermitage Hotel they would know where I was. Well, the minute I got through the door I put on glasses which I didn't wear up until that time and pulled my hat brim down; and I went out on the sidewalk on the other side of the Hermitage and watched them. They were just like a bunch of dogs after a fox or something...and I watched them hunt me. The minute I got inside the Hermitage lobby I just strolled through. Nobody ever noticed me going through. If I had run everybody would have known where I was.[17]*

Burn then went to the law office of a friend. She was a major supporter of woman suffrage. She drove Burn in her Packard to Shelby Park:

> *While we were out at Shelby Park, they were trying to get into my room at the Tulane, and trying to find me all over town, but I was just out driving around enjoying myself. I stayed gone until five or six o'clock. When I got back they had adjourned for the day and they couldn't do anything about it. It was just luck the way I got away.[18]*

Harry T. Burn Jr. later served as a page when his father was a state senator. The elder Burn gave his son a tour of the capitol and told him exactly what happened on August 18, 1920. He told his son that his escape along the ledge was a "damnfool" thing to have done. The younger Burn, speculating on the possible reason for such apocryphal stories about the day of the vote, wrote, "Odd how 'events' take on a life of their own!…One has to remember that the special legislative session of 1920 was in August, which then as now was the slow news season."[19] Oh, how I miss my late cousin's wisdom!

The younger Burn remembered attending a reception at the Hermitage Hotel with his parents in the 1950s. "A very elegantly groomed Nashville matron remarked to my father that her mother had taken her as a child in 1920 to see the historic happenings at the capitol and she had watched the mob chase my father through Capitol Plaza.…My father replied: 'Madam, those were interesting times.'"[20]

Shortly after the legislature acted, Burn called his mother long-distance informing her of his deciding vote to ratify the amendment.[21] It is unknown exactly from where he called her. It is unlikely he called her from the capitol.

According to Burn, Luke Lea received a tip that the publishers of the *Chattanooga Daily Times* and the *Nashville Banner* were planning to print stories on their front pages the next day accusing Burn of bribery. Lea then went to talk to Burn at Major Daughtry's house around midnight. Lea took Burn to the printing offices.[22] Burn made a statement to the newspaper and concluded by saying "No human being has made any propositions to me."[23] Lea's *Nashville Tennessean* put the article with his statement on the front page of the paper that morning.[24] The paper aided him by helping him release a statement about his innocence before he was even accused elsewhere in the press. The *Chattanooga Daily Times* led with the headline "Burn Deserts Cause of Antis Under Pressure" and "Dragged into Anteroom Bodily by Joe Hanover."[25] The front page of the *Nashville Banner* reported that a Davidson County judge charged a grand jury with investigating reports of "improper lobbying."[26]

The *Knoxville Sentinel* also defended Burn in an article on August 19 debunking the charges of bribery. "Charges of attempted bribery…were made in two affidavits published today…two men claimed to have heard Joe Hanover, Major Daughtry, and others tell Burn that they 'would give him anything in the world that he wanted and that it would make him the biggest man in Tennessee, and I understood Hanover to say it would be worth $10,000 to him.'"[27] Burn later recalled:

I always thought that if they had any basis at all for what they were saying it was because I remember that Joe Hanover…after the vote was cast, came up the aisle and put his arm around my shoulder and said "Harry that was the most valuable vote you have ever cast. In a man's lifetime that will be worth more to you than anything you have ever done" or something of that sort.[28]

Joe Hanover strongly supported the amendment. He led the influential Shelby County delegation, which had introduced the resolution to vote on the amendment. Burn later recalled Hanover as a friend and said that he had no improper motive in his statements before the vote.[29]

One report claimed that just before the roll call vote where Burn broke the tie, Burn was "literally dragged out of his seat and taken into the adjoining room occupied by the State Printing Commission."[30] Margaret Bruce, a clerk in the printing commission office, also accused Hanover of bribing Burn and claimed to have reliable witnesses.[31] She also claimed that she had made her stance on suffrage known and felt that her position at the capitol was "in jeopardy" because she refused to wear the yellow rose.[32]

The *Chattanooga Daily Times* printed another false report on August 20, claiming that Luke Lea helped Burn climb out the window of one room and scoot across the ledge to enter through the window into another room. The report claimed that Lea and Burn met with Hanover and others in order to bribe Burn to change his vote.[33] Although it is true that Burn climbed out a window and scooted along the ledge to another room, he did so alone, after the final vote, to escape the sergeant-at-arms and get away from the capitol.

Hanover called for an investigation into the newspapers' accusations once a quorum was present in the legislature. Burn concurred with Hanover. The paper labeled the pro-suffrage legislators "grafting scoundrels." Hanover said these charges were "absolutely false, cowardly and unjustified."[34] "These charges are no more than a clumsy effort to blackmail or embarrass friends and supporters of the rights of women."[35]

Showering Burn with praise, Hanover said, "Were I a painter and had a commission to go out and paint the picture of an honest man I could find no better model for that picture than Harry Burn of McMinn County."[36] Hanover blasted the bribery accusations. "The man who wrote it is a liar and knew he was not writing the truth."[37] Major Daughtry, having heard the conversations between Burn and Hanover, said that Hanover "did not at any time intimate to Mr. Burn that he would be paid any amount of money or that he would be given any other consideration for his vote."[38]

Senator Candler, without hesitation, jumped to Burn's defense. He did not tolerate the bribery accusations being charged against his fellow McMinn Countian. "Harry, I have known you all of your life. I know you voted your convictions....Don't let these dirty scoundrels shake you." Candler later told others, "Terrible pressure has been put on me to try to influence Burn's vote. I refused. Had I actually seen Burn take money I would not believe it, for he isn't that sort of man, and the present charges are too ridiculous for utterance."[39] Emphasizing that Burn could not be tempted with money, Candler said, "He is a director in the textile woolen mills of Niota, vice president of the Niota bank...and is involved in other business interests in Niota."[40]

"He was always a friend," Burn later recalled about Candler. "Even after he made his bitter speech against suffrage and I cast the deciding vote for it, it never affected our close ties."[41] H.M. Willson, a Niota Democrat, said, "I do not agree with Harry Burn politically, but I will swear that nobody paid him to change his vote."[42] The anti-suffragist Judge Brown of McMinn County said the accusations did Burn a "great injustice."[43]

The legislature convened that morning, Thursday, August 19. Burn sent a statement to the clerk's desk and asked for it to be read:

I desire to resent in the name of honesty and justice the veiled intimation and accusation regarding my vote on the suffrage amendment as indicated by certain statements, and it is my sincere belief that those responsible for their existence know there is not a scintilla of truth in them. I know they are false, and I feel that my association amongst you has enabled you to know me well enough that you unanimously join me in resenting the same.

I want to take this opportunity to state that I changed my vote in favor of ratification because:

I believe in full suffrage as a right;
I believe we had a legal and moral right to ratify;
I know that a mother's advice is always safest for her boy to follow, and my mother wanted me to vote for ratification.
I appreciated the fact that an opportunity such as seldom comes to mortal man—to free 17,000,000 women from political slavery—was mine.
I desired that my party, in both State and Nation, might say that it was a Republican from the mountains of East Tennessee, the purest Anglo-Saxon section in the world, who made National Woman's Suffrage possible at this date; not for any personal glory, but for the glory of his party.

H.T. Burn[44]

Burn (*above right*) shakes hands with Anita Pollitzer on the steps of the state capitol. *Burn family.*

He was bribed…his mother asked him to…he followed his conscience—there were many reasons speculated as to why Burn voted to ratify the amendment. Some newspapers speculated another possible motivation. This one involved another woman, but it was not his mother.

Burn was in a relationship with Myra Reagan in 1920. Reagan was from a prominent McMinn County family and lived in the historic General Reagan home (now called Reagan Station), a few miles northeast of Niota. Her grandfather was the former state senator and nineteenth-century railroad pioneer James Hayes Reagan. Both the Burn and Reagan families suffered great losses in the Civil War. Her grandfather Reagan served as a Confederate general and died after his release from a Union prison. Myra Reagan's mother, Elizabeth, was Febb Burn's closest friend. Myra Reagan's niece Ebie Padgett remembered her aunt as a "daredevil."[45] Like Burn, she was outspoken. After earning a master's degree from the University of Tennessee, Reagan taught nutrition to rural families in Georgia. She was well known for her generosity.

Burn and Reagan's relationship eventually ended, but not before the press erroneously reported their engagement and sensationalized her role in influencing his deciding vote. The *Knoxville Sentinel* proclaimed, "Next year

Myra will move up one station and her last name will be Burn. And she is AB-SO-LUTE-LY a suffragist! So you see, there are lots of reasons why Harry Burn voted that 'aye' vote that enfranchised millions of women."[46]

Harry T. Burn Jr. described their relationship as an "understanding" and that their families wished for them to marry more than they wished to marry each other.[47] Padgett recalled her mother telling her about Burn and her Aunt Myra. "Mr. Burn had scheduled a photo session which included her. The problem was he hadn't asked her about it. I'm sure had she known she would have worn her best dress and had her hair carefully styled."[48] She became very upset with Burn.

In an interview, Burn said, "In regard to suffrage my mother caused me to take the view I did. I have always been for suffrage as a matter of moral right, but had planned to vote against, thinking that I would thereby represent a majority of constituents, until I received this letter. I voted for it, casting the deciding vote and I expect to stand by it."[49] Many years later, Burn said, "The letter from mother merely provided further impetus."[50]

The antis did not give up easily. Several anti legislators left the state attempting to prevent a quorum. This would prevent the Speaker of the House and the Speaker of the Senate from signing the resolution. Burn later described their departure from Tennessee as a "hegira."[51] Most of them fled to Decatur, Alabama. "The general gossip at the time was, they hoped to find a time when the entire number that had voted for it, or the majority of those votes, were away from the Capitol and they could come back…and try to rescind, or repeal, the vote," Burn later remembered.[52]

Leading antis immediately moved to declare the vote to ratify the amendment unconstitutional. Threatening a legal challenge, they once again dragged out the "oath violation" argument. The grand jury convened on Friday morning, August 20, and began to hear witnesses.

People from not just Tennessee but all over the country began wiring to Burn in Nashville as soon as they heard the news of his deciding vote to ratify the amendment. Former U.S. senator Newell Sanders wired, "You covered yourself with glory today."[53] Former governor Ben Hooper wired, "History will approve your action."[54] Will H. Hays, chairman of the RNC, also wired his thanks to Burn.[55]

Two of the congratulatory telegrams from McMinn were as follows:

Congratulations thanks from Athens friends.[56]

Stand firm believe women district will elect next term.[57]

Burn holding a sheaf of telegrams.
Tennessee State Library and Archives.

A telegram from John W. Bayless of Athens on August 19 stands out in particular:

> *Voting for suffrage enrolled your name among the immortals. Stand firm.*[58]

The congratulatory telegrams from Niota were as follows:

> *Your friends believe in you stick to your guns and don't let any dirty bunch put it over on you.*[59]

> *All of us in our hometown are delighted you supported woman suffrage do your upmost until all danger is past....*[60]

Everybody wild you put it over stick to it to death.[61]

Congratulations you may proceed with the upmost assurance of our confidence.[62]

Febb Burn sent a telegram to Abby Crawford Milton at the Tennessee League of Women Voters headquarters on August 19:

I congratulate you upon victory that has been won I am proud that my son had a vote in this victory making session I thank you very much for the invitation to see the ratification completed but sincerely regret I cannot be with you.[63]

Three of the telegrams from McMinn condemning Burn were as follows:

The women and men of McMinn County are almost unanimous against suffrage amendment will you not represent them and not Wilson and Roberts and Northern women and lobbyists....[64]

I have canvassed over five hundred of your friends since Sunday and have yet to find a single one of them that want you to vote for the amendment don't disappoint them again change your vote....[65]

At a meeting of the McMinn County bar grand jury...it was unanimously resolved that you be requested to vote to reconsider suffrage amendment and vote against ratification people of county stirred up and request you represent them instead of outsiders.[66]

Burn's Uncle Bill Ensminger wired his nephew from Rockwood:

Have been unable to locate you by phone...accept my congratulations as the good people of TN are behind you. Signed Uncle.[67]

Most out-of-state telegrams to Burn came from angry women from the Midwest and Northeast. A telegram from New Jersey predicted a "deathblow for the Republican Party."[68] Telegrams from Massachusetts warned that ratification "killed the chance [the Republicans] had to win the south"[69] and that woman suffrage would cause "chaos."[70] A woman from Maine wired, "Vote to preserve the womanhood of our country."[71] A telegram from New York City wrote that Burn's vote "may invalidate the coming Presidential election."[72]

Burn received a few telegrams from out of state congratulating him on his deciding vote. Suffragists in Seattle wired, "Congratulations we send most cordial thanks,"[73] and a group of Democrats in New York City wired, "Your support of the Nineteenth Amendment wins you the heartfelt thanks…of women everywhere."[74] A telegram from Ohio thanked Burn for "completing one of the greater reforms in our history,"[75] and a West Virginia woman wired, "Women everywhere are thanking you."[76] "Suffrage is right don't weaken," wrote a Kansas woman.[77]

Burn wired his mother back in Niota on August 20:

> *On their return from Nashville Photographers of New York papers may stop over there. Thought best to let you know if you cannot come to Nashville leaving there tonight. I will try to leave for Niota tomorrow pm. Am tired but ok fight apparently won but settled tomorrow. Harry.*[78]

Febb Burn wired back that she was too ill to travel to Nashville but told him that photographers could call her.[79]

The *Chattanooga Daily Times* ran an article on Saturday August 21 titled, "The True Story of Harry Burn." H.C. Adler of Nashville claimed that Burn spoke with him in the lobby of the Hermitage Hotel after the session had adjourned and everybody had left the capitol. Adler claimed that Burn said, "Well, I don't think you think as much of me now as you did before my vote." Adler said he had heard nothing about alleged bribery at the time but told Burn that his vote did not look "clean" and that it would be "difficult" to explain. Adler said he was "charitable" to Burn because he was just a "boy." Adler claimed that Burn then said, "I have a telegram from my mother, asking me to vote the way I did." Adler asked to see the note and claimed that Burn was called away by friends and quickly left the hotel before showing him the note.[80]

Adler then claimed he set up a time to meet with Burn again later that day in a more secluded area in the hotel. When Burn allegedly met with Adler for the second time, Adler told him he would reserve judgment until after hearing more evidence. "Boy, I said, 'show me the letter or telegram, or both, and I will undertake to defend you both publicly and privately.'" Adler claimed that Burn made no attempt to produce the evidence. Adler claimed he then told Burn that he had neither the telegram nor letter. "Don't, boy, don't add lying to whatever other wrong you may have done." Concluding his story, Adler said, "That boy, is not a bad boy, he shows evidence of good training, but he is weak and was led astray by men stronger and more dominant than he at a most crucial time in his career."[81]

The same morning, Febb Burn received an uninvited guest at Hathburn. Mrs. Ruffin G. (Anne) Pleasant, wife of a former Louisiana governor and a renowned anti-suffragist, was in hysterics after Burn's vote. She made her way down to Niota on Saturday, August 21, arriving between the hours of 7:00 a.m. and 8:00 a.m. EST. Pleasant stayed at Hathburn for three hours attempting to convince Febb to call her son to demand he take back his vote. "If you knew what kind of predicament your son was in in Nashville you will urge him to change his vote…no mother would stand by her son if she knew that he had broken his pledge."[82]

Febb Burn defended her son, insisting that he had broken no pledge. Pleasant showed her a list of names, asking, "Do you know his signature?" Febb replied, "I don't know anything about all the legal part of this matter, but I do know that my son has voted his honest conviction and I know he believes in me and in my rights as his mother and as a woman."[83] Pleasant hoped to get Febb to call her son in time to vote with the antis before the legislature convened later that morning. "My quick answers made her cry," Febb said.[84]

Febb Burn showed remarkable patience to her rude guest, but after nearly four hours, she asked her to leave. "The lady said that [Pleasant] was her name, but she did not act like the meaning of the word, for she was not in a pleasant mood when she was here," Febb remarked. Before leaving, Pleasant said she was going all around Niota to stir up sentiment against Burn. "She went to Athens from Niota," Febb said.[85] She proceeded to wire her son:

A woman was here today who claims to be the wife of the Governor of Louisiana and secured an interview with me. She tried by every means to get me to refute and say that the letter to my son was false. This letter is authentic and was written by me. You can refute any statement that any party claims to have secured from me. I stand squarely behind suffrage and requested my son to stick with suffrage until the end. This woman was very insulting to me in my home and I had a hard time to get her out. Mrs. J.L. Burn.[86]

The legislature convened at 10:00 a.m. with all of the pro-suffrage legislators present. T.A. Dodson of Sullivan County, who nearly went home on a special train to see his infant (who was thought to be dying), stayed to

Burn (*center*) poses for a photo with Harriet Taylor Upton and the Republican legislators who voted for suffrage. *Burn family.*

ensure that enough pro-suffrage legislators could defeat the reconsideration motion. Only nine anti-suffrage legislators were present, with the remaining thirty-eight still in Alabama attempting to prevent a quorum.

Speaker Walker did not have enough antis in attendance to aid him in his procedural ploy. His pending motion to reconsider expired at noon. He ordered the sergeant-at-arms to make a list of those absent, find them and force them to come to the capitol. R.K. Riddick of Shelby County made the motion to reconsider the amendment. Walker claimed that the motion was "out of order" due to the lack of a quorum (two-thirds of the House membership), but he was powerless to stop them. The resolution to reconsider failed with 0 ayes, 49 noes and 9 present and not voting.[87]

Later that afternoon, back in Athens, Mrs. Pleasant spoke at the courthouse, claiming that the building could barely hold the massive crowds. She baselessly claimed that "sentiment is fully ninety percent against suffrage" in every town in the county and that many people were signing the petition regardless of political affiliation.[88] B.J. Hornsby, a prominent McMinn County Republican, signed the petition. Pleasant believed that suffrage should have been achieved through state action and not a federal amendment. "Many women who had formerly declared for suffrage said they hadn't understood the difference between federal and state action, and that they were now opposed to ratification," she said.[89] Pleasant sent the petition to Speaker Walker requesting that he read it on the floor of the House.

Later that day, Burn rode back home to Niota. He took the same special train that had been chartered for T.A. Dodson to get home and see his sick child.[90] Fortunately, his child recovered.

Chapter 6

REELECTION CAMPAIGN AND SECOND TERM

B urn later remembered receiving a "satisfactory" reception upon his first
visit back home after casting the deciding vote:[1]

> *If there was any personal antipathy or bitterness in Niota I never knew
> it. Bill Snyder, my mother's double first cousin…was the blacksmith and
> was my guard when I was campaigning for my second term. He carried
> his horseshoe hammer in his hip pocket and stood behind me…when I was
> making speeches. He always said that if anybody tries to bother me he
> was going to reach over my shoulder and hit them in the forehead with the
> hammer. I never did have anybody try to attack me physically after I came
> back. But I especially never was concerned about Niota.*[2]

The late Effie Lones was ten years old when Burn returned home that day.
"I went because everybody in Niota went. He made a speech, but it didn't
mean anything to me. I was ten," Lones later recalled.[3] She went on to work
as a teacher. Many years later, she spoke with Burn in Niota. "I hear you are
going to run for mayor," he told her. She replied that she had never thought
of such a thing but remarked that she would be a good one.[4] The idea stuck
in her mind.

Governor Roberts signed the resolution on Tuesday, August 24. Two days
later, it arrived in Washington, D.C., where U.S. Secretary of State Bainbridge
Colby made his proclamation. The Susan B. Anthony Amendment—the
Nineteenth Amendment—officially became part of the U.S. Constitution.

Antis like Candler never learned how much their behavior hurt their own cause. A newspaper column defending Burn from other newspapers that misrepresented his statement to the legislature on August 19 stands out in particular. The column made an astute observation about the antis' behavior:

> *Perhaps it comes harder to the morning paper because Burn's mother wrote him the letter she did after reading the bitter speeches that were being made against suffrage. The Antis were hoisted on their own petard. They stirred the woman's heart in that mother and she wrote at once to her son to ask him to help Mrs. Catt put the "rat" into ratification. The incident is one of the most soul stirring in American history.*[5]

Antis continued spreading false reports that a strong majority of McMinn Countians opposed suffrage. The *Tri-Weekly Post* criticized reports printed in the *Chattanooga Daily Times* that Burn's home county "is seething with rage at the ratification of the Nineteenth Amendment....In its usual fashion and fanaticism the Times indulges in a lengthy defense of the runaway red rose members....That is what a lean country newspaper published in the county where the Times assures us sentiment is so strong against suffrage thinks about ratification and the law-breaking lawmakers now willing away their time in Decatur."[6]

"I am happy simply because I followed my conscience. It kept telling me 'women are people, and this is a government By the people'....So I made the choice. I preferred to disappoint some of my constituents than be false to what I know is right," Burn told the *Knoxville Sentinel*.[7] He said that although his vote for suffrage may doom him to "political oblivion," he was happy nevertheless.[8] Burn later explained, "On that roll call, confronted with the fact that I was going to go on record for time and eternity on the merits of the question, I had to vote for ratification."[9]

The *Knoxville Sentinel* celebrated ratification:

> *There is a young man from Niota,*
> *who for precedent cares no iota,*
> *he sprung a surprise,*
> *when he flopped to the "ayes,"*
> *and enraptured the feminine voter![10]*

A West Tennessee lawyer wrote a poem to Burn:

> *A baby salon from Niota,*
> *became quite a somersault voter,*
> *he found himself able,*
> *to vote twice to table,*
> *and then he turned suffrage promoter.*[11]

The *Boston Herald* celebrated ratification:

> *Harry T. Burn of McMinn,*
> *The man who said, "Women shall win!"*
> *His "aye" told the story;*
> *Fate set him in glory—*
> *Harry T. Burn of McMinn!*[12]

A letter written by "A Democrat" in the *Semi-Weekly Post* of Athens praised Burn:

> *He has been a good boy from his birth. James Burn, his father, was as good*
> *a man as ever lived at Niota, and his mother is an excellent woman. Since*
> *his father's death, Harry has been a faithful and obedient son to his mother.*
> *He would not have sold out under any condition. He doesn't need the money*
> *that bad. When he studied the matter over he had voted according to the*
> *dictates of his conscience....I say three cheers for Harry Burn! Instead of*
> *running him for representative, I am for running him for governor.*[13]

Correspondence of all sorts continued stuffing Burn's mailbox from people who realized the enormous impact that his vote for suffrage would have. They knew that the story of his vote would become a story of legendary proportions. Despite the county being split on suffrage, many of his friends expressed confidence in his chances for reelection.

D.C. Watts, of Niota, wrote:

> *I have been at several different places since I saw you last and think business*
> *is picking up some in your favor for November. The largest complaint is the*
> *dog and road question and I think the dog question is going to blow over...*
> *bear in mind you can't please everyone and do things as you think best...we*
> *are with you just the same.*[14]

Percy Warner and John Graham, both of Chattanooga, wrote:

> *In my opinion, you have had the greatest opportunity that falls to man to have, and your vote shows that you have taken advantage of this most extraordinary opportunity…have no fear as to the outcome. The greatest movement ever known to mankind or to womankind is behind your vote, and it makes no difference what they say…time will fully vindicate your action. In so far as McMinn County is concerned…I know that the large majority…of the county will stand by you through thick and thin. In so far as the charges they are trying to trump up against you, do not let them bother you in the least…history will tell in the years to come that Harry Burn of McMinn County, Tennessee was the liberator of thirty million women.*[15]

Niota Postmaster Fannie M. Burnette wrote:

> *Hurrah for HT Burn and equal suffrage!….Niota is surely, justly proud of you and what you have done for the state and even the nation at large.…I for one am now craving the privilege of voting for you for legislator, congressman or whatever you aspire to be.*[16]

Wade H. Cord, of Charleston, Tennessee, wrote:

> *Of course we don't know what happened when the ladies locked you up in the room, but they are talking it around here that they kissed and hugged it in you and you changed your vote…you are the greatest woman's man in the country today.*[17]

S.O. Welch, McMinn County delinquent poll tax collector, wrote:

> *I note with much pride your vote for suffrage and in casting your vote as you did have doubtless done more for man and woman kind than it will ever be possible for a Representative from the good County of McMinn to do again.*[18]

George Schultheiss, of Philadelphia, Pennsylvania, wrote:

> *Permit me, a Democrat, to congratulate you.…I always thought that as women, as well as men, had to live accordingly to laws, that women, as much as men, had the right to a voice and vote in government affairs.…*

Keep up the good work and when you become governor, I shall congratulate you again.[19]

S.O. Welch sent another letter:

The Antis will try to persuade you to not be a candidate in November, but do not pay any attention to them, you will not be defeated but I would prefer honorable defeat to disgraceful withdrawal, besides sentiment is already turning in your favor...you will be elected beyond a shadow of a doubt.[20]

J.R. Yates, of Cincinnati, wrote:

Having known your father James Burn by having dealings with him more than twenty years ago makes one believe that like him you acted honestly and true to the dictates of your conscience and in the interests of rights and justice.[21]

Anita Pollitzer wrote:

We know what some of you people who stood by us are going through.... With kindest regards to your mother, whom I wish I had met.[22]

Burn's Aunt Mattie Sykes also wrote her nephew a letter of gratitude. She told him his Uncle Bill was proud of him even though he was opposed to woman suffrage.[23] Sallie Ensminger, Burn's septuagenarian widowed grandmother, lived with her daughter Mattie and son-in-law.

Febb Burn invited her brother, Bill, over for a visit a few days after the suffrage vote. He said that when he arrived at Hathburn, it "was alive with visitors from all sections of the country." He recalled "several newspaper men who went to write a complete history" of his nephew. Some visitors even carried away some baby clothes that Burn had once worn! Others cut away pieces from the house, the trees and fences and carried them away as souvenirs.[24]

In addition to swarms of visitors, Febb Burn received numerous phone calls congratulating her for taking a stand in the letter to her son. Reporters wanted to interview the mother who saved suffrage. She granted numerous interviews to newspapers across the country. Some of them came to interview her in person. Nellie Kenyon described Febb: "[She] has a kind, sweet disposition."[25] One paper described Febb's everyday life at Hathburn:

Life is no burden to her; it is a real joy for her to work for her children. Industry has become a habit with her, and she likes it. From morning until night she is on the go milking the cows, churning the milk, cooking, cleaning the house, or making or mending clothes for the family, teaching the children, or reading to them. The Burn home is full of love and joy. They are typical old time American people.[26]

"I was born on a farm and will die on one if I have my way," Febb Burn said. "My life has been a delightful one...the loss of my little girl and my husband gave me great grief, but I am thankful I have two fine boys and a dear girl."[27] The *Nashville Tennessean* described her as a "quiet country woman." Febb told the paper, "I am glad that he loved me enough to say afterward that my letter had so much influence on him....To be honest and true is Harry's motto, and I am sure he was not paid to vote for the suffrage amendment, as he has been charged by the antis. He would have gone back on the kind of blood that was born in him to have done such a thing."[28]

Febb Burn continued, "I did not know how Harry was going to vote. I had been watching the newspapers closely, hoping and praying that he would vote aye. I thought at the time that Harry would vote for it, though he never told me definitely just how he intended to vote."[29] She added, "I suppose there was never a mother who didn't think her children the handsomest and smartest in the world. Of course I am proud of Harry."[30] She cared not what others thought of her. "Some of my neighbors, I understand, have said they are sorry for me....I don't need any sympathy. I am proud of my son. He has covered himself with glory."[31] She said his stand on suffrage "will go down in history as the proper one." One paper reported, "She has no fear of mass meetings, protests, or social or business ostracism."[32]

Discussing suffrage, Febb Burn remarked, "Suffrage has interested me for years. The names of the leaders are familiar to me. I like the militants as well as the others."[33] She added, "I believe it is just a matter of rights. I have taken very little interest in the campaign...but I did know that the contest was on in the Tennessee legislature....I never worked for it or belonged to an organization that did."[34] She also noted, "I think suffrage will purify politics and I am for progress. I have hired hands on my farm...who pay no taxes, yet they are permitted to vote. But I do pay taxes and have not had any hand in my country's affairs."[35]

Reporters from all over the country called to interview Febb Burn, the mother who saved suffrage. *Burn family.*

Febb Burn said that she wrote the letter after reading "the bitter speeches of Senator Candler and others against suffrage."[36] She discussed the letter:

> *They say it was my letter which made him change his vote. It probably influenced him, but I want everyone to know that Harry is the kind of boy who thinks and acts for himself. Perhaps I shouldn't have used slang in my letter. But it struck me that Mrs. Catt and the other suffragists had struggled so long to get their "Rat" into ratification that someone ought to lend a hand when they need it most. I'm proud to say my boys and I are pals. And I felt that Harry would see me smiling at him when he read that—and know his mother was with him and in what we both knew was right. If I hadn't felt sure he was at heart in favor of suffrage I should not have urged him to say the "aye."…Politics is such a horrid mess! Just see how Harry has been attacked and hounded ever since he cast his vote for ratification. Such injustice will be rarer when all women vote.…Women are not perfect, but they are more fearless than men.… They get results quicker.*[37]

"I'm for suffrage and I expect to go to the polls and vote for the Republican ticket," Febb Burn remarked.[38] She discussed her late husband, Jim Burn, and the effect his passing had. "He [Harry] has always told me since his father died four years ago that he wanted to do something to bring his mother into national prominence. He told me just before…the legislature was called to act on suffrage that he hoped to realize his dreams for me before the end.…He loves good books. Especially he is fond of the biographies of the big men. I believe they are where he got his ideas of wanting to make me nationally known."[39]

Febb Burn discussed her reading habits. "In going over the papers I try to see it all. I was very much interested in the fight in the Senate over the peace treaty. I read all that President Wilson said about it. I felt for him.…Shakespeare is a favorite. Otho and I almost committed 'Macbeth' to memory last year."[40] Febb said she "did not spare the switch" in teaching her children their lessons. "The classics please me, those that have touches of humor are the best. I like 'Much Ado About Nothing' and 'Merry Wives of Windsor.'"[41]

Febb Burn received high honors for her role in saving suffrage. The *Toledo Blade* reported that national suffrage leaders proposed a memorial in honor of Mrs. J.L. Burn. "They say that she, by a stroke of her pen, set the women of the nation free and they feel that fitting honors should be paid her."[42]

Carrie Chapman Catt wrote to her and said she could always be proud of her son.[43] Febb received several letters of congratulations, including one from the Illinois Equal Suffrage Association:

> *You must be proud to have a boy who, although he has gone out into the world, is still ready to take advice from his mother, and in turn we must realize that your son must be proud of you as a mother because you have reared him in such a way that he can respect and appreciate your advice. Please convey to him our thanks for the service he has rendered the women of the United States.*[44]

News of Febb Burn's letter drove some antis out of their minds. They wrote disapprovingly of the pride that Burn took in the story about Febb's letter. "A man old enough to be a member of the Tennessee legislature who, having made up his mind on an important issue, shifts to the other side as a result of having received a letter, shouldn't advertise the fact."[45]

An irate anti wrote to Febb Burn:

> *Dear Madam: If you can find any comfort in knowing your young son betrayed the confidence of his neighbors and Constitution or in knowing he violates his oath, or to be branded in the eyes of the world as a grafter, or in selling his vote, then you are a strange kind of mother. He has ruined himself and disgraced his family for life.*[46]

On August 30, one of the last days of the special session, the anti-suffrage legislators returned from Alabama. The events of that day could possibly explain, in part, how the apocryphal mob chase story came to be. After the legislature adjourned at 3:00 p.m. and took a roll call, Speaker Walker directed the sergeant-at-arms to go arrest any absent legislators and bring them in.[47] They were trying to make a quorum and vote to reconsider the resolution (even though the U.S. secretary of state had already certified the amendment). Multiple newspapers reported that a sergeant-at-arms found Burn and brought him in. Burn allegedly escaped again, out the window, after which two sergeants-at-arms chased him down the street. They never found him, and Speaker Walker failed to make a quorum.[48]

The special session adjourned sine die on Saturday, September 4. Burn went full steam ahead into his reelection campaign. Very little newspaper records survive from McMinn County during this period, but the *Chattanooga*

Daily Times and the *Chattanooga News* covered the campaign more closely than any major newspapers in Tennessee.

An anonymous McMinn County woman penned a letter to the *Chattanooga Daily Times*. "The women of McMinn County are not over proud of the matter of their recent so-called emancipation." She condemned the "disorderly and unseemingly lobbying and scrambling" at the capitol that led to ratification. She claimed that "hisses and screams" interrupted the voices of the anti-ratificationists. She asserted that "a great bulk of mothers and wives of the county were busy at home performing those necessary and sacred duties peculiar to their positions," while the ratificationists were "a relatively small number of neither mothers nor wives" and were "arrogating to themselves the prerogative of being representatives of all women of Tennessee." She regurgitated the argument that those voting for the amendment had violated their oath to the state constitution by taking action before the 1921 session. She mocked the poems that praised Burn. "He's the darling of the ladies. And his oath can go to hades." She claimed that, on the whole, the women of McMinn County were not "clamoring" for ratification. She blasted the outsider lobbyists, saying they hated the South and that the matter had been decided locally. She claimed that 80 percent of the county was opposed to the amendment. She claimed Burn was "pale and trembling" at the time of his vote. She ended the letter expressing her fears of equality for "Negro women" and that the outsiders were forcing their ways on an unwilling people.[49] The letter demonstrates the lasting effect that the Civil War had on McMinn County as far as a half century after the war's end. McMinn County was still torn apart. But whether or not it was divided enough to prevent Burn's reelection was still too early to ascertain.

Burn attended a banquet in Knoxville for suffrage leaders on September 21. "The New Citizenship" was the keynote of the talks that evening. Tennessee suffragist Lizzie Crozier French also attended. Burn told her that it had been a great privilege for him to finally support suffrage and that he emerged from the fight with a "clear conscience."[50] Burn addressed the banquet:

> It is with much pleasure that I salute those who have acquired "The New Citizenship" as fellow citizens in the truest sense!...The opportunity given women of America, of Tennessee, of Knoxville, and to the individual, to assist in placing higher standards in the political world, and to institute needed reforms, will not be neglected. The interest being manifested proves this assertion to be true....Do not understand me to predict great reforms

as sweeping the country in a short period, but that with the ballot as a weapon the correcting measures will gradually be applied to the entire citizenship, men and women.... The credit for the great reform that produces the opportunity for the women to share her portion in the struggles that will be fought by means of the ballot, belongs to the women themselves, and it is to them that the suffrage service medal should be given....I am pleased that fate gave me an opportunity to have a small part in making Tennessee "The Perfect 36th"...right ultimately triumphs and if Tennessee had not acted then some other state would have done so.[51]

Burn told the audience that the majority of the men in the legislature made Tennessee "a Guiding Star to the women seeking political freedom." He also told the audience to expect further rights for women to quickly follow.[52] He would soon author a successful bill protecting further rights for mothers.

Abby Crawford Milton attended a ceremony at the McMinn County Courthouse on September 27. She presented Febb Burn with a yellow satin badge from the Tennessee League of Women Voters (LWV) for her "distinguished service" during the ratification of the Nineteenth Amendment.[53] "The women of the nation owe Burn a debt, and it is up to the women of McMinn County to pay it," said the Tennessee LWV.[54] The *Chattanooga News*, a pro-suffrage newspaper operated by Mrs. Milton's husband, George, always covered Burn favorably.

J.H. Jones, Burn's opponent in the general election, ran as an independent. A former Democrat, he campaigned with Governor Roberts in Etowah, a Democratic stronghold in McMinn. Several voters could not tell if Jones was targeting Republicans or Democrats during his campaign against Burn.[55]

An ad for Jones ran in the local newspaper implying that lobbyists would not influence him. In a thinly veiled shot at Burn, the ad proclaimed that Jones would not be liable to "tears and hysterics, fits of paleness and trembling, with after the excuse of 'Oh I was so young that I was overcome by the great pressure on me.'" Taking advantage of the split throughout the district on the issue of woman suffrage, the ad claimed, "We think Mr. Jones would first ascertain what the people of the county wanted, and how they stood on the question, and then vote that way." The ad concluded in praise of Jones as not being "the candidate of any ring or clique," having "no blemish on his name" and that he was "non-partisan."[56]

State Senator Candler supported Burn and campaigned for him. Burn is "as honest as the day is long," Candler said defending his legislative protégé.[57] Candler was also seeking reelection.

Women in McMinn County campaigned heavily for Burn. Once the three-day registration period concluded, more than nine hundred women had registered to vote in Athens, Etowah, Niota and Englewood by mid-October.[58] Registration was not required for voters in rural precincts. After reports surfaced claiming that McMinn women had no interest in voting, many supporters from both political parties working to reelect Burn quickly refuted these charges. "Women of both parties are his enthusiastic supporters," the *Chattanooga News* reported.[59]

Not all McMinn County women supported Burn for reelection, in part due to the heavy influence of anti-Burn propaganda. One report noted, "They seemed to feel that the charge that he had been paid $10,000 for his vote was true. Some women were…against him on the ground that he had not gone to war."[60] Harry T. Burn Jr. later wrote, "He thought at the time that his vote had ended any hope of a political career."[61] Some Republican politicians in McMinn prevented their women's organization from endorsing him.[62]

Mary Moody, chairman of the McMinn County LWV, actively campaigned for Burn. The local Democratic Party asked Moody to resign from her leadership position because of her support for him.[63] Mrs. Stubbs, the wife of a dean at Tennessee Wesleyan College and a Democratic activist, led a bipartisan group that Burn credited with saving his seat and his political career. According to the *Chattanooga News*, there was "an attitude throughout the campaign by male Democratic leaders to discourage the women of their party from doing anything in the campaign."[64] It was clear that if Burn were to be reelected, it would be through the efforts of the citizens of his community and not the local party organizations and leaders.

A few weeks before the election, the *Chattanooga Daily Times* printed another story about the affidavits claiming that Burn accepted bribes in exchange for changing his vote. He later said that it published the story "thinking it would hurt me in my run for a second term."[65] One report said that the *Chattanooga Daily Times* "had poisoned the people's minds… and tried to keep him from reelection."[66]

On October 20, Burn heard U.S. Senator and Republican presidential nominee Warren G. Harding speak in Chattanooga. The Hardings extended Burn their heartfelt thanks for his deciding vote to ratify the Nineteenth Amendment. Florence Harding said, "Is this Harry T. Burn?…I have heard so much of you, and I want to congratulate you for your stand on ratification…and on the fight you made for your convictions."[67] Burn told the future president and first lady of the United States how the antis had been running a "campaign of misrepresentation and abuse" against him.[68]

Despite the opposition's efforts, Burn remained confident in his belief that he would be reelected. "Although there is a bitter fight against me, I don't think it will make much headway. The women are with me, and I expect to be elected."[69] The *Chattanooga News* reported that the "rings" of both parties opposed his campaign.[70]

Desperate to defeat Burn, some of his opponents attacked him for his lack of service overseas in the Great War. An Athens man wrote a letter to the *Chattanooga Daily Times*:

> *Why not take up Mr. Burn's war record? Although I cannot speak with absolute authority, I think that he was exempt from service because he was a telegraph operator at the City of Niota. When the opportunity came, however, for making the race for the House of Representatives, this necessity for his services did not prevent his running. Why did the people of McMinn County vote for this man while their sons were away in France—many of them more needed at home than he—doing their bit to uphold the honor of their country?...Are they going to cast their votes for him, thus setting the seal of approval on his past action—an insult...to those of us who went over and did our best in defense of the flag and for the peace of the world?*[71]

The *Knoxville Sentinel*, after an interview with Febb Burn, reported that Burn had "volunteered twice during the war, but was kept home by his state for his skills at the keyboard."[72] But the *Chattanooga Daily Times* criticized McMinn voters for not electing a veteran to represent them in Nashville. "And by that show their appreciation of merit rather than by their present action seem to prefer honoring recalcitrance and slackery." It claimed that Burn violated his oath by voting for the amendment. "The women of McMinn who, we have been told, are going to do their bit in 'purifying politics' to defeat him. Politics cannot be purified by advancing and honoring those who pollute it." The paper claimed that McMinn voters would vote Burn out of office: "Mr. Burn may be ever so agreeable a young man; he may be ever so genial and companionable, but the people of McMinn County cannot afford by solemn vote to approve the nullification of the constitution....The ladies who are going to advocate his cause may be willing to overlook his politics because he is a 'suffragist,' but the people of McMinn County will hardly regard the suffrage as being paramount to the majesty of the constitution."[73]

One day before the general election, the *Chattanooga Daily Times* published one last hit piece on Burn. The subtitle of the headline read, "Boys Who Did Bit in Great War Want to Know Why Harry Stayed at Home": "Mr. Burn has been working day and night to hold his party vote and succeed himself in the lower house. He has left no stone unturned to overcome the great wave of criticism which followed his disregard of the petitions and resolutions, letters and telegrams that poured in on him from his home people during the suffrage fight in Nashville....His friends of both sexes have been working overtime in his interest." The piece relished in Burn's reelection struggles: "An amusing feature of this race is that generally a Republican candidate for representative in this county has such a walkover that it is not necessary to make a canvass." The piece emphasized how Dr. Gus Shipley, chairman of the McMinn County exemption board during the war, gave a speech critical of Burn in Etowah. Dr. Shipley, a "strong Republican," dismissed his excuses for not going to war. The doctor had seen both of his sons serve in France. The piece reported that Burn responded to these criticisms by pointing out that had the voters had a problem with him they would never have elected him to the legislature in fall 1918, right as the war concluded. "There are a great many ladies who had sons and brothers in the war who have been heard to say that they would not vote for Burn in spite of the fact that he cast the deciding vote on the suffrage question."[74]

The *Chattanooga Daily Times*' relentless attacks on Burn's lack of service in the Great War extended beyond its opposition to woman suffrage. The publisher had been chairman of the Draft Exemption Board for Tennessee. But as one report pointed out, the chairman did not object to Burn's exemption when the war was on, but after Burn's vote for suffrage, he blasted him as a "slacker."[75]

The *Chattanooga News* published a defense of Burn the day before the election. Criticizing the "campaign of defamation" against him by the "malignant foes of suffrage," the paper also pointed out that he had been duly elected in 1918 despite his not having served overseas in the war:

> *Mr. Burn was a farmer; the nation needed food; he was a skillful telegraph operator; railroads were crying for men to keep their wires open....It is indeed surprising that it takes a vote on suffrage to bring forth Mr. Adler's opposition to Mr. Burn's exemption from war service.*[76]

The race turned out to be tighter than Burn had anticipated. The *Chattanooga News* reported on November 3, 1920, that at first "it was thought he had lost his race."[77] Early reports showed him trailing in the vote tally. He was then reported to be leading by fewer than 100 votes.[78] After the late returns came in, he had defeated Jones by 285 votes.[79] Burn would return

Febb Burn's voter registration card. *Calvin M. McClung Historical Collection.*

to Nashville for a second term in the House—2,387 McMinn Countians turned out to vote for him.[80] Turnout was high, especially for the time.

Governor Albert Roberts lost in his bid for reelection to Republican Alfred Taylor. As mentioned previously, Alfred Taylor was the brother of the late governor Robert Love Taylor. Bob Taylor defeated his brother Alf in the 1886 gubernatorial contest, referred to as "The War of the Roses" (a name that is sometimes used to refer to the fight to ratify the Nineteenth Amendment in Nashville). State Senator Candler, despite his bitter opposition to suffrage, also won reelection. Candler would go on to serve in the state legislature for many more terms and remained involved in McMinn politics until his death.

Republicans won sixty-three seats in the U.S. House of Representatives and ten seats in the U.S. Senate, dominating every region of the country except for the South. Warren G. Harding was elected president of the United States. Voter turnout across the country increased by 8 million, although only 32 percent of eligible women turned out to vote, less than half of that of men. Not all women wanted to vote right away, but voter disenfranchisement prevented many women from voting, especially black women. Universal suffrage was still far from complete.

Reporting on Burn's victory, *The Athenian* noted, "We are also particularly well-pleased at the re-election of Harry T. Burn as a member of the legislature for McMinn County. He is a young man of ability, made a good representative in the last session...we feel like shouting 'Hurrah for Burn!'"[81] The *Hamilton County Herald* also celebrated Burn's reelection:

"Poor Harry Burn" as he was designated by the Chattanooga Times following his vote on the suffrage amendment, has been reelected to the legislature by the voters in McMinn County. This is in direct opposition to the instructions given out by the "Mourning Times" to the voters of McMinn County. The result means the repudiation of the denouncement of Mr. Burn made through the news and editorial columns in the Times. It means that his action of the legislature when he voted for the ratification of the Nineteenth Amendment, has been approved by the people who elected him to office![82]

Former U.S. senator Newell Sanders wired Burn his congratulations.[83] Burn also exchanged letters of congratulations with Governor-elect Alfred Taylor.[84] The RNC wrote to Burn:

I am gratified to read in the news dispatches today that the discreditable campaign waged against you by the Democrats failed to defeat you. In my speeches I have often referred to your courageous and splendid stand, which resulted in Tennessee ratifying the suffrage amendment, and to the support given to you in your stand by your noble mother. I have never understood the reasoning of men who felt themselves mentally stronger and more fit than their mothers; not to excuse those who would laud the Revolutionary slogan that "taxation without representation is tyranny" yet refuse to apply the same principle to women.[85]

The *Chattanooga News* wrote to Burn:

I am most pleased that you have been returned by a considerable majority. It is very fine proof of the confidence your constituents have in you. If the News contributed anything to your victory I am very glad.[86]

Burn began his second term in the House when the 62nd General Assembly convened on Monday, January 3, 1921. Now one of the most famous members of the legislature, he used his influence to introduce even more bills than in his first term. He introduced seventeen bills, House Bills Nos. 9 through 25.[87] Most of these bills aimed at repealing or amending existing laws. One of the bills recognized and protected rights for women previously denied for decades.

Burn followed through on his promise to introduce a bill to repeal the dog law passed during the 1919 session. His repeal bill, House Bill No. 13, easily passed the House of Representatives on January 20.[88] The Senate later tabled the bill. But a series of bills were later passed that exempted fifty counties from the dog law, including McMinn County.

A bill to redistrict the state was the first of his many attempts to reapportion the state legislature. The bill provided for redistricting of the state's senatorial and floterial districts, as well as its House of Representatives districts. He demonstrated forward thinking on many issues throughout his career. He foresaw the problem of reapportionment needs that would not be addressed until almost a half century later.

Under his redistricting bill, McMinn, Monroe, Bradley and Polk Counties would be placed in the same Senate district. Also, McMinn would have one representative, while larger counties, such as Shelby and Davidson, would have as many as six or seven representatives.[89] Burn knew that giving the urban counties more representatives than the small rural districts would make representation more equal. The bill failed to become law. Under his failed bill, the four southeasternmost counties would have become the Seventh Senatorial District.[90] (He would go on to represent this eventual district many years later.) But he also wanted factors other than population to be considered when reapportioning Senate districts. He would be present to address this controversial issue again many years later.

Among the bills Burn introduced included one to provide no voter registration for certain counties. Two bills stand out among his barrage of bills: one to provide for the appointment of women as state guardians and another to provide for additional voting precincts in McMinn County. The latter bill became law, making it easier for Burn's fellow McMinn Countians to get to the polls back home.[91]

Burn voted aye on several bills allowing his home counties to issue bonds for improving roads and schools. At the urging of former governor Roberts, he introduced a bill to provide revenue for state highway construction.[92] In February, he voted for an unsuccessful bill to incorporate Vonore, a small city on Tellico Lake in northern Monroe County.[93] He would later represent the people of Vonore in the State Senate.

Cracking down on vice, Burn supported another bill to "make possession of gambling paraphernalia presumption of guilt."[94] The Senate tabled the bill. He also voted aye on a Senate bill to fix the tax on cigarettes[95] and a bill to provide a minimum fine for violation of liquor law.[96]

Burn wished to offer an amendment to a bill that made it unlawful to perform any work on Sunday. The bill did not apply to necessary public utilities or necessary acts of charity. Punishments included a fine and jail time. He wanted the bill to "provide that provisions of this act shall not apply to persons who are members or communicants of churches or religious associations or organizations which do not observe the Sabbath on Sunday, and who have observed such other day, when the carrying on of their regular vocation or business does not interfere with the proper observance of Sunday as the Sabbath by those so believing and practicing, and when the business is not of a public or quasi-public service."[97] After a few amendments the bill failed, with Burn voting no.

Burn voted on several bills for Confederate veterans. His maternal grandfather, Confederate veteran Tom Ensminger, is buried in Niota. Burn voted aye on a bill to enlarge cemeteries at the Confederate Soldier's Home[98] and supported a bill to increase pensions for Confederate soldiers.[99] In April, Burn voted no on a bill "to require all voters to pay poll tax."[100]

Burn's "Equal Guardianship" bill was the standout bill of his second term. Endorsed by the Tennessee LWV, Burn's House Bill No. 10 was drafted to "repeal section 2492 of the Code of 1858, which provides for the appointment of guardians of infants."[101] The old law allowed fathers, in the event of their death, to will away their legitimate children to anyone, without the mother having a say in the matter.

Abby Crawford Milton, chairman of the Tennessee LWV, said, "Under the old law a father could will away his child, without the mother's consent, perfectly legally. Such a thing is unspeakable in modern civilization."[102] The bill made women legal co-guardians of their children. Mrs. John Lamar Meek claimed that the bill "is humanly just and right."[103] Mrs. W.E. Wheelock said, "I think the old English law, which was founded on the solidarity of the home, should not be interfered with, but strengthened, but inasmuch as this proposed law removes the ability of a father to dispose of a child to the exclusion of the mother, it is good, for that is an injustice that could be corrected."[104]

The Equal Guardianship bill passed the House in February in a 65–5 vote.[105] Governor Taylor later signed it into law. Burn took particular pride in this bill. On a document written in 1962, he listed this bill, along with his vote to ratify the Nineteenth Amendment, as the two accomplishments he was most proud of in his entire legislative career.[106]

The legislature adjourned in April. Of the thirty bills introduced by Burn during the session, Governor Taylor signed fifteen of them into law. Burn ended his two House terms batting .500 or higher in getting his bills to become law.

Chapter 7

ROCKWOOD AND SWEETWATER ATTORNEY

B urn declined to run for a third term in the Tennessee House of Representatives in 1922. He later stated he had "always believed in two terms except for constitutional conventions."[1] Having served on three committees as a legislator, he became interested in law.

"After I came back home I began to read Gibson's Suits in Chancery and Caruthers's History of Lawsuit. I became fairly familiar with them. I started a correspondence course and got along very well with it."[2] Burn took the course through the American Correspondence School of Law out of Chicago. Still working for the Southern Railway, he studied law while working at the telegraph office in Strawberry Plains.[3]

Burn was prepared to attend Cumberland University Law School in Lebanon, Tennessee, before an alternate opportunity arose. He received a job offer in nearby Rockwood. A small city in western Roane County, Rockwood is north of Niota. Like Niota, Rockwood is situated just below a ridge. Walden Ridge, stretching northeast seventy-four miles through East Tennessee, towers over the city. The view from one thousand feet atop the ridge features magnificent views of the Ridge and Valley Appalachians of East Tennessee. On a clear day, the Appalachian Mountains can be seen. Just over the ridge to the west past Cumberland County is Middle Tennessee.

Rockwood was founded as a company town in 1868 and grew up around the Roane Iron Company. As it was replete with iron ore and coal and located close to the Tennessee River, and with anticipated railroad development plans, former Union general John T. Wilder knew that the site would be an ideal location for industry. Wilder and Hiram Chamberlain led development of the Roane Iron Company. Wilder is credited as the city's founder, but it is named for William O. Rockwood, the first president of the company. Other major industries soon developed in the city. While Birmingham, Alabama, grew to become a large steel city in the South, Rockwood earned the nickname "The Little Pittsburg of the South." The Roane Iron Company's blast furnace produced pig iron. Burn's move to Rockwood began his long love affair with the city.

Burn (*above*) sits with his Uncle Bill Ensminger in the 1920s. *Burn family.*

Burn had to pass the bar exam to get the job. The firm of Wright, Haggard, and Wright was on retainer at the First National Bank. Timothy A. Wright was bank president and Uncle Bill's attorney. At the time, Uncle Bill worked as a cashier.

Burn passed the bar exam and was admitted to the Tennessee Bar Association in spring 1923.[4] His great nephew Jack Burn remembers how his uncle enjoyed telling the story of how he was able to forego law school by passing the bar exam. Uncle Bill helped Burn pay for a room at the Mourfield Hotel during his residence in Rockwood. In return, he would chauffer his uncle around town, frequently taking him fishing.

The *Nashville Tennessean* celebrated Burn's move to the city with the headline "Suffrage Hero Enters Rockwood Law Office."[5] When he began his job at the firm, the name became Wright, Haggard, Wright, and Burn. Shortly after he moved to Rockwood to begin his new career, Timothy A. Wright sadly passed away. The firm hired a new partner and changed its name to Haggard, Jennings, Wright, and Burn. Burn worked in the commercial collections department. The firm's major clients included the First National Bank, Roane Iron Company, Rockwood Mills and Southern Cities Power Company. Business was good for the firm for the first few years.

In 1924, Burn decided to devote himself full time to law. He tendered a letter of resignation from the Southern Railway Company. Responding to Burn's resignation, the chief dispatcher from Knoxville wrote, "We regret to give up such a good man as you…your name will be remembered for years to come by the Railroad Company as well as your associates."[6] A valued employee, he would return to railroading many years later.

Burn continued his involvement in local and state politics. In February 1924, Roane County Republicans elected him to serve as their delegate to the Republican National Convention.[7] In May, he attended a Tennessee Republican Party meeting in Knoxville with other delegates. As the convention prepared to adjourn, he "sprung a last minute sensation."[8] He moved that the convention endorse former governor Alfred Taylor as the party's nominee to challenge Governor Austin Peay. Burn had got on well with Taylor during his second term in the legislature, but the delegates refused to endorse the seventy-six-year-old former executive. After Burn helped circulate petitions all over the state, Taylor qualified as a candidate for the nomination. Captain Thomas F. Peck of Etowah won the party's nomination for governor.

Later that year, Burn was elected to serve as a delegate from Roane County to a state constitutional convention that was never held. His opportunity to amend the Tennessee Constitution would eventually come. He would be vindicated in his desire for long-overdue reform in the state.

Thirty miles southwest of Rockwood on the Tennessee River is the city of Dayton. In 1925, all eyes were on Dayton as the "Scopes Monkey" trial began. Interested parties sieged upon the small Rhea County city as John Scopes faced prosecution for violating state law by teaching the theory of evolution. The prosecution team included future Tennessee circuit court judge Sue K. Hicks, future U.S. Senator from Tennessee Tom Stewart and, most famously, perennial populist presidential candidate William Jennings Bryan. Rhea County native John Randolph Neal Jr., along with Clarence Darrow, represented Scopes. Burn attended one day of the trial.

Many years later, Burn purchased the book "Six Days or Forever?" by Ray Ginger. He gave the book to his son and left a note inside the front cover. He described sitting for a few minutes in the jury box while the jury was excused. "Darrow and Bryan were about eight feet apart. I was in the row behind them about halfway between them," he wrote. If there was something exciting taking place close by, Burn was usually there.

Having turned thirty in late 1925, rumors began to spread about Burn running for governor in 1926. The *Rockwood Times* had not only falsely

Rockwood, Tennessee. *Tennessee State Library and Archives.*

reported that he planned to run, but also included a photo of him in Cuba with a group of women in bathing suits.[9] His attorney charged that the article was printed "much to the plaintiff's chagrin and humiliation."[10] He sued the paper for $500. The editor/publisher of the paper at the time was Hammond Fowler Jr.

Burn and Fowler Jr. quickly became close friends. If anyone in Burn's time could be aptly referred to as "Mr. Rockwood," it was Hammond Fowler Jr. Born and raised in Rockwood, his family owned the *Rockwood Times*. After graduating from Cumberland University Law School, he served as counsel for many organizations in town. A legendary orator and active citizen, he went on to become a major public figure.

Fowler also found success in state politics. In 1934, he became the first Democrat since the antebellum period to win election to the State Senate representing McMinn, Bradley, Roane and Anderson Counties. "He was a staunch Democrat and very fixed in his opinions," State Senator Ken Yager remembered.[11] But, Fowler once said of Burn, "He is the only Republican

I could ever vote for!"[12] Gerald Largen recalls how Burn and Fowler would "exchange barbs" with each other. Their constant exchanging of insults confused those who did not understand their friendship. Largen even suspects that their 1926 lawsuit could have been a staged attempt to increase their own publicity![13]

In summer 1926, a young Cumberland University Law School graduate named Winfred Earl Michael approached Burn in Rockwood. By this time, Burn and Haggard operated the law firm. Michael told Burn that he would like to cooperate with him in opening a law office in Sweetwater. Michael worked with Haggard and Burn for a time as an associate. In 1927, Burn bought a law library from a Kingston lawyer and bought office space in Sweetwater. He left town to open his own law office with Michael, his first partner in the firm. Known formally as "W.E.," Michael's friends called him "Mike." Michael, a decade younger than Burn, became an active Sweetwater citizen, serving as city attorney for several years.

Sweetwater is Monroe County's largest city, situated only a few miles northeast of Niota on U.S. Highway 11. Incorporated in 1875, Sweetwater has been and still is a predominately agricultural and industrial town. The

The view from Burn's Sweetwater law office in the Scruggs Building. *Monroe Archives.*

111

city lies primarily in the Sweetwater Valley. Burn and Michael was, for a time, the only law firm in town. Sweetwater is a more populous city than Madisonville, the Monroe County seat. Sweetwater's population at the time was 2,200.

Burn and Michael, Attorneys operated as a general practice and specialized in municipal debt readjustments and corporate reorganizations. Burn traveled to Washington, D.C., frequently during his legal career. The *Sweetwater Valley News* once reported that Burn "is known as one of the most successful attorneys of East Tennessee and his firm has an extensive practice throughout this section of the state."[14]

Shortly after Burn relocated to Sweetwater, Rockwood declined. After decades of prosperity, the company town lost its powerhouse industry when the Roane Iron Company closed its doors in 1932. But, Burn would not forget about Rockwood.

Burn became an uncle to two nephews and one niece during the 1920s. His brother Jack married Olive Reed Arrants on June 15, 1921. They had two sons, James Edwin in 1922 and William Hoyal in 1924, and a daughter, Sara Virginia, in 1926. William was my grandfather. In 1928, Burn's grandmother Sallie Ensminger passed away in her mid-eighties.

Chapter 8

CAMPAIGN FOR GOVERNOR

A fter almost a decade out of office, Burn made a return to the game in a grand fashion. Now age thirty-four, he entered the race for governor of Tennessee. This time, it was for real. Republican Herbert Hoover had been elected president of the United States in 1928, increasing speculation that a Republican had a good chance of winning the governorship in 1930.

Governor Henry Horton was considered a vulnerable incumbent. He had been Speaker of the Senate before becoming governor upon the death of Governor Austin Peay. Narrowly reelected in 1928, Horton deposited millions of dollars in state funds in the bank owned by Luke Lea and Rogers Caldwell, his political allies. Rumors began to spread about "serious financial straits" before the 1930 election.[1]

Tennessee had elected a Republican governor in 1910 and 1920. Both hailed from East Tennessee. Would it happen for a third time in 1930? Prominent Knoxville Republican and future congressman John J. Jennings Jr. denied rumors that he would run for governor. He claimed that a housecleaning must take place before the Republicans could be successful statewide. The party "must be reorganized from the ground up," he said.[2] A grassroots candidate working as an attorney in the small East Tennessee town of Sweetwater was preparing to enter the contest.

Reports in early May claimed that Tennessee Republicans might not even have a candidate for governor. But rumors among Burn's friends had begun to spread in early spring that he was exploring a bid for the governorship. According to the *Sweetwater Valley News*, "Burn's candidacy was set afoot by his friends, without his knowledge or consent."[3] Petitions for his candidacy had been passed around several East Tennessee counties.[4] W.E. Michael, his law partner, encouraged him to run. He later said that Michael "was ambitious politically."[5] Burn said he was "seriously considering seeking the nomination" and that a formal announcement from him may be forthcoming within days.[6] On May 10, Burn told the *Post-Athenian*:

> *When in the course of events one's friends have qualified him as a candidate for the nomination of a great political party as its candidate for governor, due regard for such confidence and friendship requires that the person so honored should make a definite expression of his attitude…we will have no political pork barrel for finances, no propaganda machine and no well oiled organization. But we shall work to restore in Tennessee a government "of the people, by the people and for the people."…I favor good roads and better schools, but without extravagance. Expenses of government must be deflated to the same basis as the business of the citizens who carry the burden of taxation. I shall in the future…frankly declare my views, on our problems.[7]*

Burn's opponent for the Republican gubernatorial nomination quickly emerged: Memphis businessman Charles Arthur Bruce. Harry T. Burn Jr. later referred to Bruce, a forty-six-year-old millionaire, as the machine candidate in the primary. Known formally as "C. Arthur Bruce," he graduated from the University of Chicago and Harvard University. He spent his early career dabbling in various industries. He eventually joined the family lumber business, the E.L. Bruce Company in Little Rock.[8] The company was one of the largest lumber businesses in the world.

The Tennessee Republican Executive Committee met on June 2, with Burn in attendance. J. Will Taylor, East Tennessee congressman and a powerful member of the RNC, worked hard to ensure that no Republican primary for governor was held. By a "fluke," the committee endorsed Bruce after a mention of his name by the Shelby County delegation was mistaken as an endorsement. Burn left the meeting shortly afterward.[9] The

C. Arthur Bruce. *Memphis Public Library and Information Center.*

editor of the *Sweetwater Valley News* wrote that Burn made a mistake in not consulting with J. Will Taylor to enter the race. "As everybody knows, J. Will does not like to be ignored in anything political in Tennessee."[10]

Governor Horton's supporters acknowledged his vulnerability. A West Tennessee Democrat said that a revolt against the Horton regime was "terrific and growing by leaps." The previously successful Republican gubernatorial victories of 1910 and 1920 happened largely due to splits among Tennessee Democrats. Some speculated that Bruce, well known in West Tennessee as a highly respected businessman, could win many Democratic votes in a contest with Horton.[11]

Many Republicans disagreed with the endorsement of Bruce. J. Will Taylor's critics pointed out "significant things" about the Bruce endorsement.[12] Bruce lived as far away as possible from the First and Second Congressional Districts in East Tennessee, the state's major Republican strongholds. Some questioned the enthusiasm for Bruce's candidacy in East Tennessee and thought that Horton would struggle to win East Tennessee should the Republican candidate hail from there. That friends of Governor Horton were happy with the Republican Party's plans did not go unnoticed. Just as Jennings said, Tennessee Republican leaders did not have their house in order.

Bruce announced his candidacy on June 6. "I have never held political office and my activity politically has been of short duration."[13] He told supporters that he felt a duty to accept the invitation to run after so many of his Memphis and Tennessee friends urged him to run.[14] He said he would reveal his platform at a later date.

Despite Bruce's endorsement by the party leaders, Burn dove headfirst into the race. He described his unique campaign strategy:

> *Some politicians claim this to be a new kind of campaign in Tennessee. First, there is no campaign fund, and the advertising you see will be paid for by friends who believe in what I stand for. Secondly, the only promises that will be made are that Tennessee shall have honest, efficient and economical government and that taxpayers' money will not be wasted in building a political machine.... Thirdly, the campaign shall be a positive campaign, not a negative one. I am a candidate because I believe in certain fundamental principles and not just because I oppose certain things.*[15]

Shortly after Bruce's official announcement, a petition was filed without Burn's knowledge to qualify him as the party nominee for railroad and public utilities commissioner.[16] Burn was certainly qualified for the position, given his extensive railroading experience. A powerful position, state Republican leaders hoped that the offer would lead to his withdrawal from the gubernatorial primary. They assured him that all of his campaign expenses would be paid and that he would be running unopposed.

On June 14, Burn said he "carefully considered the suggestion" but ultimately decided to remain in the race for governor. "My conscience will let me render political obedience to the rank and file of the party and to the people of the state of Tennessee....I will fight for the right to lead the Republican Party to victory in November. I ask for the moral support of all good citizens who are disgusted with the present conditions." He concluded by utilizing the political capital from his 1920 vote to ratify the Nineteenth Amendment. "Especially will I be pleased to have the support of the good women of Tennessee. May they now use the ballot for the principles I stand for and thus vindicate my vote that gave them the right to vote."[17]

Burn anticipated that Bruce would be expecting an endorsement. "The gentleman who, I presume, will be my opponent claims some kind of endorsement. If he makes that an issue its fallacy will be exposed.... Loyal friends started this campaign and I will not desert them when a fight impends."[18]

Local politicians speculated on Burn's alleged reluctance to run because of the expense of a campaign and the time it would divert from his law practice. But these same leaders also acknowledged the increasing demand for him to remain in the race.[19] He regularly received communications from friends throughout the state urging him to stay in the governor's race.[20] At this point, it was obvious that the party leaders wanted Burn out of the race. The *Sweetwater Valley News* described his candidacy as a "thorn in the flesh to J. Will Taylor" and that it was "tearing down the little playhouse of C. Arthur Bruce."[21]

In an attempt to get Burn to withdraw from the race, Bruce met with Burn in Knoxville. According to Bruce, Taylor said that Burn had agreed to drop out. Burn denied having made that statement and told Bruce he was here to stay. Unsatisfied with Burn's answer, Knoxville's postmaster requested that Bruce meet Burn in Sweetwater to further discuss his withdrawal. Burn welcomed the request but warned them of the futility of their efforts.[22] Bruce made it as far as Lenoir City, twenty miles from Sweetwater, before turning back. They discovered heavy support for Burn in the area and became discouraged from traveling further.[23] This series of events demonstrated Burn's popularity in small towns and rural areas compared to Bruce's heavy support in urban areas.

Burn officially opened his campaign and announced his platform on June 28. At 8:00 p.m. from the front porch of Hathburn, Febb Burn introduced her son to a crowd of thousands. The *Sweetwater Valley News* reported that "the entire citizenship" of his little hometown of Niota attended.[24] Many citizens of Sweetwater, Athens, Etowah, Cleveland, Knoxville and Chattanooga also attended, crammed throughout the Hathburn grounds. Etowah native Captain Thomas F. Peck, the 1924 Republican gubernatorial nominee, also attended. Reporting on the crowd in attendance, the *Post-Athenian* wrote, "There were young and old and the percentage of interested representatives of the fairer sex was noticeable to an important degree."[25]

Burn surveyed the major objectives of his campaign, including tax relief for agriculture, limiting state highway mileage, removal of tolls from bridges, free textbooks, repeal of obsolete laws, immediate water power development, state parks and drastic retrenchment in state expenditures.[26] A former member of the telegrapher's union, Burn supported "equal and just treatment of labor and capital."[27]

Burn proposed a $10 million budget to the legislature, a reduction of the previous year's budget. He claimed that the biggest savings "will come from removing hundreds of political appointees from the public payroll."[28] Threatening to remove political appointees from the payroll was an outright declaration of war against the entrenched political establishment of the state. He immediately made many enemies with this proposal. Burn defended his tax reform proposals:

> *In the past ten years farm values have decreased fifty percent or more. It is difficult for farmers to pay interest and taxes. Relieving them of the state land tax, when and if done, is a meager effort, taxes levied by the counties for schools and roads are burdensome to agriculture in the present economic condition. Let the state allocate more funds to counties from indirect taxes and thus permit a real reduction in land taxes and curtail other expenditures on the part of the state to permit this relief.*[29]

Burn explained his opposition to tax burdens: "Especially taxes, which will produce only a limited income with high collections. It is well known that the present administration in its program of wild extravagance has endeavored to place such a tax on cosmetics and amusements."[30]

On infrastructure, Burn proposed to "limit our state highway system to 6,000 miles until that mileage has been built….With the Memphis to Bristol

Highway and the Lee Highway and others, not yet completely hard surfaced nothing but politics is served by adding blue print mileage."[31] On education, Burn advocated removing schools and their directing influence from politics: "Under the present method of administering our school system, the requirement for the directing head is that he be a good politician rather than an outstanding educator. I have in mind two women, either of whom is capable of directing our school system….Heads of institutions, also, should be appointed on the basis of their qualifications and without regard for political considerations."[32]

Burn spoke of his maternal grandfather, Tom Ensminger, the late Confederate veteran. He vowed to support Confederate pensions for soldiers who had "fought on principle."[33] He would later join the National Society Sons of the American Revolution and the Sons of Confederate Veterans.

Other prominent Republicans from the area followed Burn's speech. His close friend Hammond Fowler delivered the closing talk. A staunch Democrat, Fowler said he was "for Tennessee first" and would help Burn in every way possible.[34]

A few days after announcing his platform, Burn traveled northeast for a campaign tour in the First Congressional District. Home to the state's oldest cities, many Northeast Tennessee voters descended from the state's first settlers. Their culture of self-reliance and individualism matched well with Burn's political philosophy.

Burn campaigned in Sevierville, Newport and Greeneville. Many Republican leaders, rank-and-file Republicans and even a few Democrats welcomed him. He was pleased to discover that friends in the region had been actively campaigning for him. He garnered such heavy support from the people and party leaders in Greene County that he had to extend a planned ten-minute talk to two hours. His most eager supporters bought printed advertising and decorated their car tire covers with "Burn for Governor."[35]

Burn also visited Johnson City and Jonesborough, both in Washington County, the state's oldest county. Jonesborough is the oldest city in Tennessee. "Besieged with requests for speaking engagements," he was amazed to find the same spirit of near universal approval of his candidacy as exists in his home counties.[36] He received enthusiastic support in Unicoi, Carter and Johnson Counties. His campaign manager, W.E. Michael, said of the Northeast Tennessee visit:

W.E. Michael's law school graduation
photo. *Michael family.*

*The rank and file of the party in the cradle of Tennessee liberty have an
inherent love of freedom in political affairs and this characteristic is another
reason why Burn's appeal gets such response. They recognize in him a
native son who has political experience sufficient to quality him for the
office...but who remains aloof from all factional control.*[37]

Burn challenged Bruce to a debate in mid-July. W.E. Michael sent a
telegram to Bruce making the request. Two hours later, Bruce wired back to
decline Burn's challenge:

*I cannot see where any party good can come of a joint discussion between Mr.
Burn and myself as you suggest....I do not know of any issues that are of
sufficient public interest to justify the procedure. I stand for the same improved
conditions that I assume Mr. Burn would sponsor. I expect to leave the matter
of fitness to serve the state as chief executive to the voters in the primary, this
being the only issue I can see between Mr. Burn and myself and one that is
not properly debatable in a personal way between us.*[38]

Bruce had spent the previous few days campaigning in the major cities
of the state: Memphis, Knoxville and Chattanooga. He told newspapers he

expected to be nominated as a "matter of course."[39] Burn had been patient with Bruce's impertinent and arrogant behavior, but it would not last.

Burn continued campaigning in East Tennessee in mid-July. Being the strongest Republican region of the state, he spent much of his campaign east of the Cumberland Plateau. He visited three mountainous, rural counties: Campbell, Morgan and Anderson.

Burn returned to the northeast corner of the state, delivering speeches in Kingsport and Greeneville. He elaborated on his platform and, for the first time in the campaign, criticized his opponent. He described Bruce as "clean personally" but criticized his alliance with the "lily white" Republican faction in Memphis while simultaneously attempting to forge an alliance with Robert Church.[40] He lambasted his opponent's friendship with "Boss" Crump. He referred to Crump's machine as the "Little Tammany of the South."[41] E.H. Crump's Democratic machine was renowned for its iron-fisted rule over Memphis and Shelby County. Through the manipulation of hundreds of thousands of votes in the state's most populous county, the Crump machine frequently decided statewide elections during the 1930s and 1940s.

Burn criticized Bruce's lack of a platform and statements sharing his views on the issues. He emphasized how little Bruce had done for the Republican Party compared to him. "They say I am too young, but in political experience and service to the Republican Party I am as old as Methuselah compared with my opponent....The first time I was old enough to vote I voted for myself and was elected to represent my county in the state legislature."[42] Responding to Bruce's claims that he was the only businessman in the race, he pointed out how he had been, before the age of twenty-one, an executive of the Niota Water, Light and Power Company, Crescent Hosiery Mills and the Bank of Niota.

In late July, Burn ventured into his opponent's territory. West Tennessee—a flat, sparsely populated and heavily Democratic region—does not resemble Burn's homeland. He campaigned in Memphis, the state's largest city. Although few Republican voters resided in the region, he worked hard to solicit their votes.

Bruce made his first speech of the campaign season in Chattanooga on July 22. Before a small crowd of about 150 people at the Hamilton County Courthouse, he delivered what the *Chattanooga Daily Times* called "one of the strangest political speeches ever heard in Chattanooga."[43] He spent one hour discussing not the issues but instead listing his qualifications he believed a governor should have: education, business ability, legal training and motives for seeking office.[44]

The Bruce campaign set up exhibits to showcase his diplomas and several business awards. "The state needs a businessman at its helm," he insisted.[45] Downplaying the perception of political ambition, Bruce claimed he had no idea of entering the race until his friends urged him to run. "I am not and never have been a seeker after political office. Whatever service I can render must of necessity be along business lines." He claimed to be a novice. "I appreciate that I am inexperienced in politics and inexperienced in making political addresses."[46]

Bruce also touted his legal education as an invaluable asset for a state's chief executive. Downplaying his wealth, he admitted that he might be considered "moderately well-off....My wife and I and all our family are just plain folks. We live simply in a modest home in Memphis. We do not have social ambitions."[47]

Bruce still refrained from touching on the issues. "I am not unmindful of the fact that the citizens…are interested in my stand upon individual issues in the state, but I feel it is proper that I should reserve my opinions on these issues until after I am the regular nominee of the party, following the primaries, and if the primaries result in my nomination."[48] Bruce concluded his first and only major speech, saying, "I hope I have given those of you who have not known me a better picture of the man to whom you might delegate the task of chief executive."[49]

As the primary election drew closer, Burn increased his attacks on Bruce. He cautiously separated Bruce the man from Bruce the candidate. He never stooped to personal attacks during the campaign. After hearing reports that there would be no Republican primary in some West Tennessee counties, he focused on building support in the larger counties of the region.[50] He visited several cities in the region, including Henderson, Lexington and Huntingdon. He spoke to a crowd of three hundred supporters in Selmer. In a speech in Jackson, he criticized Bruce's non-political speech:

> *My opponent opened his campaign in Chattanooga Tuesday night but discussed no issues. Instead he displayed certain school diplomas. While I have no Ph.D. degree, I would gladly meet the learned gentleman in a joint debate. When I recently challenged him he hastily answered with a hundred-word telegram when the single word "no" would have sufficed. I know that the rank and file of the party is with me in my fight. The politicians should no longer receive my opponent, however much they may want some of his money for campaign purposes. They could and should tell him candidly that as the nominee for governor he would only be able to lead*

the party to ignominious defeat in November. His lengthy declaration that he is a great man…can be generally accepted, but it is indubitably true that he displayed no political wisdom in deserting his former party allies to merge with the Memphis Machine?[51]

Bruce said very little during the remainder of the campaign. In a rare speech, he actually touched on some issues. Discussing the high cost of highway building, he criticized Governor Horton's administration's "mammoth political machine" and advocated "efficiency, economy and honesty in government."[52] His remarks were almost word for word a replica of a recent Burn campaign ad. "I should have copyrighted my platform at the opening of my campaign, since my opponent has now appropriated it to his own use," Burn said in response.[53]

The Roane County Friends of Harry T. Burn ran an ad one week before the primary election. The top of the ad featured a photograph of Burn next to a box with a question mark inside of it representing Bruce. "An unknown millionaire from Memphis who boasts of the endorsement of Bob Church and the friendship of Ed Crump." The text for Burn read:

The Republican Party of Tennessee can elect a governor this fall if its nominee is HARRY T. BURN. A clean, courageous young East Tennessean with a record of 14 years service to his party. Not a millionaire, but a capable businessman familiar with the needs of Tennessee. The only Republican candidate who had the courage and candor to go to the rank and file of his party and tell the state where he stands on vital problems confronting us. IF you want a nominee who reads telegrams about bathing the poodle dog instead of discussing issues, and who relies on the support of the Memphis machine rather than the mass of the people—DON'T VOTE FOR BURN.[54]

In a speech in Cleveland four days before the primary election, Burn called Bruce "a straw candidate, a stool pigeon in the hands of the Memphis political machine to perpetuate the Horton machine in power." He stressed his desire to stop the "hand-picked" candidate.[55] His campaign ad in the *Cleveland Herald* invited voters to hear his speech at the courthouse. "Ladies especially invited."[56] He did not shy away from courting the votes of women.

With the primary election two days away, Burn made the closing speech of his campaign in Knoxville. Speaking before 125 people in ninety-five-degree heat, he blasted Bruce for his "last minute trickery" to gain an advantage. He described how Bruce attempted to "hitch his campaign to Congressman J. Will Taylor's through the use of illegal instruction cards."[57] Typically, instruction cards have a sample ballot with all candidates for the party's primary. He claimed that instruction cards in the Third Congressional District included only Bruce's name.[58]

Elaborating on his platform, Burn further emphasized his support for land tax relief through reducing state expenditures and expressed his opposition to "blueprint mileage" to the state's highway system to "pay for political debts." Taking the schools out of politics was reiterated. The forward-thinking Burn promised a revision of the Tennessee code to remove "ox-cart and slavery laws in the radio and automobile age." Referencing a portion of the state employees, whose positions he vowed to terminate, he said he would remove "a hoard of inspectors who usually go about harassing merchants."[59] His remarks on reducing the number of state employees drew a prolonged applause.[60]

Republican Men:
Nominate this man from the "hills of East Tennessee" and win with him in November on his platform of honest, efficient and economical government!

Republican Women:
This man's vote in the Tennessee legislature in 1920 gave you the right to vote. For bringing you political freedom he asks no favors, but he solicits your support for the principles for which he fights!

Republican Primary, August 7, 1930

Harry T. Burn
FOR GOVERNOR

"Burn for Governor" campaign flyer. *Burn family.*

Burn was equipped with quick wit. "I wonder where my opponent's platform is? I have been trying to find it for six weeks."[61] He criticized Bruce for listing his ability to play the mandolin and playing a feminine role in a college play as qualifications for being governor. He recalled his humble beginnings, discussing his predawn awakenings to feed pigs and five-mile walks to hang railroad switch lights as a teenager while Bruce learned to play the mandolin.[62]

Republican women of Knoxville held a luncheon for Burn at the Hotel Farragut. Several prominent Knoxville Republican leaders attended. In his speech, Burn emphasized the importance of honesty in all lines of human activity. He spoke of learning of the importance of honesty in his experience as a lawyer and that he predicated his campaign on honesty and consistency. He told the audience:

Honesty in everything has been my motto in life. While in the legislature I cast the deciding vote for woman suffrage, and was willing to take the consequences, although political expediency indicated a vote against woman suffrage. But later events proved that I was rewarded for following the dictates of my conscience. I may not win the nomination at this time, although I firmly believe I will. But if I lose now I believe I will eventually be successful. I am basing my candidacy on honesty and I am sure that honesty will win out in the end.[63]

That same day, Congressman J. Will Taylor, the powerful Republican congressman from the Second District (including Burn's home counties), stated that he had wished to avoid holding a gubernatorial primary in order to "save the state money."[64] Contradicting an earlier report, the Tennessee Republican Party announced its intention to hold a primary "in every county of the state."[65]

In the issue one day before the primary election, the *Rockwood Times* ran an editorial entitled "Church-Crump-Bruce or Burn?" Burn was complimented as a "successful young lawyer, bank director, farmer, businessman and legislator." Readers were warned of the imminent and inevitable loss that Bruce would suffer at the hands of incumbent Governor Horton should he be the party nominee. Burn was praised as "having lived 35 years among the common people of East Tennessee, who is one of them, who knows their problems and their needs, and is far more available as a party nominee than a millionaire member of Memphis country clubs, whose whole time is given to his vast business enterprises in Mississippi and Arkansas…who has probably not been in more than ten county seats in Tennessee in his life, who did not even become a resident of Tennessee until after Burn had made a commendable and brilliant name for himself by his various activities." Readers were implored to dismiss the "pessimistic, defeatist propaganda that Burn hasn't any chance." Burn was given a nickname: "the plucky warrior of Republicanism." Bruce was criticized for "clinging to the coattails of the mighty J. Will Taylor," for "stealing the very words of Burn's constructive platform" and for the use of "trick" instruction cards that tried to tie Bruce's candidacy to the well-known and popular Republican candidates in East Tennessee. Readers were assured that Bruce's actions down the home stretch proved that the "trend was toward Burn." The editorial concluded by encouraging readers to go to the polls to vote for Burn in a "tidal wave" that will "wash over the mountains and overcome the crooked vote that will be marked up against him by the Church-Crump-Bruce bipartisan alliance in Shelby County."[66]

Bruce's well-financed campaign ran ads in major newspapers throughout Tennessee. An ad in the *Knoxville Journal* urged voters to "Put Bruce and his business ability in the Governor's chair" and stated he was "not a politician."[67] The *Memphis Press Scimitar* reported that Bruce was "confident" he would win the nomination and that he "expects to get an almost unanimous vote in Shelby."[68] The *Nashville Banner* referred to Bruce as the choice of the "organization" element of the Republicans and predicted a "poor second place" showing for Burn.[69] The *Commercial Appeal* reported that estimates of Republican turnout in Shelby County would not exceed 2,800 votes.[70]

Election Day returns came in slowly throughout the state, particularly in the rural precincts. Burn trailed Bruce 20,200 to 13,960 as of noon the day after the election, with only one-quarter of precincts reporting.[71] Burn's supporters hoped he would pull ahead after all of the rural precinct results came in.

That morning, Burn spoke to the *Rockwood Times* on the telephone. "On the basis of the returns as just reported, I am not conceding the nomination to my opponent. I am confident that later returns from East Tennessee will give me sufficient votes to assure me a victory in the primary."[72]

Unfortunately for Burn, once all of the results were tallied, the race was not even close. Bruce finished the primary election with a nearly two-to-one vote margin of victory over Burn for the Republican gubernatorial nomination. The final tally on record for the August 7 primary election lists 60,447 votes for Bruce and 32,815 votes for Burn, with Burn winning only fifteen counties.[73]

Burn performed well in McMinn County, receiving 2,133 votes to Bruce's 436 votes. He also won the adjoining counties of Monroe, Meigs, Loudon and Roane. He lost Bradley and Polk Counties, both bordering McMinn. His heaviest losses came in the major cities and in the rural Democratic Middle and West Tennessee precincts. He lost Hamilton County 1,783 to 1,149; Knox County 4,935 to 1,857; and Davidson County 1,567 to 95. He lost especially big in Bruce's home county of Shelby, receiving only 206 votes to Bruce's 7,379 votes.[74]

Some counties in Middle and West Tennessee did not even hold a Republican primary due to typically low turnout in the region.[75] Prominent Republican leader Howard Shofner later stated, "There was no concerted effort to bring out the Republican vote outside the First and Second Congressional Districts."[76] Burn had just learned that winning a primary

The results of the 1930 Republican gubernatorial primary. Burn won the counties in dark gray, Bruce won the counties in light gray and the counties in white held no primary. *Map by Justin White.*

is nearly impossible without strong support from party leaders. But he still refused to concede the race.

The front page of the *Rockwood Times* on August 14 read, "Frauds in Shelby Give Bruce Lead in GOP Primary."[77] By this time, Bruce had a four-thousand-vote lead over Burn, with thirty-four of the ninety-five Tennessee counties reporting. The four largest counties, as well as all East Tennessee counties, had reported their complete results.[78] Burn anxiously awaited more counties to report, even though many of them held no Republican primary. He was clinging to false hope.

The *Rockwood Times* also ran an editorial on its front page entitled "The Plucky Warrior Wins."[79] The paper claimed that once all of the votes were tallied, Burn would win with a majority of three to four thousand votes. It reported that even his closest friends and advisors looked at his campaign as a noble but futile effort. It revealed that he had raised very few campaign dollars and that he had little organization consisting only of a handful of loyal friends across the state. The paper bragged on East Tennessee delivering every Republican governor since the end of the Civil War. It reminded readers of Memphis's reputation of "unblemished election frauds." It also questioned the unbelievably large number of votes cast for Bruce in Shelby County. After referring to Bruce as "this angel of sweetness and light" and the "epitome of virtue, honor and honesty in politics," the piece blasted Bruce for claiming to be the nominee with only 20 percent of the precincts reporting the day after the election. It predicted that Bruce would lead the party to "dismal, overwhelming, utter defeat" in November. It concluded with the question of whether or not the Republican Party would tolerate his being defrauded out of the "fruits of his victory" and if the rank and file would even get behind Bruce in the general election against Governor Horton.[80]

Burn, no stranger to political controversy, contested the race. He filed a petition with Howard Shofner, the chairman of the state Republican executive committee. Burn made many allegations about the primary election. Some of his claims have been substantiated.

According to Burn, there was "no call for a primary in 30 or 40 counties in Tennessee."[81] Many of his supporters claimed that the results in the precincts of Shelby County were padded. "There was no legal election in Shelby County. About 1,000 votes were cast and 7,000 certified."[82] Allegedly, Bruce's vote in Shelby County was larger than that of the entire Republican vote cast for Calvin Coolidge in the 1924 presidential election.[83] The petition filed by Burn also claimed that the chairman of the Shelby County primary board instructed election officers to return the ballots and scroll sheets to him after the election without counting or tabulating them.[84]

The *Rockwood Times* reported on several communications received by the Burn campaign alleging corruption, including prominent Memphis Republicans claiming that at least five thousand fraudulent votes were cast against him in Shelby County, that Bruce's lumber trucks were hauling black citizens from Mississippi to vote in Shelby County[85] and that Burn representatives in Nashville found only one precinct open.[86]

Much to Burn's chagrin, Bruce seemed to have won the majority of votes in East Tennessee, claiming a 1,694-vote lead. Burn vehemently denied this, pointing out that the Crump machine had amended Section 130 of the state code to include Van Buren, White and other Middle Tennessee counties in East Tennessee.[87] "My opponent's headquarters admits that I carried the First Congressional District, the only section that has given us a Republican governor since the Civil War. My majority there is much larger than they concede."[88] He claimed that machine politics made the Knox and Hamilton County primaries a "farce."[89] "The question of spurious instruction cards used in the Third Congressional District and passed to voters with the official ballot must be satisfactorily determined," he said.[90]

Burn declared himself the party's gubernatorial nominee. He outlined his plans for the general election campaign against Governor Horton, who had been renominated. "In truth, I am the nominee of the rank and file of the Republican Party." Burn, consistent with his campaign's indefatigable theme, said, "I have not congratulated Mr. Bruce as yet and am conceding nothing pending further investigation."[91] Justifiably frustrated, Burn did not see his own arrogance in claiming victory.

Two of Burn's claims have been verified. He provided evidence of illegal instruction cards being used in the Third Congressional District. Official records of the final vote tally prove that he was partially correct that several counties held no primary. Twenty-one counties showed no votes cast for governor in the primary.[92] But with those counties being heavily Democratic, it is highly unlikely he would have received a significant number of votes there to swing the nomination his way.

"Mr. Bruce ran well in the Democratic sections of Tennessee…he had the machine politics working to bring things up for him."[93] Burn asked, "On last Saturday, five days after the official results should have been forwarded to…the secretary of state, about twenty counties had reported. Why the holding out of the other counties? The friends of the would-be nominee controlled most every primary board and those politically wise know what has transpired. The cancer of Shelby County corruption is spreading eastward."[94]

When Burn arrived in Nashville to contest the results, two of Bruce's emissaries requested to speak with him when he was checking into his hotel. He refused to speak with them. They tried to convince him to withdraw his contest of the election results. The two emissaries referred to him as "Governor."[95] W.E. Michael and Hammond Fowler represented him in the contest.

Burn and Michael submitted a plethora of further evidence of corruption in the primary election. An investigation concluded that a stenographic error had mixed up Burn and Bruce's votes in Carter County. This error ballooned Bruce's overall lead, giving him a victory in the First Congressional District, the only district Burn was thought to have won. The committee refused to correct this error.[96]

Affidavits from Claiborne County relayed under oath stories of vote buying, votes cast by underage persons and the handing of marked ballots out to be taken into the booths. The committee dismissed these claims, saying they lacked evidence that corruption existed to give Bruce an advantage. Even two marked ballots given out by Bruce workers were submitted as exhibits, only to be dismissed by the committee.[97] Burn read a telegram he had just received from the Shelby County court clerk explaining that the ballots and the election records of the county had not been filed according to law. He claimed to be unable to give a list of specific names of precincts in Shelby County due to the recent destruction of election records. A.V. McLane, U.S. attorney and Bruce's counsel, objected to Burn's reading of the telegram from the Shelby County court clerk. "So you are afraid to let this go into the record, are you?" Burn snipped. "No," replied McLane, "but we don't want you to have the benefit of any cheap notoriety." Burn then accused McLane of being connected with the "crooked work" in the Davidson County primary.[98]

The committee also refused to hear evidence of voter suppression from Davidson County. One prominent Republican woman residing in the Belle Meade section spent several hours searching before she finally found a precinct. She and her family voted for Burn. The ballots were allegedly destroyed after she left.[99] Burn alleged that, just as in Shelby County, no ballots or tally sheets from any Davidson County precinct was filed as required by law. His attorneys examined voter lists in the county, discovering they did not match with the number of registered voters in the county.[100] W.E. Michael explained:

> *Mr. Bruce also stated…that he did not desire the nomination if tainted with a fraudulent vote. Will he tell us why the tally sheets, poll lists, and ballots in the Shelby County Republican Primary are not available for inspection? The law requires one set of returns to be filed with the county court clerk, another with the secretary of state as soon as can be canvassed. That date was August 11, 1930. This is August 27, 1930. His committee that was supposed to pass on the contest was afraid to go into the facts I was ready to produce. I would have embarrassed some of the committeemen.*[101]

"I intend to get justice, and if I cannot get it here…I am going to get it in the courts of Tennessee," Burn warned the committee.[102] On August 27, the Republican state board of primary election commissioners, in a near unanimous vote, dismissed Burn's petition contesting the election.[103] One committee member, E.C. Alexander of Elizabethton, voted "present." In accordance with a previous Tennessee Supreme Court ruling, Howard Shofner stated, "The only evidence admissible would be that showing specifically that illegal votes were cast for one or the other candidates."[104] Bruce's attorneys claimed that Burn's allegations were indefinite and not specific. They also claimed that all of Burn's claims could be allowed and Bruce still would have won the primary by more than 20,000 votes. W.E. Michael fervently denied these claims.[105] The *Rockwood Times* reported on investigations that found that less than one-third of Tennessee counties had complied with the law in holding the primary election and filing the returns. The results from these eighteen counties gave Burn 16,044 votes to Bruce's 14,641.[106]

Burn took no further recourse. C. Arthur Bruce had defeated him in the Tennessee Republican gubernatorial primary by a 27,632-vote majority. The *Knoxville News Sentinel* reported that the Bruce-Burn contest went "almost unnoticed in the fire of the Horton-Gwinn affair."[107] Burn's campaign against Bruce was not the only contested election. There were also accusations of election fraud in the Democratic primary for U.S. Senate. W.E. Michael "vigorously" protested the decision. "I realize that I am speaking to a committee which, to a large extent, has expressed an opinion."[108] Burn then commented on his inability to prove specific charges in Shelby County "when the records are withheld."[109]

The *Rockwood Times* refused to accept Bruce's nomination in an editorial entitled "The Steal Is Ratified."[110] It described the committee's hearing "about as fair and impartial as the trial of an aristocrat by a Jacobin tribunal during the Reign of Terror in the French Revolution....Had Mr. Bruce won fairly, or had he even shown a tendency to resent the methods used by his supporters to seize the nomination....Burn would today be preparing to take the stump on behalf of the candidacy of his opponent."[111]

It is possible that the Tennessee Republican Party did not want to seriously challenge Governor Horton and wished to nominate Bruce without going to the trouble of holding a primary. Bruce delivered a brief speech expressing his gratitude and claimed that prospects for a Republican victory at the polls in November were "never brighter."[112] Bruce went on to face Governor Horton in the general election. He counted on independents and dissatisfied Democrats to bring him victory. "I will put the best I have into this campaign. I have dropped my business completely," Bruce claimed.[113] Republicans continued to slam Horton for his role in the Bank of Tennessee controversy. They were overconfident about their prospects to win back the governorship for the first time since 1920.

Burn had pointed out to voters that Bruce was known as a "lily white" Republican in the Memphis area. Despite this, Bruce attempted to court the support of the influential black leader Robert Church. A Republican, Church instead supported Democrat Governor Henry Horton. Former KKK members campaigned for Bruce, and he refused to speak before black voters.[114]

Bruce lost to Horton in a forty-three-thousand-vote blowout.[115] Tennessee Republican Party leaders learned that Bruce was not the candidate to lead them to victory after all. It would be another four decades before Tennessee would elect a Republican to the governor's office. (Bruce would go on to win the Republican gubernatorial nomination again in 1940, losing in another blowout to Governor Prentice Cooper.)

After Horton's reelection, Burn criticized Bruce for only receiving half as many votes in Shelby County compared to the primary. He called the efforts of Taylor and Bruce in the election an "abject failure."[116] He called for the resignation of J. Will Taylor from the RNC:

> *Again the voters have emphatically repudiated a hand-picked candidate for governor....Having killed the Republican Party in Tennessee, will the czar now provide a decent burial or will he like a vulture seek to feed upon the corpse? Since the rank and file of the party continue to show their determination to have nothing to do with candidates offered by Mr. Taylor, I suggest that a decent consideration for the welfare of the party would prompt his resignation.*[117]

One year after his gubernatorial campaign, Burn became an uncle for the fourth time when Jack and Olive Burn's last child, Jacqueline LaRose, was born in 1931. This period began Burn's longest time out of office. After his disheartening gubernatorial campaign, he needed a break. He continued practicing law in Sweetwater and would not run for office again until after World War II.

Chapter 9

MARRIAGE AND FAMILY

Approaching his thirty-eighth birthday, Burn exchanged vows with Mildred Rebecca Tarwater on the evening of October 25, 1933, in Rockwood. The twenty-six-year-old bride was from one of the most prominent families in the city. Captain James F. Tarwater, her ancestor and former employee of the Roane Iron Company, founded Rockwood Mills in 1905. Like the Burn family, the Tarwaters were successful hosiery manufacturers.

The wedding ceremony, of "outstanding social interest" according to the *Rockwood Times*, took place at the First Christian Church.[1] Burn's younger brother, James L. "Jack" Burn, served as the best man. Burn's groomsmen included Hammond Fowler and W.E. Michael. Burn's sister Otho Burn performed at the ceremony.[2]

The union was not to be. Some had their suspicions that the marriage would not last. After the couple left the altar as husband and wife, Burn's Uncle Bill Ensminger turned to a friend and said, "The party is over and the war has begun."[3] Eddyth Ensminger, Uncle Bill's wife, later said her husband had "a sense of humor that few people ever possessed."[4]

Burn and Tarwater did not remain married for long, separating after a year and a half. They divorced in December 1935, producing no children. Tarwater sued him for the divorce, charging non-support.[5] Burn had actually been a supportive husband, but divorce at this time required a legally valid reason. They had problems they could not reconcile. Burn did not offer opposition in the suit. Admirably, Burn and Tarwater remained on good terms.

Burn and his first wife, Mildred Rebecca Tarwater, sit in front of their McCaslin Avenue home in Sweetwater. *Burn family.*

The 1930s continued to be a depressing decade for Burn. After a failed bid for the governorship and a failed marriage, the Great Depression devastated his communities. Burn and Michael worked extensively in the municipal bankruptcy proceedings of the 1930s.

Real estate values declined rapidly throughout the decade. Unable to collect sufficient revenue from property taxes, several municipalities defaulted. Burn and Michael represented Sweetwater during its struggles in this period. Michael completed a study of the city's financial condition. The city defaulted on $565,000 of bonded indebtedness. "In 1932 that was an enormous amount of money," Michael later explained.[6] He told the city commission about "a bill under consideration in the Congress providing relief for bankrupt cities and towns." He suggested that the bill might help them "settle our creditors and at the same time preserve some degree of local pride."[7] Sweetwater became the first municipality in the country to file for bankruptcy under the Wilcox Municipal Bankruptcy Act in 1934.[8]

Michael traveled the country meeting with bondholders. Burn served as chief counsel, writing the briefs and arguments. "I drafted the pleadings in federal court....Mr. Michael did most of the traveling and I did most of the office work," Burn later remembered.[9]

Decades later, while researching Rockwood's history, William Howard Moore consulted Burn. After meeting, Burn took him to a cemetery in

Cardiff, a small community near Rockwood that had been devastated by the Panic of 1893. Burn "bemoaned the 'broken dreams' of the people buried there," Moore remembered.[10] Burn and Michael also assisted Hammond Fowler when he represented Rockwood during its bankruptcy struggles. "You just don't know how desperate the situation was in Rockwood," Burn later recalled. "You couldn't sell a piece of property for anything at all."[11] William Howard Moore described Burn and Michael's accomplishments in helping Rockwood as a "surprisingly little heralded *tour de force*."[12] Burn and Michael worked tirelessly to help municipalities and individuals with their financial struggles during the Great Depression. Not only that, but they also did it for little compensation.[13]

The U.S. Supreme Court ruled the Wilcox Municipal Bankruptcy Act unconstitutional in 1936. Fortunately for Sweetwater and Etowah (also represented by Burn), the ruling did not force them to scrap their reorganization plans. The two cities, along with Rogersville, were the only three cities in the state to benefit from the law.[14] Michael's plan to help Sweetwater worked, at the very last minute. "As soon as all of this was worked out we happily disposed of the old bonds and coupons by cosigning them to flames. The next day after the bonds were destroyed the Supreme Court...decreed that the act under which we had proceeded...was unconstitutional."[15]

Burn served as the city attorney for Niota for a time, and Michael continued to serve as the city attorney for Sweetwater. In October 1936, after ten years as partners, Burn and Michael dissolved their legal partnership. The split was amicable, and they remained friends, for a time.

The genealogy bug bit the Burn family in the early 1930s. Burn joined the National Society Sons of the American Revolution in 1931, beginning a long and extensive affiliation with the organization. His ancestry tracing back to Samuel Blair, a veteran of the Battle of Kings Mountain, qualified his membership.[16]

Febb Burn started researching the Ensminger genealogy and discovered that her family also descended from American Revolutionary War veterans. Her ancestor Henry Ensminger qualified her for membership in Daughters of the American Revolution.[17] Her genealogy research proved invaluable in the writing of the first chapter of this book.

Burn began searching for unanswered questions relating to the origins of his family before they arrived in the New World. After the decade's midway point, things began to improve for him. On July 3, 1936, the steamship *Laconia* left Boston. Burn was a passenger on the ship, bound for Liverpool. This trip was to be the first of many international travels in his lifetime. He was starting an extensive tour of several European nations throughout the summer. He visited the United Kingdom, France, Germany, Switzerland, Belgium and the Soviet Union.[18] Researching Burn genealogy partially motivated his journey. He hoped to find evidence of his family's possible connection to the Scottish poet Robert Burns (which has never been verified). Harry T. Burn Jr. insisted that the family name has always been "Burn," while his cousin James L.E. Burn believed it might have been "Burns" at one time.

In Dumfries, Scotland, Burn visited with members of the Robert Burns family. He visited two homes formerly occupied by the famous poet. He visited the Robert Burns farm on the River Nith, where the poet wrote several of his verses. Although he rarely drank alcohol, Burn also visited the "Hole in the Wall," the famous "loafing and drinking place" of Robert Burns.[19] While in Dumfries, Burn also attended the sheriff's court. He admired the way the sheriff handled a group of tourists who had been drinking while driving. He recalled the "twinkle" in the sheriff's eyes when he discussed the judgment.[20]

In London, Burn was granted a seat in the gallery at the Palace of Westminster. He listened to a meeting of Parliament. He also visited the old law office of Charles Dickens.[21]

While in the Soviet Union, Burn visited the beaches of Sochi and the Red Room in Leningrad. The friend of a Soviet government official took Burn to many places "off the beaten path." He also visited factories and wheat farms. He remarked that he wondered what would happen should the communistic plans of Stalin be found "not infallible." He referred to the state-owned newspapers as "little more than propaganda sheets."[22]

Burn visited Berlin and several towns in Switzerland. He stopped off in Manheim, Germany, to visit his cousin Peter Ensminger. He then sailed along the Rhine to Cologne. After traveling through Belgium and France, he boarded the *Queen Mary* back to New York.[23] Burn later said the trip was a wonderful experience. When he arrived back home in early September, he was a single man, but not for much longer.

Burn's Uncle Bill Ensminger gave his nephew a great opportunity to gain more experience in the financial sector. Beginning in the mid-1930s, Burn began serving on the board of directors of the First National Bank of Rockwood. Uncle Bill had worked his way up to bank president.

In the late 1930s, Burn invested in the Sweetwater Bank and Trust Company, becoming the majority stockholder. He later became president but did not perform the day-to-day operations of the bank.[24] His affiliation

Febb Burn successfully
managed the Hathburn farm.
Burn family.

with this bank ended in the 1940s. His brief involvement with the Sweetwater bank provided him with an experience that prepared him for a future career in finance.

Febb Burn continued running the Hathburn farm, just across the railroad tracks from Jack's farm, called Edgewood. Hathburn was a general farm, the principal crops being corn and tobacco. Some farm families and occasional outside help assisted her on the farm.

Visitors enjoyed Febb Burn's delicious biscuits, cooked with lard. She would lie down on her fainting couch to take a short nap in the mornings while the biscuits cooked. When the biscuits were done, her dogs would bark to wake her up and let her know! The late Effie Lones remembered Febb as "one of the most gracious people in the world." She enjoyed eating Febb's biscuits with hot butter and brown sugar.[25]

According to Harry T. Burn Jr., Febb Burn "had no sense of fear....She lived alone in a large, isolated house, but if there was a noise in the middle of the night at the barn, she went to see what it was. This would be unthinkable and foolish in the 21st century."[26]

Burn's younger siblings took different paths in life. His brother, Jack, was more entrepreneurial than political. After managing Miller's Department Store in downtown Athens, he founded and operated Burn's Cash Store in Athens for many years. He did all of this while still operating his farm. In 1934, he left the store to begin managing Crescent Hosiery Mills in Niota, ensuring that a second generation would be involved in operating the mill. Walter L. Forrest, the older brother of Burn's uncles John I. and J. Ben Forrest, managed the mill for the first three decades of operation.

Jack Burn kept the hosiery mill running through the Great Depression while also running his farm. The mill even turned a profit during some of the darkest years of the Depression. Harry and Jack Burn secured seats on the mill's board of directors for their Uncle Bill Ensminger, who helped the mill secure a substantial loan from Hamilton National Bank in Chattanooga.

During World War II, the rationing of war materials threatened the mill's very survival. Jack Burn went to the federal government's War Production Board and convinced it to allow the mill to obtain the yarn it needed. He told the board the mill would not sustain operation without the yarn and explained the devastating effect that the mill's closure would have on Niota.

Under Jack Burn's leadership, the hosiery mill racially integrated its workforce several years before federal government action. A disgruntled employee approached him after his announcement of racial integration at the mill. Harry T. Burn Jr. proudly recalled his uncle's telling of the conversation. An employee told Jack that she would not work alongside black workers, using a racial slur. Jack told her the mill was integrating whether she liked it or not.

Those who knew the jovial Jack Burn remember him as a "pistol" and a "cut-up." He liked to pull tricks while walking through the mill. He would place a quarter and a sock on the floor when no one was watching. He would then hide and watch to see if anyone picked up the items. More often than not, someone would pick up the quarter but leave the sock. He would then emerge from his hiding place and ask, "Why did you leave the sock on the floor? The sock is as valuable as the quarter." As easygoing as he was, he liked a tidy workplace.

Jack Burn's devotion to the mill was unwavering, but like his mother, he had a lifelong passion for farming. For photographs, he frequently wore

Left: James Lane "Jack" Burn. *Right:* Olive Reed Arrants Burn. *Burn family.*

overalls with a business suit because he wanted people to know he was a businessman *and* a farmer. Although he would only live to meet one of his six grandchildren, they all posthumously referred to him as "Daddy Jack." His wife, Olive "Ollie" Arrants Burn, taught elementary school in Niota for many years. Her grandchildren and students called her "Aboo."

Peggy Clark Torbett grew up in a home next to the mill. She described Jack Burn as a "good-hearted man and very generous." She recalled how much he loved to farm. "One time he let us stay in our home without paying rent for six months," she fondly remembered.[27] Bill Clark, Torbett's brother and my best friend Geoffery Suhmer Smith's grandfather, loved to go fishing with Jack in Mouse Creek when he was a boy. Bill has told me many times how my great-grandfather Jack Burn treated him "like I was a part of his family."

Otho Burn was a decade younger than her brothers. After graduating from East Tennessee State Normal School in 1924, she taught in Mount Pleasant, Tennessee, for three years. She earned a BS from East Tennessee State Teachers College and a MA from the University of Tennessee before she started her career at Tennessee Wesleyan in 1930.[28]

Otho Burn loved to entertain for everyone, especially brides and the women's club.[29] She worked with the club to build a library in Athens. She participated in many community activities, but her greatest passion

Burn's nieces and nephews in 1933. *Left to right*: James L.E. Burn, Jacqueline L. Burn, William H. Burn (the author's late grandfather) and Sara V. Burn. *Burn family.*

was singing. She aspired to be an opera singer, studying at the Nashville Conservatory of Music and the Cincinnati Conservatory. She had a "concert quality soprano voice," Harry T. Burn Jr. later wrote.[30] "The staff at the Cincinnati Conservatory unsuccessfully urged her to pursue a professional career in music, particularly grand opera."[31]

Ultimately, Otho Burn chose to follow her passion for education. She taught at the Methods and Practice school at Tennessee Wesleyan College, eventually becoming the principal. "People loved her at TWC," Mintie Willson remembered.[32]

Otho Burn married Robert Rhea Hammer in 1936. The couple married in Virginia after Otho performed in Washington, D.C. Rhea Hammer owned a hardware store in Athens. Carolyn Hutsell Pemberton remembered Otho's devotion to helping foreign students.[33] Otho's nieces and nephews called her "Aunt Tat."

"Otho was very musical," Mintie Willson recalled. "She was a lovely lady and well liked." Willson laughed as she recalled how much her late husband, Hugh M. Willson, admired Otho when he was growing up. "Hugh was mad that she married and moved to Athens....Otho and her friends were always so nice to me," Willson fondly recalled.[34]

William Vestal grew up across the street from the Hammers. He remembered hearing her play the organ while he played in the front yard of his home. According to Vestal, Otho Hammer enjoyed having children over to visit and was never worried that the antique furniture might get damaged when they ran around her home.[35]

Judy Townsend remembered how badly Otho Hammer wanted to have kids. Otho and Rhea adopted a young girl from Korea named Mimi. "Otho was like a second mother to me," Townsend fondly recalled. Townsend's father was a close associate and friend of Rhea Hammer's. According to Townsend, Otho could keep the attention of the entire room. "She was very supportive of everyone, and I have heard no one speak badly of her to this day," Townsend said.[36]

A young teacher from New England named Ellen Folsom Cottrell said, "I've gone into the wilds," as she drove down to Athens, Tennessee, in her Ford Model T.[37] She had accepted a position at Tennessee Wesleyan College teaching speech and physical education. She started her new job in fall 1936 and quickly befriended Otho Burn Hammer.

Born in 1908 and raised in the Boston neighborhood of Roxbury, Cottrell played tennis and enjoyed hiking. The youngest of three children born to Charles and Carolyn Cottrell, her family had roots in Rhode Island. She

Above: Otho Virginia Burn Hammer. *Burn family.*

Opposite, inset: Ellen Folsom Cottrell. *Burn family.*

studied speech at Leland Powers School of the Theater in Boston before earning her undergraduate degree in English, speech and history from Westminster College in New Wilmington, Pennsylvania.[38] A lifelong teacher, she taught while working toward her undergraduate degree. She spent a summer studying in the United Kingdom and Continental Europe. She did graduate work at Boston University and the University of Virginia. An outstanding communicator, she could get by in French and earned certificates to teach English, speech and history.[39]

Cottrell directed several plays at the college and helped with women's athletics. Through her new friend Otho Burn Hammer, she met a forty-one-year-old attorney named Harry T. Burn. The recently divorced Burn had just returned from his European tour. A whirlwind romance resulted. Burn had finally found the love of his life.

Harry T. Burn and Ellen Folsom Cottrell drove down to Rossville, Georgia, on Valentine's Day 1937 and got married. Richard Cottrell Bourne, her nephew, said that he was not at all surprised that Burn and his Aunt "Ellie" wed so quickly after meeting. "She had a very vivacious personality," Bourne recalled.[40] The couple had one child. They welcomed their son, Harry Thomas Burn Jr., on October 22, 1937. They called their son "Tommy" during his childhood years. Richard Cottrell Bourne remembered family gatherings in New England:

> *I remember Harry Sr. as a gregarious, always very well dressed man—very business-focused and exhibiting "southern charm." He was devoted to Ellen and to Harry Jr. He fit in so very well with Charles T. Cottrell, the consummate "Boston attorney"! Although obviously devoted to Harry Jr., Harry Sr. was not inclined to engage with Harry Jr. or us cousins in our childhood activities or antics....Harry Jr. gravitated toward absorbing family history and places of interest, especially in Jamestown, as we came to appreciate in later years.*[41]

J. Polk Cooley remembered Ellen Burn as a classy lady. "I thought that Harry was domineering with his son and was frequently directing him in his decision making," recalled Cooley, "but he could not do the same with

Ellen!"[42] According to Bill McFarland, Ellen was always dressed nice. "She was always so polite," McFarland recalled.[43]

Mintie Willson remembered Ellen Burn as very bright and outgoing. "She was attractive and seemed younger than she really was." Willson recalled that she was her son's staunchest supporter. "They had a wonderful relationship."[44] Paul Willson, Mintie Willson's son, remembered how intelligent and well-spoken Ellen was. "She was universally liked and respected. I feel blessed to have known her."[45]

Former Athens mayor Ann Scott Davis remembered Ellen Burn as the epitome of a southern lady. "She was gracious and strong, but not forceful." Davis recalled how often Harry Jr. quoted his mother and how influential she was in raising him. "She was supportive of her son, but was not hesitant to tell him when he was wrong."[46]

Upon the entry of the United States into World War II in 1941, Burn served his country in the war effort at home. Being too old for the armed forces, he returned to the service of the Southern Railway in 1942, working in the operating department in the Knoxville Division. "After Pearl Harbor I went with the railroad as a relief agent, and left Bill Howe in charge of my law office. He was an associate."[47] Burn handled train orders and supervised employees at the larger stations in the Knoxville Division. He later wrote that he did "emergency work, day or night." He gave up his "lucrative law practice" and wrote that it was "a privilege to make that contribution to the war effort."[48] He was also chairman of the first USO drive in Monroe County.

Growing up in Sweetwater during the war, Tommy spent time with his "Nannie" Febb. Unfortunately, she would not live to see the end of World War II. Her elder sister, Mattie E. Sykes, had passed away in 1941 at the age of sixty-eight. In 1943, Febb began experiencing heart trouble. After a lingering illness, Febb Ensminger Burn passed away at Epperson Hospital in Athens on June 18, 1945, at the age of seventy-one.[49] She was survived by her brother, Bill, three children and five grandchildren. At the time of her passing, she was a member of the Niota United Methodist Church. My grandfather William H. "Bill" Burn, who had served on the USS *Warrington* (DD-383) in the Pacific Theater, was still serving in the navy overseas at the time of his grandmother's passing.

Above: Febb Burn with her youngest grandchild, Harry T. Burn Jr., in 1938. *Burn family.*

Opposite, inset: Harry T. Burn Jr. was called "Tommy" as a child. *Burn family.*

Three months after Febb Burn passed away, Japan surrendered and World War II finally came to an end. "After they dropped the bomb on Hiroshima, I had been working nights for the railroad and working my law office in the day, and my health got rather poor, so as soon as the war's end was apparent I became inactive with the railroad."[50] He practiced law in Sweetwater for the remainder of the 1940s.

Perhaps the only historical event connected to McMinn County as nationally renowned as Burn's 1920 vote for the Nineteenth Amendment occurred in Athens in 1946. This event and its consequences greatly affected Burn's next venture into politics. Known as the "Battle of Athens," it, too, related to the right to vote.

The Battle of Athens occurred as a result of a culmination of frustration that had built up in McMinn County for several years. The Democratic Party's fortunes began to improve in the 1936 election. Etowah Democrat Paul Cantrell won a close election as sheriff. Like their Republican predecessors, McMinn Democrats installed their own political machine. They soon developed connections to the E.H. Crump machine in Memphis.[51] By 1942, Georgia native Pat Mansfield had won election as sheriff and Cantrell had won election to the State Senate.

By the summer of 1946, several GIs had returned home to McMinn County from service in World War II. Having just risked their lives to fight tyranny and protect free and democratic government, they decided that it was time to end the corruption in their home county. A group of GIs, made up of Democrats and Republicans, ran for the county government offices. The group was determined to end the Democratic Party's machine. They campaigned through the summer of 1946.

The GIs knew that they had a tough fight ahead of them. In the 1938 primary election, a fight resulted in a stabbing death.[52] Etowah Democrat George Woods, elected as state representative in 1940, secured legislation in 1941 to reduce the number of voting precincts in the county from twenty-three to twelve.[53] Woods became Speaker of the Tennessee House of Representatives in 1945. In 1943, three McMinn County election officials were convicted of election fraud in a federal court. The court found that they used "the color of their office to deprive certain citizens of their right to vote in the 1940 general election at a rural school polling place."[54] The three election officials closed the precinct at 10:00 a.m. after only forty people voted. They took the ballot boxes with them allegedly "to keep the peace" after a fight broke out.[55] In 1944, George Spurling, who had been deputized on the spot by Sheriff Deputy Minus Wilburn, murdered Earl Ford. A Seabee from neighboring Meigs County, Ford had committed no crime.[56]

The GIs had bipartisan support, and the machine saw its power slipping away. On election day, August 1, 1946, Sheriff Pat Mansfield's deputies engaged in various voter intimidation tactics at precincts throughout the county. When GI poll watcher Bob Hairrell objected to a teenager being permitted to vote, Sheriff Deputy Minus Wilburn blackjacked him and took him to jail. Sheriff Deputy Windy Wise shot Tom Gillespie, a black man, allegedly because he was voting at the wrong precinct. Fortunately, he survived his wounds.

When the polls closed, Sheriff Mansfield, State Senator Cantrell and several deputies absconded with key ballot boxes and left for the county jail. There, they could count the votes outside of public view. The GIs had good reason to believe that Sheriff Mansfield and his deputies were manipulating the ballots in their favor. This time, Mansfield was running for State Senate and Cantrell was seeking the sheriff's post again.

A small group of GIs and their supporters concocted a risky plan to ensure that the votes would be "counted as cast." They gathered several guns (mostly from the local armory) and headed for the jail. At the time, the jail stood on White Street between College and Hornsby Streets, one block away from Tennessee Wesleyan College. After fortifying their positions on a hill across the street from the jail, the GIs demanded that the sheriff and his deputies hand over the ballot boxes so a fair count of the votes could take place. After the sheriff refused to hand over the ballot boxes, shots were fired and the two sides exchanged gunfire for several hours.

The GIs knew that they had to get the ballot boxes and prove they won the election. If they failed, they would go to prison for insurrection. After the GIs threw dynamite at the jail, the sheriff and his deputies finally surrendered and handed over the ballot boxes at approximately 3:00 a.m. Miraculously, no casualties resulted in the conflict. A fair count of the votes took place. After fraudulent tally sheets were thrown out (some of which were marked 15-1 for the machine candidates), it was proven that the GIs had won by a two-to-one margin.[57] Knox Henry, who had served in the North African campaign, was elected sheriff. State Representative George Woods, a member of the county election commission while simultaneously serving in elected office, certified the election results.

The Democratic Party's machine had been ousted from power in McMinn County. The incident made the front page of the *New York Times* (falsely reporting that Sheriff Mansfield had been killed). Even former first lady

R. Rhea Hammer and Otho Burn Hammer. *Burn family.*

of the United States Eleanor Roosevelt commented on the incident in her newspaper column.[58]

The effects of the Battle of Athens reverberated all over the county, even down to the city government. Every member of the Athens city board of mayor and aldermen resigned his post. In the September 1946 referendum vote for the city government, Burn's brother-in-law Rhea Hammer won election as mayor of Athens, receiving more than nine hundred votes.[59] No longer fearful of the voter intimidation and election fraud they had endured for the past several years, voter turnout in Athens was double what it had been in the previous city election.

Had these events not transpired, it is unlikely that Burn would have been elected to represent his home counties in the State Senate. After the machine was ousted, elections were competitive again in the county. In November, Republican J.P. Cartwright won election as an independent to represent the Seventh Senatorial District. The 1947 state legislature passed a successful bill establishing the county council–county manager form of government for McMinn, a reform model that would be emulated by other local governments. To reduce the potential for corruption, the Sheriff's Department switched to a strictly salary-based income. With the machine overthrown, the stage was set for a return to public office for Burn.

Chapter 10

FIRST TERM IN THE STATE SENATE

Two years after the Battle of Athens, and almost two decades after his failed gubernatorial bid, Burn made a remarkable political comeback. No longer a bachelor and youthful political novice, the seasoned middle-aged attorney was married and raising a son. His law office in the Scruggs Building, situated beside the railroad tracks on Morris Street, had neighbors in a bank, a restaurant, a paint store, a furniture store and a pool hall. According to Joe Sherlin, employees of the woolen mill frequently walked across the street after work to play pool and eat dinner.[1]

Ellen Burn taught in the Sweetwater City Schools. "She was an excellent teacher and a fine person," remembered Joe Sherlin, one of her high school students. "Mrs. Burn helped us build our confidence, especially when we practiced public speaking."[2] She later earned a MA in English and speech from the University of Tennessee, with a concentration in dramatics.[3]

Burn announced his candidacy for the State Senate in summer 1948. The Seventh Senatorial District consisted of McMinn, Monroe, Bradley and Polk Counties. Due to its recent history of election violence, the district was nicknamed the "Bloody Seventh."[4] Previously, McMinn and Bradley Counties were in the same Senate district as Anderson and Roane Counties. Herschel Candler and Hammond Fowler had both represented the district in the past. In 1945, machine politicians in McMinn County secured legislation to revise the district's boundaries.[5] The son of longtime Polk County political boss Burch Biggs lost a legislative contest in 1944. As a result, Polk and Monroe Counties were moved from the staunchly

Republican Sixth Senatorial District (that included Knox County) to the Seventh District, controlled by the Democratic machine in McMinn County.

In an open letter to voters, Burn stated his support for temperance, financial integrity, schools and new industries. The citizens of Sweetwater would soon find out how serious he was about temperance. He also vowed to devote his efforts to "obtaining a bridge over the Tennessee River at Watts Bar" between Meigs and Rhea Counties.[6]

Congressman Estes Kefauver of Madisonville was running for the U.S. Senate. W.E. Michael ran for the Republican nomination for the Third Congressional District's open House of Representatives seat. Burn's former law partner was now a prominent Sweetwater attorney with his own practice. "He was a fine citizen of the community," Joe Sherlin remembered.[7] Nancy Baker recalled Michael as "colorful and intelligent."[8]

Like Burn, Michael also supported clean elections. "When a citizen is deprived of his or her right to vote, as has been done many times in the past few years in Monroe, McMinn, and Polk Counties, that citizen has lost his contact with, and participation in, government. When governments are elected or entrenched, by violence, intimidation and fraud they are not representative governments of the people but become gangster governments and under them no person is safe in his life, liberty or property."[9] Anticipating the community's renewed confidence in the election system, the *Daily Post-Athenian* ran the headline "Record Vote Seen for McMinn with Clean Election Forecast."[10]

In the August 3, 1948 primary, Republican voters in the Seventh Senatorial District voted in a landslide for Burn. He defeated the incumbent, State Senator J.P. Cartwright of Athens, and challenger John Hoskins of Etowah for the Republican nomination. Burn won Monroe County with "an avalanche of votes."[11] He also won the district's largest county of Bradley. Hoskins won McMinn County, while Cartwright won Polk County.[12]

Burn and his family in the mid-1940s. *Burn family.*

While McMinn, Monroe and Bradley Counties held peaceful elections, violence at the polls in Polk County proved to be a harbinger for the many troubles Burn would soon face as state senator. Three men were killed and two others injured in election violence throughout the Copperhill area of Polk County. One election official was shot dead after the lights were shut off while he was counting votes. Another man was murdered in an ambush.[13] Dozens of National Guardsmen were called in to impose a curfew. In the presence of several witnesses, the ballots were counted, and the Democrats lost the election to the Good Government League (GGL), a nonpartisan political organization allegedly in favor of reform. The Burch Biggs machine was losing its grip on Polk County politics after years of dominance. During the peak of its power, Biggs-backed candidates received thousands of votes in the county, while their opponents would often tally fewer than fifty votes.[14]

Burn faced off against attorney Winston Prince of Cleveland in the general election. On November 2, 1948, the southeastern Tennessee community elected Burn to the State Senate. His margin of victory over Prince exceeded 4,000 votes. He won Prince's home county of Bradley 2,727 votes to 1,824 votes, having won nearly every precinct in the county.[15] The *Daily Post-Athenian* reported that Burn "swept Winston Prince completely out of the picture" in his 1,300-vote victory in McMinn County.[16] Burn's election to the State Senate came exactly thirty years after his election to the Tennessee House of Representatives in 1918. Statewide, the governorship went to Democrat Gordon Browning and Estes Kefauver won election to the U.S. Senate.

Unsuccessful in his bid to flip the Third Congressional District from blue to red, W.E. Michael lost the U.S. House of Representatives race to James B. Frazier Jr. But Michael eventually won election to the Tennessee House of Representatives, serving three terms in the 1960s. His son, Van, practiced law with him in Sweetwater. (Van became the lead developer of the Lost Sea, a popular tourist attraction in Monroe County.)

Burn thanked voters in the local papers. "I will strive to represent the entire district and my actions will not be governed by political considerations."[17] He added, "I shall support a constructive program of a non-political nature."[18] One of the most respected public figures of his time, a man who walked away from two elected offices when he could have been reelected numerous times, still could not avoid sounding like a politician by promising to be non-political.

On December 11, the State Senate Republicans elected Burn as their floor leader. "It will not be the attitude of the Republicans in the Senate to

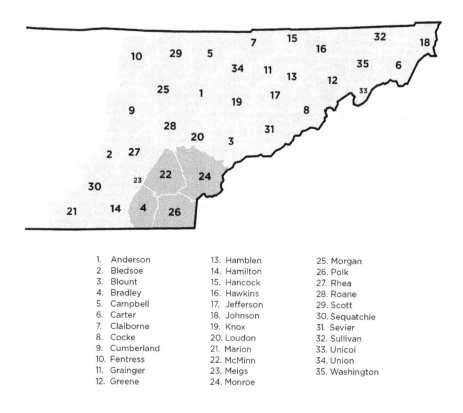

1. Anderson	13. Hamblen	25. Morgan
2. Bledsoe	14. Hamilton	26. Polk
3. Blount	15. Hancock	27. Rhea
4. Bradley	16. Hawkins	28. Roane
5. Campbell	17. Jefferson	29. Scott
6. Carter	18. Johnson	30. Sequatchie
7. Claiborne	19. Knox	31. Sevier
8. Cocke	20. Loudon	32. Sullivan
9. Cumberland	21. Marion	33. Unicoi
10. Fentress	22. McMinn	34. Union
11. Grainger	23. Meigs	35. Washington
12. Greene	24. Monroe	

The Seventh Senatorial District. *Map by Navigation Advertising, LLC, Murfreesboro, Tennessee.*

adopt obstructionist tactics. We will support measures of the Browning Administration, which we approve. However, we are going to maintain our identity as we can play our proper part as the Republican minority," Burn said.[19] He would get on well with Browning, and the two had some ideas in common.

The 76th General Assembly began its session on Monday, January 3, 1949. On January 7, the Speaker of the Senate announced the appointment of the pages. Tommy served as one of three new pages.[20]

Throughout the session, Burn introduced several bills to amend the charter of several cities in his district. In the era preceding "home rule," cities relied on the state government in much of their decision-making. Cities would sometimes have to wait until the legislature was back in session to pass a private act to address a local problem. Home rule would soon become a reality in Tennessee. Burn would be there to see it through.

Burn and ten other senators introduced a successful bill to provide for a state educational system.[21] He introduced a series of bills to authorize schools to purchase and loan textbooks for Monroe, McMinn and Bradley Counties. He introduced an unsuccessful bill to authorize free schoolbooks for Polk County.[22]

Burn worked with colleagues to introduce a bill to provide bonuses for veterans of World War I and World War II.[23] Unfortunately, the bill did not pass, nor did a bill that he supported to increase pensions to widows of Confederate veterans.

Not only did Burn support laws to recognize suffrage for all citizens, but he also always managed to be in office to vote on such matters. He introduced a series of bills to provide permanent registration for voters in Monroe, McMinn and Polk Counties.[24] All three failed to pass. But the legislature made progress toward universal suffrage. A bill abolishing the poll tax statewide in primary elections became law. Also, women, the blind, disabled veterans and people over fifty became exempt from the poll tax.[25] Burn voted for all of these bills.[26]

A strong supporter of sin taxes, Burn introduced a bill to regulate and tax the sale of beer in certain counties.[27] One of these bills would have doubled the tax on beer and liquor. Neither bill became law. His prohibitionist tendencies had not mellowed in the decades after his vote to ratify the Eighteenth Amendment. He supported a bill to hold local option elections on beer in certain counties.[28] The bill eventually became law. He consistently supported bills that recognized the right of localities to vote on issues affecting them.

The most impactful laws passed during Burn's first term in the State Senate worked to ensure clean elections for all Tennessee voters. Governor Browning spearheaded a series of election reform bills based on an eight-point program by the Tennessee Press Association (TPA): universal permanent registration of all voters, requiring the use of standard metal ballot boxes with locks except where voting machines are used, forbidding any office holder or candidate in a current election or primary from serving as an election commissioner or primary board member or in any capacity as an official at the polls, revising absentee voting laws to safeguard against fraud and requiring that all sessions of elections commissions and primary boards be open to the public and a record kept of same.[29]

Burn and other State Senate Republicans said they were "for the governor" in the drive to achieve election reform.[30] Memphis political boss E.H. Crump, scared of losing his power, fiercely opposed these reform bills.

Fortunately, his power diminished by the day. Governor Browning, a fellow Democrat and former ally of Crump, lead the way to take down the Crump machine once and for all.

Beginning in the early 1900s, E.H. "Boss" Crump had served as mayor of Memphis. He later won a term in the U.S. Congress. He eventually became a millionaire political boss, not serving in office but controlling who served in various positions. From 1932 to 1948, he virtually decided statewide elections through the manipulation of hundreds of thousands of Shelby County voters in the era of the poll tax. Some characterize Crump's regime as "benevolent," citing the increased public services in Shelby County during his reign. But his violations of individual rights and abuses of power cannot be excused. One reporter was beaten for "getting too close to election fraud."[31] Crump refused permits to new businesses that refused to buy insurance from his company.[32] Crump's actions were rooted in his lust for power and wealth through dishonesty and extortion.

The Committee on Privileges and Elections studied the TPA proposals. One senator spoke to people in the less populated communities who informed him that multiple voting is practiced there as well as in cities. Where no registration is required, the same people voted in town and then went out and voted in one or more county polling places.[33]

Burn helped develop a bill to prohibit government employees from serving as election officials. Exemptions included schoolteachers and members of the legislature. The bill barely passed in the Senate. He also pushed for the measure to permit judges to witness the marking of ballots. The measure passed 20–6. State Senator R.B. Ragon Jr. of Chattanooga opposed these bills. "We have trouble finding people to serve in holding elections as it is!"[34] Burn thought back to the recent event in his home county when he responded to Ragon. "Three years ago the newspapers of the state were full of stories about the Battle of Athens. Armed deputies and the sheriff carrying ballot boxes off to change them precipitated that battle. I hope to high heaven you pass this bill to keep men like that away from the ballot box!"[35]

Critics of the bill claimed that it would interfere with the secret ballot and that it would discourage the blind and illiterate voters. Burn called these claims "exaggerated and misconstrued" and said that judges were needed to witness and ensure that voters properly marked their ballots. "All this talk of making the vote public is just plain hooey!"[36] State Senator Don Lewis of Elizabethton said, "I can't understand why you gentlemen oppose something that will promote clean elections."[37] That Burn advocated passionately for clean elections and to crack down on election fraud comes as no surprise to anyone from McMinn County. Discussing the new laws, an assistant clerk remarked to Burn that "[w]hen the politicians realize just what this legislature has done to the election laws they will think a long time before permitting irregularities. I would certainly be afraid to have a part in any monkey business."[38]

McMinn County has another connection to women in government and support for suffrage rights: State Representative Mary Shadow. From Meigs County, McMinn's neighbor to the west, Mary's sister Muriel was married to C. Scott Mayfield. Founded in Athens, Mayfield Dairy Farms is one of the most successful industries in McMinn County's history. In her early twenties, Mary Shadow served as floterial representative for Rhea and Meigs Counties. At this time, she was also the state's lone woman legislator.

Inspired by the needs of her rural county, Mary Shadow introduced a universal registration bill in the Tennessee House of Representatives. She responded to critics who claimed the bill was not wanted in small rural counties. "I come from a small rural county and we certainly want to be included in a permanent registration bill."[39] Shadow was serious about enacting reforms that would relieve Tennessee communities of this constant threat to clean elections. She felt inspired to run for office after studying political science in college and hoped to inspire the younger generation to the needs for more safeguarding of election privileges and duties.[40] Two voter registration bills eventually became law, including one providing for permanent registration in counties with more than 50,000 people in population and towns and civil districts with more than 2,500 people in population.[41]

Governor Browning signed the main points of the TPA's clean election program into law, including Burn's bill to forbid all public officials (except for teachers and state legislators) from serving as election officials. A new law required election commission meetings to be open to the public and to keep records. The new laws ordered the use of metal ballot boxes and allowed election judges to witness the marking of ballots.[42] Burn told the *Sweetwater Valley News*:

> *If two or more join to violate any election law such will be considered a conspiracy punishable as a felony. This is the first time in Tennessee history that one could be sentenced to the penitentiary for stealing the birthright of his neighbors…as the Senator from McMinn County, scene of the "Battle of Athens" of 1946, and Polk County, scene of the "Battle of Polk" in 1948, I was pleased with the progress made toward safeguarding the ballot box and the rights of our citizens to have their votes counted as cast.*[43]

It did not take Burn long to ignite controversy in Sweetwater over his local legislation. Monroe County representative Homer Johnson introduced a bill to ban the sale of beer, wine and other alcoholic beverages in Sweetwater.[44] Burn staunchly supported the bill.

Continuing his fight against what he perceived as vice, Burn was involved in a lawsuit against the operators of a café business that had been selling beer without the landlord's consent. He tried to get the business evicted from the building. At this time, selling beer without the property owner's consent in Sweetwater violated the law. Upset with the city government for not enforcing the law, he said he would not hesitate to vote for what he thought was right if he believed a local official was wrong. He said it was a moral issue. "I take my stand on the side of right and common decency." He claimed there was "so much misinformation" being spread around about the "so-called beer bill."[45]

W.E. Michael vehemently opposed the beer bill, and his friendship with Burn began to strain. Michael responded to Burn's remarks in a rare letter to the editor in the *Sweetwater Valley News*. He took his former law partner head on. "I never try my lawsuits in newspapers….Sweetwater voters decry the decision of Representative Johnson of turning Sweetwater over to your tender mercies."[46]

Michael represented the café operators that sold beer without the owner's consent. Pointing out the bill's unpopularity, Michael said that Burn had obviously not spoken to many constituents. He continued calling out Burn:

> *Some question your motive. The moral issue is whether or not one who is elected to serve in a representative capacity should betray the trust imposed in him by his party and the people who elected him to use his office for his own personal benefit. This type of legislation will do irreparable damage to our county and our party. It appears you have destroyed any opportunity to accomplish anything worthwhile. You are not proposing bills you discussed in the campaign that will benefit the county and state. I regret this very deeply.*[47]

Joe Sherlin remembered hearing a story about the controversial beer bill. "Harry was meeting with local ministers about the beer bill. Somebody delivered a case of beer to Harry's office. 'Mr. Burn, here is the beer you ordered.' Harry was so mad he ran down the stairs and out the door chasing after the delivery boy to find out who sent him the beer!"[48]

Main Street in Sweetwater. *McMinn County Historical Society.*

After an absence from the State Senate during the controversy over his Sweetwater beer bill, Burn explained:

> *I was suffering from "localitis," which is especially prevalent in Polk, Bradley, and Monroe Counties. McMinn County may expect an invasion of the epidemic when bills now being prepared are sent to the representative from that county. The "disease" is most virulent in Sweetwater—still the best small town in America. A symptom of this disease is high blood pressures on the part of the Senator and Representative, which reflect still higher blood pressures on part of some constituents. Many people back home say the disease is closely related to the foot and mouth disease, in that a legislator opens his mouth and puts his foot in it. There is no quick cure for this "disease." The suggestion that newly enacted legislation can be revised at the next session obtains no results for the simple reason that the person to whom the suggestion is made is morally sure there will be no next session for the one making the suggestion. Fortunately, our constituents are good Americans and accept democratic processes, but time is the only known cure for "localitis."* [49]

After meddling with Sweetwater citizens' beer, Burn attempted to change the city's boundaries. He introduced several city limit expansion bills in the State Senate. But his visions for a growing community could not always be reconciled with the citizens of his communities. Many citizens and local government officials in these cities opposed his expansion efforts.

Sweetwater, though larger than Niota, was a small city, home to almost four thousand residents. The population had doubled since 1920. Burn wanted it to continue its growth. In many of her 1920 interviews, Febb Burn proudly shared her son's ambitions to help his community grow.

Burn proposed a bill to expand the Sweetwater city limits.[50] It included a referendum for the citizens to vote on the issue. As he had always done, he thought big. The bill would significantly enlarge the city's boundaries. "If the bill passes, Sweetwater will be the only town in the United States fronting on both the Atlantic and Pacific Oceans," W.E. Michael said.[51]

Burn believed that the city limits bill would benefit Sweetwater because of the impending new sales tax refund. Based on the results of the coming 1950 U.S. Census, Tennessee cities over a certain population would receive a sales tax refund. Burn wished for Sweetwater to qualify, but it was up to him to convince the people to agree.

The beer bill, if passed, would permit beer to be sold on the one block of Railroad Street between Morris and Chestnut Streets. It included a prohibition on selling beer within eight hundred feet of churches and schools and a requirement for vendors to own their own buildings or get permission from the owner to sell beer. Michael continued ridiculing Burn's Sweetwater bills:

> *The city limits will be the equator on the south, the rising sun on the east, the Aurora Borealis to the north, and the Promised Land in the west... and the only oasis on this great desert will be the block on the east side of Railroad Street between Morris and Chestnut.*[52]

The city commission asked Governor Browning to veto the beer bill. Burn defended the bill from those claiming it to be unconstitutional.[53] Michael disputed Burn's claims that the café required a license and the property owner's permission to sell beer.[54]

Burn got into another public feud in the newspaper, this time with Sweetwater citizen Harry Hall. Hall discussed a public rally "to decide if the majority of citizens want his legislation." Hall claimed that Burn said he would not attend the rally because "all public rallies are crowded with bums and hoodlums." Hall questioned Burn's courage to face the citizens.[55] Responding to Hall, Burn said:

> *A referendum at the ballot box is the only solution.... The tirade of Harry Hall...will impress no one who knows that for years he was a darling of the Washington politicians, presumably with his snout in some parasitic pursuit. During the New Deal era he advised members of Congress how to run the federal government. Now he condescends to tell the elected representatives of the City of Sweetwater how they should vote on local legislation. He says he likes me personally but has fought me for ten years. It may have begun years ago when I was on the side against him in a case. After years supporting New Deal-ism he began positioning himself for a political job if Dewey was elected. I never said all public rallies are crowded with bums and hoodlums. I said that such meetings were invitations for agitators to misrepresent the facts and for some demagogue to take charge. I will not walk into traps that enemies are so eager for me to step in to.*[56]

After several revisions, Governor Browning signed the Sweetwater city limits bill into law. But the city government remained dissatisfied with the bill. Burn's permanent registration bill for Monroe County failed to become law.

Burn discussed the legislature's accomplishments in the *Sweetwater Valley News*. He discussed the state's new education and road programs. He said it was easy to criticize the legislature but also acknowledged that sometimes criticism is warranted. "Service in the legislature does not transform an individual into Utopian perfection nor into an ogre....Every dictator has climbed into power by first striking at the representatives of the people in the legislative branch."[57] He did not take criticism well on this issue, as evident by his inappropriate remarks inferring that criticism of the legislature precedes dictatorship.

Burn also criticized Boss Crump of Memphis: "In Tennessee for years we had one man on the banks of the Mississippi pulling wires behind the scenes. In Sweetwater we recently had two or three individuals who thought they could control legislation behind the scenes. They did not 'know' Governor Browning. They did not use the methods of reason and persuasion. They attempted to take control of legislation behind the scenes. You should be thankful that their efforts failed."[58]

The entrance to Burn's second-floor law office in the Scruggs Building (New Block) in Sweetwater. The building still stands. *McMinn County Historical Society.*

Burn took pride in what he and Governor Browning accomplished in diminishing the power of political bosses like Crump who had engaged in voter manipulation for decades. He had reason to be proud of the laws he developed with Governor Browning, but he made a mistake comparing dissenting Sweetwater citizens to a figure like Crump. Harry T. Burn Jr. later wrote that his father "had a very thick hide in the courtroom and the political arena."[59] But Burn's handling of the criticism of his Sweetwater bills proved to be an exception to that.

Burn discussed his vote to authorize a referendum to hold a limited constitutional convention in Tennessee. "The first vote I ever cast was for a constitutional convention....I was elected from Roane County to be a delegate in 1924 at a convention that was never held due to lack of sufficient support required in the constitution....I want to bring home rule to all municipalities on all questions. Local legislation should not be the responsibility of the General Assembly, as it is now."[60] He knew that amending Tennessee's constitution would help the state move forward and improve.

When Burn introduced a bill to expand the city limits of his beloved Niota, a repeat of the Sweetwater controversy ensued. The city commission clashed with Burn over the bill for several weeks. It had the "little community in quite an uproar," according to the *Daily Post Athenian.*[61] Several hundred Niota citizens held a meeting expressing their opposition to the bill. Although Burn did not attend the meeting, McMinn County representative G.L. Aderhold said he would not support any bill unless a majority of Niotans found it "satisfactory."[62]

W.T. Conar, city recorder, staunchly opposed the bill and engaged in a public feud with Burn in the *Daily Post-Athenian.* Burn accused opponents of spreading "falsehoods and deliberate misinformation" about the legislation.[63] He strongly implied that Conar only opposed the bill to create publicity for himself because he had plans to run for local office. Burn assured voters that the bill would not be voted on in the legislature if Niotans did not approve it in a referendum.[64]

Under the bill, Niota's new boundaries included moving the northern boundary to the McMinn-Monroe County line, the southern boundary about six hundred yards north of the Athens city limits, the western boundary to Marshall Hill and the eastern boundary up on the ridge. Burn claimed the proposal would increase the city limits by 20 percent while adding two dozen new houses.[65]

Conar, referring to Burn as the "great stalwart of democracy," claimed Burn had a misconception of what constitutes a democracy "of the people, by the people, and for the people."[66] He scolded Burn for refusing to discuss the issue publicly with the citizens. Continuing to deny that the proposed bill included a referendum on the issue in Niota, he said he wondered if Burn considered himself a "ruler" and Niotans as his "subjects."[67]

Burn also wished for Niota to qualify for the sales tax refund. The city had insufficient funds for paving roads, and the refund had the potential to bring in the city thousands of dollars. He worried that an increase in the city's property tax would be inflicted on the citizens should the city not qualify for the sales tax refund.

Burn responded to Conar's characterization of him as "dictator-like": "If my efforts to cooperate with those who are trying to regain tax money already paid and to get it back every year for the next ten years is 'dictation,' then the word has a new meaning....Furthermore, I have absolutely no fear of political reprisals."[68]

"He is so determined that Niota will be a big city that he would stop at nothing to beat opposition," Conar replied.[69] Conar expressed his fear that Burn would revise the bill to include a city manager so he could get rid of the city board and city recorder. "I agree with him that he has no fear of political reprisal for he is politically mad."[70]

Burn had dreamed since childhood of growth for his hometown. But Conar and other Niotans wished for the city to remain small. Burn and Aderhold worked together on revising the bill. "Niota will have a slight extension of the city limits."[71] Telephone calls and reports from Niota revealed that many residents were not happy with the proposals. The city commission remained opposed to the city limit expansion "whether it be large or small."[72]

The bill passed both chambers of the legislature. Burn denied that he ever received a petition or even one written objection to the bill. "The enactment of the bill completed my legislative program, both general and local, one hundred percent."[73] Shortly before the bill passed, the Niota city commission dismissed him from his longtime position as city attorney. The hometown hero had gotten the boot. Despite all of his conflicts with constituents over his proposed city limit bills, he always worked carefully to ensure that every bill had an option for a local referendum on the issue.

Although Cleveland already had enough people to qualify for the sales tax refund, Burn still supported growth for his district's largest city. Stuart Park, East Cleveland and the Lusk subdivision would all be annexed by the city under his bill.[74] The residents of these areas petitioned the city requesting incorporation, wishing to have access to the city's police, fire, road and school services. The city commission unanimously supported the plan. They reached a compromise with Bradley and Polk County's floterial representative, Frank Lowery, including a referendum for the five thousand people in the areas proposed to be annexed. The bill later became law.

Burn and Lowery both introduced bills in their chambers to levy a 10 percent tax on retail beer sales in the city of Cleveland.[75] If you wanted to have easy and cheap access to alcohol without having to drive far away to obtain it, it was best to not live in a district represented by Harry T. Burn. The bills failed to become law.

Inspired by the system in Hamilton County, Burn introduced a bill for permanent voter registration in Bradley County. Under the bill, only one permanent registration would be required the following August. The bill required the county election commission to set up an office in the courthouse. Each voter would get a card after registering and would only be required to reregister if they missed six consecutive primary or general elections.[76] Bradley County's leaders disliked the bill and requested its withdrawal, claiming that it imposed "too great a cost and is too cumbersome for Bradley."[77] They complained about the bill's provisions requiring an election commission office in the courthouse and the employ of a full-time registrar. The bill failed to become law.

By the end of the 1949 session, Burn had introduced 103 bills, and Governor Browning signed 21 of them into law. Burn's problems in Monroe County did not go away after the legislature adjourned. The Monroe County Republican Party disclaimed the Burn-Johnson legislation at its June meeting. "Our representatives acted as individuals on their own behalf and not as representatives of the G.O.P. of Monroe County."[78] Later that summer, the Monroe County Republican Party reelected W.E. Michael as chairman. Immediately after the vote, Burn and several of his supporters got up from their chairs and left the meeting.[79]

Burn attempted to set up a full-time election registrar in the old Bradley County Courthouse. *Ridley Willis Collection, Cleveland Public Library History Branch and Archives.*

Michael humbly accepted the nomination, remarking that many others deserved the position. Burn claimed that he had no interest in the position. "Eventually the decent element of the party will learn what Sweetwater Republicans already know. Then they will correct the situation."[80] He considered running for circuit court judge but ultimately decided to seek reelection in the State Senate.[81] The controversy over some of his local legislation ensured that he would face a challenger in the 1950 primary. A challenger emerged from Athens.

Chapter 11

SECOND TERM IN THE STATE SENATE

W.L. Ledford of Athens challenged Burn for the Republican nomination for the Seventh Senatorial District in the summer of 1950. Ledford campaigned on a promise to "not pass any ripper bills to tear up your county."[1] Frank Lowery, the Democratic representative for the floterial district of Bradley and Polk Counties, had pushed through successful bills in the 1949 legislature changing the Polk County government. The bills removed the power of the county's quarterly court and created a county commission. Critics of such bills called them "ripper bills."

Burn emphasized how he had no argument with Lowery on local legislation. He had demonstrated a good working relationship with Democrats who held ideas in common with him, including Governor Browning. He reminded voters that he preferred to defer to the county representatives on local legislation.

Burn said he did not have "a program for local legislation in any county." He instead focused on statewide issues. "I will devote my efforts principally toward obtaining for East Tennessee a fair portion of the membership of the Senate and House of Representatives. Under the present apportionment we are denied that basic right."[2] He foresaw the need for reapportionment in Tennessee long before the state was finally forced to address the issue. He ran campaign ads touting his record on "schools and roads."[3]

The *Cleveland Daily Banner* reported that observers questioned Burn's chances of reelection. Predicting that he would not carry Bradley County, they also reported on "strong opposition" in his home county of Monroe.[4]

RE·ELECT

HARRY T.
BURN
——STATE——
SENATOR
Republican Nominee · · Second Term
Tues., Nov.7

Campaign poster from Burn's State Senate reelection campaign in 1950. *Burn family.*

Several Niotans had not forgiven Burn for his attempt to expand their city limits. It looked as if he would be facing another challenging reelection.

Burn defeated Ledford in the August 3, 1950 Republican primary. He lost Bradley and Monroe by more than five hundred votes each. But he doubled Ledford's vote in McMinn and defeated Ledford ten to one in Polk.[5] The front page of the *Daily Post-Athenian* read, "It looks like Tennessee has had its first peaceful August election since the war."[6] Burn thanked primary voters in the local papers. Possibly referencing the controversy over his bill to expand the Niota city limits, he said, "I deeply appreciate their endorsement of my record in the 1949 General Assembly."[7]

Burn began his campaign against the Democratic nominee Vance Davis of Benton, a former judge. The *Daily Post-Athenian* reported that the State Senate race was "the hottest race in McMinn."[8] Davis ran ads promising to support the needs of farmers and veterans. He vowed to never pass local legislation that the people opposed and to "work in harmony" with county representatives.[9]

Burn ran more ads in the *Daily Post-Athenian*, including "Vote for Harry T. Burn. Support a McMinn County boy!"[10] He also expressed his support for widening Main Street (U.S. Highway 11) through Sweetwater into a four-lane highway. "By working together we should obtain such a highway as a part of the state system."[11]

The Good Government League (GGL) of Polk County endorsed Frank Lowery for floterial representative of Bradley and Polk Counties and Vance Davis for State Senate. Lowery, formerly a Democrat, stood for reelection as an independent against Thomas Johnston, a Democrat and a disabled World War II veteran, and John "Buck" Arp, a Republican. As discussed previously, Polk County had recently ousted Burch Biggs, a corrupt sheriff connected to the Crump machine in Memphis. Many of the county's problems persisted even after Biggs's ouster. Burn reminded voters about the corruption in the Polk County treasury. He accused Davis and Lowery of trying to return to power the local officials who were "responsible for the deplorable condition of the county treasury."[12]

Burn told Bradley County voters that he was running a "hands-off Bradley County" platform.[13] He said he would consider no bills providing for changes in the city or county government without first having submitted such proposals to the people. "Choose ye next Tuesday whom ye will serve, the taxpayers with their great burden of taxation, or the politicians who act as if your money was theirs," Burn said.[14] He had no tolerance for waste, fraud or abuse.

Burn explained his proposal to make Bradley County's Pike Road superintendent an elected position. His reason was because of the superintendent's power over purchasing. "A man who spends as much of the taxpayers' money as the road supervisor ought to be elected by the people," he claimed.[15] It was said that the position had been controversial and often used as a political weapon. He accused Davis of "seeking out individuals and making agreements with them rather than by taking his plans to the public" and condemned their "vest-pocket politics."[16]

The *Cleveland Daily Banner*'s editorial board praised Burn. The board complimented his "clear and forthright statements" during the campaign. In contrast to Burn, the paper criticized the "ambiguous" Lowery and Davis.[17]

Burn defeated Davis on November 7, 1950, winning reelection to a second term in the State Senate. He won McMinn, Monroe and Bradley Counties.[18] He would now be working with two new state representatives: Abe Trew and Beverly Wood, who were elected to serve as the McMinn and Monroe County Representatives, respectively. Frank Lowery won reelection as the floterial representative for Bradley and Polk Counties. Governor Browning easily won reelection. The *Polk County News* reported that Davis's loss was the first loss for a GGL candidate since its creation in 1946 and that the election "was quiet all over the county with less than half the voters voting."[19]

One week after the general election, the front page of the *Polk County News* reported the bombshell that would reverberate in the county for years to come. "Fraud Charged in Polk Vote" read the headline on November 16.[20] The defeated candidate for floterial representative, disabled World War II veteran Democrat Thomas Johnston, obtained an injunction restraining the Polk County Election Commission from disposing of election records. He contested the election on grounds of fraud in the canvass of votes. It

THE POLK COUNTY NEWS

Vol. 67—No. 38   BENTON, TENNESSEE, NOVEMBER 16, 1950   PRICE FIVE CENTS

Fraud Charged in Polk Vote

Lewis Receives Election Post

W. A. Lewis, leader of one faction of the Polk County Quarterly Court and Polk county campaign manager for Governor Gordon Browning was appointed a member of the Polk County Election Commission last week. Lewis succeeds Frank I. Lowe who resigned to make an independent race for representative.

Lewis' appointment created a great deal of comment in local politics, because he had recently been adjudged by Chancellor Glenn Woodlee as the duly elected chairman [in a term in office] by county court and as such would carry on the duties of the chairman until a chairman was elected. Also it was reliably reported that Lowery ...

Jake Higgins

I have been reminiscent this week, recalling memories long since almost forgotten. I have been recalling the old Bob Tay-

BULLETIN

Thomas Lynn Johnston, Cleveland Democrat, defeated narrowly in the Nov. 7, general election in his run against Frank D. Lowery, Ocoee, independent, for the office of floterial representative, Wednesday obtained an injunction restraining Polk County Election Commission from disposing of election records pending outcome of Johnston's contest on grounds of fraud in the canvass of votes last Monday.

The injunction, answerable to Chancellor Glenn W. Woodlee, in the latter's court here, was issued by Circuit Judge L. D. Miller, of Chattanooga, on application by Johnston.

Johnston's bill impounded all records, including those of poll taxes, absentee votes and others, involved in the election, along with scroll and tally sheets.

It was contended by the plaintiff that revisions made in the election tally were part of an alleged fraud which accomplished Johnston's defeat at the hands of Lowery, incumbent running on an independent ticket. Lowery's pre-canvass majority in Bradley and Polk Counties was

Burns-Johnston Charge Wholesale Fraud

Charges of "glaring, wholesale fraud" were leveled at Polk County election officials Monday by State Senator Harry T. Burn and Thomas Lynn Johnston, Democratic nominee for Floterial Representative from Polk and Bradley counties, who brought the charges after witnessing the official canvass here Monday.

Late Monday afternoon Johnston served notice of Frank D. Lowery, that he would contest Lowery's election before the House of Representatives when it meets in Nashville in January 1951.

... Burn who was barely ... by a small 67 majority in ... ... making up the ... ... district, stated

Although he still won reelection, news of election fraud in the 1950 Polk County general election made Burn furious. *From the* Polk County News.

appeared the GGL was involved in the fraud, attempting to win back power recently lost to the Democrats.

Among the records impounded included poll tax receipts, absentee votes, scrolls and tally sheets.[21] After witnessing the canvass results, Johnston called it "glaring wholesale fraud" and said that Lowery had more than doubled his majority in Bradley and Polk Counties.[22] The State Senate contest between Burn and Davis was allegedly "a reduction in a four county majority of more than 700 votes for Burn to 67 votes."[23] Although Burn still won reelection, he called for a federal investigation. He was absolutely livid. He told the county election commission:

> *I have seen with my own eyes—and those of you who are witnesses here have also seen—the most brazen, barefaced attempt, to steal an election, in the history of Tennessee....I urge you, gentlemen, in the name of common decency, and honesty, not to make yourselves parties to this palpable fraud by certifying these returns. There were so many irregularities apparent on the record that two election commissioners voted to adjourn the canvass without certifying the returns.[24]*

Burn and Johnston charged that ballots were improperly marked, that illegal absentee ballots were cast and that ballot boxes were unlocked.[25] Burn offered to appear before the GGL Executive Committee to "present evidence that fraud was perpetrated in the election."[26] GGL chairman Robert Barclay ignored his offer.

The Polk County election commissioner admitted that the scroll sheets were altered and that the total was changed to benefit Lowery. He also said that several ballot boxes were unlocked when brought from the vault of the election commission on the day of the official count. Lowery's attorney requested to examine the scroll sheets and other records.[27] The courts could not find a parallel case. "This is probably the first time such a case has come up for decision" in Tennessee history.[28]

The Tennessee House of Representatives announced its intention to try the contest in January. A joint committee of the House and the Senate would have final disposition of the state's election contest and would likely order a complete recount of the election records. Burn got his wish when a U.S. attorney stated that the Polk County situation was the subject of "active inquiry" by President Truman's Justice Department.[29] By legislative order, the records of the votes were removed to Nashville for investigation.[30]

Before he was sworn in for his second and final term in the State Senate, Burn and three of his East Tennessee Republican colleagues drafted a redistricting bill. The bill attempted to address Tennessee's long-overdue reapportionment needs. The state legislature had failed to follow the state constitution by not reapportioning since 1901.

Burn reached out to the delegations from Tennessee's four major urban centers. He believed that the urban centers and the region of East Tennessee, all of which had grown in population recently, would benefit from more adequate representation. State Senator Don Lewis of Elizabethton said, "We believe it would give East Tennessee better representation."[31] Many rural legislators voiced their opposition to the bill, claiming that their counties "would suffer considerably from reapportionment."[32] This sparked the beginning of an urban-versus-rural clash that would remain unsolved for years, but it was not for a lack of trying on the part of Burn and his colleagues.

"I realize that any reapportionment will be on a partisan basis, and that the Democratic Party in power could tie larger Democratic counties to every district so that reapportionment would be a sort of gerrymandering proposition," Burn said. However, he claimed that the state constitution must be upheld and that the legislature would have to "let the chips fall where they may" in the redistricting process.[33] Senator Lewis said, "I represent 172,000 people in my district, and that's too many." Knox County was split into three Senate districts, each representing approximately 75,000 people. "Proper representation under the 1950 census would be less than 100,000," Lewis added.[34]

State Senator Glenn Yoakum of Taswell remarked that the bill could "mean about a 35 percent increase in Republican representation in the legislature." Referencing the recent population growth in the region, Yoakum claimed that "59 percent of taxes in the state are paid by East Tennesseans." He knew that his district was underrepresented compared to districts in other parts of the state. "I represent seven counties in the Senate....Gibson County in West Tennessee, which has a Senator of its own, is only a little larger than one of mine."[35] State Senator Henry Butler of Pigeon Forge also chimed in: "The cities will gain tremendously from reapportionment....I stand to lose a little myself by it, but I think it should be done. I think it's best for the state."[36] Burn said, "Davidson County would probably have twice its present representation" under proper reapportionment. But the urban delegations were reluctant at first to support the bill. Burn also pointed out that the heavily Democratic counties of Anderson and Sullivan in East Tennessee would make considerable gains.[37]

The 77th General Assembly began its session on New Year's Day 1951. Tommy, Burn's now thirteen-year-old son, again served as a page during the session. Senate Republicans nominated Burn for Speaker of the Senate.[38] He was not elected to the position.

Burn and a colleague introduced another bill to provide for local option elections relative to beer.[39] This bill, like the one he introduced in the previous session, failed to become law. He voted aye on a successful bill to levy a tax on retail sales of beer.[40]

The State Senate sent a bill to Governor Browning requiring that one year of U.S. history be taught in high school. Burn supported the bill.[41] He also supported a successful bill permitting women to serve on juries.[42]

In light of the ongoing Polk County election fraud investigation, Burn introduced a bill to regulate the handling of election returns.[43] The bill failed to become law. In response to accusations of communist infiltration in the government, Burn worked with colleagues to introduce two bills: to prohibit subversive persons from occupying state positions of trust and to prohibit subversive organizations and activities in the Department of State.[44] Neither bill became law.

After weeks of investigating the election fraud charges in Polk County, the joint committee of the legislature found no irregularities in Bradley County, but in Polk County "it was an entirely different story."[45] The committee was unable to conclude that Polk County held a valid election.

Evidence proved that more than two hundred unregistered persons were shown to have voted.[46]

Precedent from the Tennessee Supreme Court noted that "if illegal voters participate in an election in sufficient number to change the result had they all voted one way, the courts will declare such election completely void."[47] The joint committee said, "When we apply this principle to our contest, then Lowery's illegal votes are subtracted and Johnston becomes the winner…we see no alternative except to report to this body that our judgment in this election so far as Polk County is concerned, was void, and we recommend a new election be called."[48]

Burn testified during the investigation. Due to the expense involved of transporting witnesses to Nashville for their testimonies, a hearing took place in Benton (the Polk County seat).[49] Burn took to the witness stand first. He talked about the difference between the vote totals in the official canvass and the totals announced on election night. Election officials substantiated his claims.[50]

Some witnesses claimed in testimony to not having voted despite their names appearing twice on the scrolls. Others testified to having voted once, but their names appeared twice on tally sheets. Johnston's lawyers produced evidence that two persons listed as having voted were dead.[51]

The testimonies had concluded by February, lasting almost a week. The *Polk County News* reported that Benton became the stormy center of the most "spectacular election contest on record" and one that attracted national attention. "Observers agree that whatever changes were made to the votes were changed after the night of Nov. 7 when the unofficial canvass was announced."[52]

On February 15, the joint committee's report passed by a 72–3 vote in the House of Representatives to unseat Lowery.[53] Johnston took the oath of office to become the floterial representative for Bradley and Polk Counties. Keeping his promise to voters, Burn waited to introduce local bills until the Lowery-Johnston election was decided. "I prefer to wait until I can confer with the seated representative."[54] He praised the *Cleveland Daily Banner* for its coverage of the Polk election fraud investigation and trial. "I wish to heartily congratulate the Daily Banner for its courageous and unwavering course in interest of good government and honesty in public affairs.…It should give pause in the future to those who might connive or conspire to attain public office through fraudulent methods."[55]

After Johnston was sworn in, Burn immediately demanded a Polk "housecleaning." He said he would remove Barclay from the county commission unless he "kicks the rascals out."[56] He charged that Barclay was present at the Ducktown precinct on election night with a county employee who took part in ballot stuffing. "Why does he not want the thieves prosecuted?" Could it be because he is trying to protect some of his political bedfellows? If they do not go, he will go."[57] GGL chairman Barclay was furious:

> *There has never been in the state of Tennessee a grander steal of an election than was pulled right there in the state capitol. All of this is the direct result of the blank, unreasoning, immature man that animates our present state. By his Hitler-like, dictatorial personality and his childlike reaction to what he deems is due him, but is not given him, he set out on sounder basis than purely vengeful spite to wreck Polk County. He is largely responsible for the acts of the General Assembly when it ran roughshod over the majority of Polk Countians.*[58]

Burn and Johnston, determined to clean up Polk County government, demonstrated that election fraud would not be tolerated. Johnston proceeded to introduce a bill to abolish the Polk County commission.[59] Governor Browning signed the bill, returning power to the county court. Another bill created the office of county attorney.[60] Burn and Johnston also introduced bills to repeal the county school board and place the election of a new school board and road supervisor in the hands of the county court.[61] Finally, to break a deadlock on the county court, Burn and Johnston introduced successful legislation to incorporate Ducktown. This gave the Democrats a five-to-four majority on the newly enlarged county court.[62]

The *Cleveland Daily Banner* criticized the Burn-Johnston "ripper legislation," claiming that it was "based upon determination to have personal revenge against political enemies." The newspaper seemingly excused the reaction of some Polk Countians to the legislation, alleging it was "stirring such great resentment that violence becomes increasingly likely....If violence does flair, the Daily Banner believes that the men who so greatly contributed to its incitement should be held equally culpable with any who may be held participants."[63] The newspaper implored Governor Browning to carefully consider his support of the Burn-Johnston legislation.[64]

Burn responded to the newspaper's criticism, including claims of the two legislators "inciting riot." Burn said, "In recent months, people of Polk County have been beaten up, shot at, and run out of the county and the perpetrators have not even been prosecuted by officeholders sponsored by the Good Government League....The legislation we have passed is absolutely essential to the proper functioning of government in Polk County."[65] He never apologized for their Polk County legislation.

Burn saw one of his Polk County bills finally signed into law. The bill provided a system of road construction and maintenance in Polk County.[66] He also introduced a bill to provide clerical help for the county judge and the county court chairman.[67] He worked to ensure that Polk County remained functional in the aftermath of its fraudulent election and borderline anarchy during the 1951 session.

During what would be his final term in the state legislature, Burn once again had the opportunity to cast a vote to amend the U.S. Constitution. He deserves praise for his remarkable political timing. The Twenty-Second Amendment was the first amendment to be ratified since 1933 (the same year the Eighteenth Amendment, which Burn had voted to ratify in 1919, was repealed by the Twenty-First Amendment). The amendment limits the president of the United States to two terms or ten years in office. The U.S. Constitution originally had no term limits for the presidency and, to this day, has none for members of Congress. An excerpt from Section 1 of the Twenty-Second Amendment:

> *No person shall be elected to the office of the President more than twice, and no person who has held the office of President, or acted as President, for more than two years of a term to which some other person was elected President shall be elected to the office of the President more than once.*

President George Washington established the two-term precedent when he declined to run for a third term in 1796. Six U.S. presidents were elected to and served two terms in the nineteenth century. Although some attempted, no former president had been nominated by a major party for a third term until Theodore Roosevelt. He ran unsuccessfully on the Bull Moose Party ticket in 1912. Woodrow Wilson also served two terms as president and considered running for a third term.

President Franklin D. Roosevelt broke precedent and made history when he won election not only a third time in 1940 but also a fourth time in 1944. In addition to their support for his ongoing New Deal programs, his supporters cited the likely imminent entry of the country into World War II as a reason to break tradition and reelect him. Roosevelt, plagued by many health problems in his life and during his presidency in particular, passed away from a cerebral hemorrhage in 1945. Although millions of

Americans adored Roosevelt, many people believed that the time had come for presidential term limits. In the 1946 midterm elections, the Republican Party regained control of both houses of Congress for the first time in nearly two decades. Congress proposed the Twenty-Second Amendment to the states for ratification in March 1947.

Ratification of the amendment took longer than most amendments typically do. Four years passed before the requisite states ratified the amendment. Tennessee became the thirty-second state to ratify on February 20, 1951. It was Burn himself who made the motion to vote on the resolution in the State Senate in late February.[68] He voted in favor of the amendment, as it easily passed both chambers of the legislature. His beliefs on serving two terms had not changed. He served two terms in the Tennessee House of Representatives and was in his second and final term in the Senate.

Minnesota became the thirty-sixth state to ratify the amendment on February 27, 1951, but it would not go into effect until President Truman left office in 1953. Upon ratification, the amendment received little fanfare. After all, it was only the twelfth time since the ratification of the Bill of Rights in 1791 that the U.S. Constitution had been amended. A likely explanation of the light media coverage owes to the perception that it was a partisan move by Republicans intending to prevent another Franklin D. Roosevelt from serving several terms again. "The amendment when proposed was generally regarded as a rebuke to the late President Franklin Roosevelt who won four terms in the White House," wrote the Associated Press.[69]

However, it must be remembered that the amendment also applies to Republican presidents. The issue was not as partisan at the media portrayed it to be. While the vote to propose the amendment was mostly along party lines in the U.S. Congress, an examination of the states tells a different story. The amendment not only passed in Roosevelt's home state of New York but also in the legislature of every southern state. At the time, the Democratic Party dominated southern politics, a region where Roosevelt was beloved.

Burn had now voted to amend the U.S. Constitution on three separate occasions in four different decades: Prohibition, woman suffrage and term limits for the president of the United States—three very different issues. His first vote attempted to control people and deprive them of their individual rights. But his next two votes recognized the rights of all people, regardless of gender, and placed limits on the most powerful governmental figure. He always managed to be in office to vote on the more impactful amendments. He would live to see four more constitutional amendments pass, two of which related to suffrage.

In another example of Burn's remarkable sense of political timing, the 1951 legislature took aim at permanently abolishing the poll tax in Tennessee. The Tennessee Constitution of 1870 gave the legislature the power to levy a poll tax. But the legislature did not make the poll tax operative until 1890. After that, voter participation among Tennessee men dropped from 71 percent to 58 percent. By 1924, by which time women could also vote, only 20 percent of eligible Tennessee voters cast a ballot.[70]

Tools of racism like the poll tax prevented black citizens and poor whites from voting. In the instances where these groups were permitted to vote, it was only by permission of power lusters. Political machines and bosses thrived in the era of the poll tax. Many political bosses in urban areas won elections through the purchase of poll tax receipts. Urban black and poor white voters could only vote under control of the political machine. The Crump machine in Memphis shrewdly used the poll tax to buy blocks of votes. W.E. Michael remembered the poll tax era:

In the 1930s and 1940s political corruption in Monroe as well as McMinn and Polk Counties was so rife that it was hardly believable now by persons who were not alive at that time. Both parties were guilty of buying votes and buying block books of poll tax receipts because the poll tax was then required before one could vote. A certified list was furnished to all election officers showing those who had paid the poll tax...any voter presenting himself to vote could present his poll tax receipt if he had one.... On election day each party had paymasters at all of the polling places. This man was furnished with money by the candidates, or party organizations, for the purpose of buying votes.... The blame for this practice should not be borne entirely by the political parties or the candidates, but they must share the blame with the voters who expected, and took, the money for voting, or who refused to leave their homes to vote until they had been paid....I have seen candidates walking up and down the street handing out $1.00 bills and standing in line with the voters and handing out whiskey just before or just after the voter had cast his ballot. Usually some stratagem was devised to be sure the voter who has been bought had voted "right." One of the methods used was to give the prospective voter a marked ballot to hide in his pocket. He was then instructed to go into the booth, pretend to mark a ballot, take the marked ballot out of his pocket, put it in the ballot box, put the blank ballot in his pocket and bring it back to the paymaster to get his money.[71]

In 1943, the state legislature passed a poll tax repeal. Included in the repeal was a permanent registration system for voters, something Burn had always supported.[72] In fact, in 1938, the McMinn County Court became the first in the state to repeal the poll tax at the local level.[73] Nineteen other county courts quickly followed suit. With several one-dollar county poll taxes repealed, some voters only had to pay the one-dollar state poll tax. Unfortunately, the 1943 state poll tax repeal did not last. The Tennessee Supreme Court struck down the legislature's repeal of the state poll tax and the permanent voter registration system by upholding a decision of a lower court in, of all places, Polk County.[74]

Determined to take down the Crump machine, Governor Browning enthusiastically supported the 1951 poll tax repeal. Without such power, Crump would no longer be able to decide statewide elections though the manipulation of hundreds of thousands of Shelby County votes. "The poll tax has long been an evil and an obstruction in the way of a free electorate," wrote the *Kingsport News*.[75]

In March 1951, Burn joined in a 29–1 vote for a House bill repealing the state poll tax.[76] Unlike the 1943 poll tax repeal bill, the 1951 bill stood a much better chance to survive a legal challenge. The Tennessee Press Association and the Tennessee LWV spent years advocating for the poll tax repeal. Victory on this issue was finally within sight in Tennessee.

The legislature cleverly crafted the 1951 poll tax repeal to ensure its survival. The *Clarksville Leaf Chronicle* explained, "The law provides that voters must pay only the poll tax for the year 1871, if it is assessed against them, in order to vote."[77] Since the 1949 legislature passed a bill that exempted voters over the age of fifty from the poll tax requirement, this bill relieved all voters of this barrier to the right of suffrage.

The drafters of the 1951 poll tax repeal knew that one more safeguard would be required to ensure a permanent end to the poll tax in Tennessee. To prevent a future legislature from repealing the repeal, the poll tax would have to be made part of the state's governing document. Burn would be there to ensure that it did.

Polk County moved closer to anarchy on March 13. Citizens of the GGL committee took over the courthouse, refusing to allow the county court to meet. This was not the first time the courthouse had been seized in the county's recent history. The GGL presented an ultimatum demanding the resignation of several office holders. Chairman Barclay had recently claimed, "The government of Polk County has all but been handed over to the Biggs Machine."[78] The GGL demanded the repeal of "obnoxious legislation."[79]

Burn and Johnston claimed that the recent legislation "is obnoxious only to political demagogues and those who are not concerned about corrupt elections" and urged Polk Countians to "refuse to yield to threats."[80] They released a statement:

> *The GGL obtained much of its vast power in Polk County through legislation. It set up a county government…and ruled by an iron hand. Assaults and intimidations have been committed without arrests. Their action in Benton is characteristic, but certainly is no indication of good government. We have no apologies for unseating those who have practiced a bold and barefaced tyranny since they took over the government of Polk County. We only attempted to liberate the good people of Polk County. One demand calls for the resignation of W.A. Lewis as chairman pro tem of the Polk County Court. Mr. Lewis is a high-class gentleman and was until recently a member of the GGL. He was elected by the people. He should continue to serve.*[81]

GGL chairman Barclay spoke at an April rally claiming that Polk County, a pro-Confederate county, was ready to secede from Tennessee.[82] Barclay called Burn and Johnston "the most contemptible liars in Tennessee" as the crowd cheered.[83] Burn replied, claiming that the "former lieutenants" of the Burch Biggs machine now in the GGL behaved like "hatchet men."[84] The behavior of the GGL in the events after the ouster of the Biggs machine proves that such corruption is not exclusive to members of one political party or faction.

The county court could not meet for several months. By April, the legislature had adjourned, leaving Governor Browning to deal with Polk County's problems. Since the court was unable to meet for so long, bills and notes against the county began piling up. Teachers went unpaid, and repairs were at a dead end.[85] Newspapers as far away as St. Louis and Chicago reported on the story.[86]

A truce was finally reached, and court was scheduled to meet again in mid-May. But on the evening of May 11, 1951, things turned deadly once again in Polk County. The victim was W. August Lewis, who had defected from the GGL the previous year. Lewis, now the Polk County court chairman, had just returned home from dinner with his family. After his family went inside, he pulled the car around back to park it. After he exited the car, three shotgun blasts struck him in the chest. The assassin had been waiting for him in the bushes next to the garage. One witness reported seeing an automobile speed from Benton around the time of the shooting. While en route to a clinic in Athens, he was asked if he knew who had shot him. He shook his head negatively and then died from his injuries, age forty-three.[87]

After Lewis's murder, things became so bad for some Polk Countians that there were reports of people wanting to sell their property and leave the county. "People are afraid to live there," the *Polk County News* reported.[88] Lewis's murder had brought about a "reign of terror" so severe that Governor Browning considered splitting up the county.[89] One plan would parcel out Polk County to its neighbors of Bradley, McMinn and Monroe Counties. The county was hundreds of thousands of dollars in debt.

A special election took place on August 11 to replace Lewis on the county court. A GGL member won election to the court, breaking the longtime 4–4 deadlock on the court. In late August, the Polk County Court met for the first time in six months, and the GGL was back in power.[90] Governor Browning scrapped his plan to dissolve and split up the county. The murder of W.A. Lewis has never been solved.

The series of events in Polk County proved to be partial inspiration for the legislature and Governor Browning to push for a system of home rule for cities and counties. Although not excusing their violent actions, Governor Browning said that he "appreciates the fact that the people of Polk County are definitely wrought up over the local legislation that has been passed. This is one definite argument that we should have had our constitution changed two years ago to place local legislation in the hands of the people themselves in each county and each town concerned." Despite Browning's lament, it was he who signed into law all of Burn and Johnston's "ripper bills." It is possible that Browning believed that state intervention in local affairs was necessary in certain situations, especially election fraud.

Thankfully, the 1951 legislature passed another bill to provide for a referendum of the people to call for a constitutional convention. Burn voted for the bill.[91] Governor Browning signed it into law, and a referendum was scheduled for the 1952 elections. Burn's chance to finally vote for changes to Tennessee's long-unaltered constitution was getting closer to reality.

Incidents such as those in Polk County in 1950 demonstrated the need for the bipartisan election reform led by Burn and Governor Browning in the 1949 legislature. The state legislature should rightfully intervene to administer justice in election fraud cases. The right to vote is meaningless without a guarantee of clean and honest elections. Several localities suffered from election fraud and voter intimidation for decades. It is imperative that the state governments, which have the power to administer elections as per the U.S. Constitution, pass and enforce laws that ensure legitimate elections. Burn believed in this passionately and always voted in favor of such bills.

During the 1951 session, the Sweetwater city commission made clear its desire to return the city limits to its 1947 boundaries.[92] "I accomplished the purpose and am willing to pull the lines back in to any point you desire," Burn had previously said.[93] It reached a compromise that altered the city limits, but not to the 1947 boundaries.[94]

Monroe County leaders requested both legislators work to secure legislation for a bond to build a new school near Sweetwater High School.[95] In response to initial fears that a property tax increase would be necessary to secure the school bond, Burn and County Representative Wood developed a new plan.[96] Appropriations received from the state sales tax rebate, for which Burn had passionately advocated, would pay for the principal and interest of the school bond.[97] The *Sweetwater Valley News* endorsed the idea of using the school bond to build a new junior high school. "Crowded conditions" and students unable to receive "personal attention" were among reasons for the need of a new school.[98] The people of Sweetwater overwhelmingly approved the school bond in a record-high referendum turnout.[99]

McMinn County's new representative, Abe Trew, had introduced a bill to allow McMinn citizens to elect school board members. Trew claimed that Burn supported his legislative program for McMinn.[100] But Burn later changed his mind about the school board bill. "It is my desire to work with the representatives of the Seventh District....But I cannot support a bill that lets the representatives legislate a public official out of office because of differences of opinion on matters of policy."[101] He insisted that Trew led him to believe that the bill would not legislate anyone out of office. After discovering that up to six of the seven members of the school board would be removed from office, he withdrew his support for the bill. "Any bill which legislates an official out of office before his term expires is...a ripper bill."[102] He made a conscious effort to keep his promise to oppose ripper bills.

Burn did not inherently oppose the General Assembly taking action to remove certain local officials from elected office. As evident from his actions in handling the election fraud in Polk County, he believed that certain situations permitted the state government to intervene and act as a check on the power of county and city governments. "If the officials have been guilty in stealing elections or condoning such frauds, then a ripper bill is fully justified," he explained.[103]

McMinn County High School, the second public high school to be organized in the state of Tennessee in 1903, caught fire in March 1951.[104]

Many citizens believed the time had come to replace the twenty-five-year-old building. On the questions of raising funds through bonds, he wished for the people of McMinn to vote on it in a referendum.[105]

Burn eventually secured legislation to give McMinn a $300,000 bond to allow for repairs and "other school building construction."[106] After repairs, the building would last another three decades before being replaced. But the relationship between Burn and Trew became strained late in the legislature's session. Not only had Burn killed the McMinn school board bill, but Trew also opposed a second bill to alter the city limits of Niota.[107] What really irritated Burn, though, was the way Trew criticized his actions in Polk County:

> *The words "Good Government League" are a halo. Apparently Mr. Trew believes that any politician heading a party of that name become a paragon of virtue, even if he condones and supports election thieves. Five years ago, the Battle of Athens was fought against election thieves. I still abhor election thieves. The fact that the stealing is done for the candidates of the so-called Good Government League does not make the thievery any more palpable to me. By his votes during this session of the legislature, Mr. Trew has indicated that he was not shocked by the acts of former lieutenants of the Burch Biggs machine who are the hatchet men of the so-called Good Government League of Polk County.*[108]

Burn and Trew pushed a bill through both chambers of the legislature that extended the Athens city limits by 10 percent.[109] Like the Niota bill, it included a referendum by the people. One of Burn's oldest political colleagues, Herschel Candler, drafted the referendum.[110] Now in his early seventies, he served as city attorney for Athens after a long tenure in the state legislature. The citizens of Athens approved the referendum. An early draft of the bill would have annexed the Midway Drive-In Theater. Located on State Highway 30 between the city limits of Athens and Etowah, the theater still operates at the time of this writing and is one of only a few drive-in theaters remaining in the country.

In Bradley County, Burn faced protests from the ten-person county court over his proposal to hand over tighter control of the county's fiscal affairs to the county judge.[111] He met with the members of the court and explained his desire to make the judge the purchasing agent to "eliminate petty graft" in Bradley County that had been "going on for years."[112] Even with his amendments to the bill, the court was still not happy with the proposal. The bill later died in the legislature. Burn proceeded to hold a general public discussion meeting on all bills in consideration affecting Bradley County during his time in the State Senate.[113] Burn faced less controversy over Bradley County legislation than in the other three counties during his two terms in the State Senate.

By the end of the 1951 session, Burn had introduced fifty-seven bills, eight of which Governor Browning signed into law. He accomplished much of what he desired, but not everything. Introduced before the session began, the redistricting bill he had cosponsored failed to pass. Many urban districts continued to be underrepresented, with rural districts still dominating the legislature. Reapportionment had been kicked down the road once again. Many years later, Tennessee would be dragged kicking and screaming to address the problem. Burn would be there to help.

After serving his home counties in the State Senate for four years, Burn and his family left Sweetwater. He was set to start a new career. A job opened up at the First National Bank in Rockwood.

Chapter 12

RETURN TO ROCKWOOD

B urn was named the new president of the First National Bank in Rockwood one week after he was reelected to the State Senate in 1950. He succeeded his uncle, Bill Ensminger, who retired after forty-five years of service. He took a pay cut to leave his law office in Sweetwater to come work as bank president. He and his family moved back to Rockwood in spring 1951, when he officially took over as bank president.

Uncle Bill married Eddyth Abbels, his sweetheart from youth, in 1950 at the age of seventy-five. He enjoyed his hard-earned retirement with his new bride. He had seen the bank through the Great Depression. Eddyth later wrote, "He was able to assist many good businessmen who might have lost their life savings without Will coming to their rescue."[1]

Harry and Ellen Burn made Rockwood their primary residence for the rest of their lives together. They loved life in Rockwood. They lived in an apartment in the Mourfield Hotel on Rockwood Street. Built in 1887, the Mourfield was Rockwood's most elegant hotel. The family attended the First Presbyterian Church of Rockwood. In the fall of 1951, Tommy started high school at the McCallie School in Chattanooga. Ellen taught U.S. history, civics and English at Rockwood High School.

James Albertson remembered Ellen Burn's high school English class. "We called her 'Granny Burn,'" he laughingly recalled.[2] Larry Bowman remembered Ellen playing her ukulele in class.[3] Before class one day, Eddie Bilbree was playing his ukulele. Ellen invited him to come in front of the class and play it with her. Bilbree had great respect and admiration for Ellen.[4]

Above: Rockwood High School. *Roane County Heritage Commission.*

Left: Faculty photo of Ellen Cottrell Burn. *Burn family.*

Anne Scandlyn Powers loved Ellen Burn's class. "She would stand on a desk and do dramatic readings during poetry lessons." Powers said that her class was never boring.[5] Full of life, Ellen had a great sense of humor. "Mrs. Burn could keep you in stiches," said Geraldine Wallick.[6]

Rockwood Street is the city's main east–west thoroughfare. During this time, Burn's bank, the high school, the hotel, the family's church and the Live and Let Live Drug Store (still in operation today) all fronted Rockwood Street. East Rockwood Street intersects with Gateway Avenue (U.S. Highway 27). West Rockwood Street passes through the residential blocks of the city underneath tall shade trees just below Walden Ridge. One of the earliest memories that Anne Scandlyn Powers can recall is walking down the sidewalk hand in hand with Burn and her grandfather. "They were both wearing suits and 'old man hats.' Mr. Burn was always dressed to the nines."[7]

J. Polk Cooley remembered first meeting Burn shortly after law school. The time had come for Cooley to purchase his first car. He asked Burn for a $1,600 loan. At first, the bank agreed to give him the loan. Burn, the new bank president, stepped in and denied Cooley's loan request, citing recent banking regulations discouraging giving loans to young people like the twenty-three-year-old Cooley. "I stood my ground," Cooley said. He

Rockwood Street, with Walden Ridge in the background. *Roane County Heritage Commission.*

told Burn he needed the loan, and he guaranteed that he would pay it back. Burn changed his mind and signed off on the loan. Cooley said it is a "fond memory" of Burn and that it was a very nice thing for Burn to have done for him.[8]

"Harry was very thorough," Cooley recalled. Cooley did lots of work for Burn's bank, especially real estate title work. The first "Please, No Smoking" sign Cooley ever saw was in Burn's office at the bank. "Harry favored the color green," Cooley chuckled. "He used green paper, green ink, and even painted the bricks outside of the bank green."[9]

According to Cooley, Burn had a lot of energy and imagination. "Harry was very studious and was always working." He had a front-row seat at Burn's political activities in the community. "Harry was smart, shrewd, and sometimes caused controversy." He said he and Burn always respected each other and remained friends despite their inevitable legal conflicts. "There was never a dull moment with Harry," he remembered fondly. "He's one to remember."[10]

"Mr. Burn was my first boss," Geraldine Wallick recalled. "He was strict, but he was a very good boss." She appreciated how Burn permitted her and the other employees to learn how to perform many different jobs at the bank. "At every staff meeting, Mr. Burn always told us: 'Nothing is permanent but change.'"[11] David Hembree worked for Burn for two years and is grateful for the Christmas bonuses he gave to the employees. "Back then, $100 paid for my family's Christmas presents."[12]

Burn earned commendations for his banking work. According to the *Daily Post-Athenian*, "He brought innovative hours and special community services to the banking business, several of which are now common practices in the financial field."[13] Jessie Jones recalled that Burn had a reputation as an "honest banker."[14] According to David Hembree, Burn would usually leave the bank each day "carrying a load of banking magazines and other banking literature." Hembree remembered Burn saying, "Hembree, we are a five million dollar bank today."[15] During Burn's fifteen-year tenure as president, the bank grew in resources from $1 million to almost $10 million.[16]

Despite Burn's honest and successful banking career and consistent support for fiscally responsible policies, the same could not be said of his personal finances. He was a poor money manager when it came to his own finances. He earned a comfortable living but was not frugal. Like other statesmen such as Thomas Jefferson and Winston Churchill, he maintained an expensive lifestyle. The family frequently dined at restaurants, traveled extensively, wore the nicest clothes and furnished their home with antique

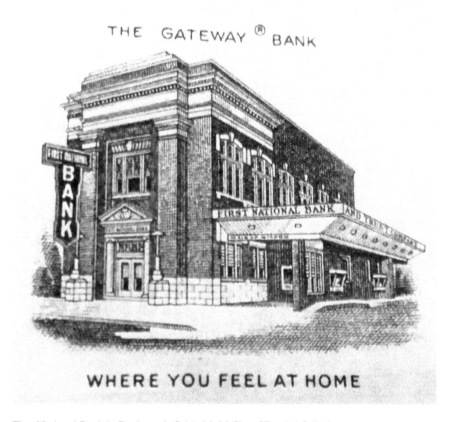

First National Bank in Rockwood. *Calvin M. McClung Historical Collection.*

furniture. Ellen Cottrell Burn, who came from a wealthy New England family, sometimes had to bail him out!

Uncle Bill Ensminger continued serving on the board of directors after his retirement. Everybody in town called Uncle Bill "Uncle Billy" and even "Old Man Ensminger." J. Polk Cooley remembered Uncle Bill sitting at his desk on the left side of the lobby at the bank. "Uncle Bill sat there and chewed tobacco….He was a character! He would shout at people walking into the bank if they were behind on their loan payments."[17] During World War II, Uncle Bill approved a loan to Geraldine Wallick's grandparents to help them purchase their home. "He was a mess," she said. "If he thought it, he said it."[18] Maurice Grief remembered the time a $100 bill went missing when Uncle Bill was still bank president. "He was really upset and looked all over for it," Grief said. When Uncle Bill got home, he found the bill in the cuff of his pants. He never wore pants with a cuff again![19]

The Mourfield Hotel. *Roane County Heritage Commission.*

Uncle Bill was truly a force of nature. Although his mother, Sallie Ensminger, lived into her eighties, he outlived his sisters and father by many years. He enjoyed the outdoors and especially loved to fish and hunt. He never had children, but he was devoted to his dogs and horses. When he was bank president, life insurance salesmen visited the bank. A handful of employees purchased life insurance policies. Uncle Bill attempted to purchase a policy but was rejected. His 110-pound weight might have been a factor. One year before his death, in his early nineties, he told the story of how he had attended the funerals of all of the bank employees who bought life insurance that day. He never did get life insurance.[20]

A few years after returning to Rockwood, Burn founded an insurance company. In operation for almost a decade, Gateway Insurance Agency Inc. sold fire and casualty insurance. Now able to make connections in the insurance business, he soon became a legal representative for the

Philadelphia-based Insurance Company of North America.[21] After all, Febb Burn had told him when he was a boy that he had the intelligence to be a Philadelphia lawyer.

Burn became involved in many organizations outside of his job as bank president. He was a joiner everywhere he went. In addition to his longtime memberships in the Junior Order of United American Mechanics and the National Society Sons of the American Revolution, he joined the Rockwood Civitan Club and became a major player in the further development of the Rockwood Ruritan Club.

Burn's involvement with the Ruritan Club demonstrated not only his desire to live in a better community but also his love for "Small Town America." He never lived in a big city. He told a fellow Ruritan member about his travels to the small towns in the extreme South, Southwest and West that were dying: "No one seems to be interested in these little towns."[22] He wished for the Ruritan National and other organizations to establish a "Small Town Foundation." These organizations "will survive only if our small towns survive," he wrote.[23] Thinking of a motto to describe the work of Ruritan Clubs, he suggested, "To Help Save and Beautify the Small Towns of America" and "Making Better the Small Towns of America."[24] He always observed small towns during his travels and frequently contacted their local officials offering to help set up a Ruritan Club in their community.

Burn's remarkable foresight extended beyond politics. The First National Bank in Rockwood opened branches in Kingston and South Harriman under his leadership. Rockwood, Harriman and Kingston are the three largest cities in Roane County. Below the triangle formed by these three cities and above Watts Bar Lake lies an area once known as Piney Grove. U.S. Route 70 now runs through the area.

Burn predicted that the Piney Grove area would soon see significant growth. He encouraged its development and even suggested a new name for the area.[25] The local government took a vote, and the area became known as "Midtown," the name suggested by Burn. Midtown became a business center, and he anticipated the business that the nearby Kingston steam plant would bring to the area. Burn wrote to a fellow banker in Georgia recommending he take the lead in organizing a Ruritan club. He told the banker how much it had helped Midtown:

> *I have helped organize five Ruritan Clubs in the past six or eight years and have seen some of them rejuvenate its community.... The Midtown Ruritan Club in less than three years obtained a new school building, a post office,*

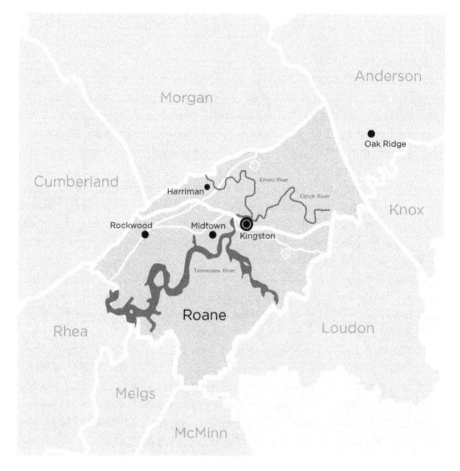

Roane County Map. *Map by Navigation Advertising, LLC, Murfreesboro, Tennessee.*

a branch bank, a water works system, and a better identity as a stop for interstate busses than the long established towns.[26]

Gerald Largen said that Burn has been "vindicated" in his foresight to develop Midtown.[27] Midtown currently has the only hospital in Roane County and is not far from Roane State Community College. It became a municipality but later lost its incorporation after a legal challenge. It remains an important region in the county.

Burn still practiced law on occasion while serving as bank president. Gerald Largen first met Burn in the late 1950s when he began his legal career. "Harry was a good chap. I liked him." Burn even offered to set up an office for him at the bank. Largen politely declined Burn's offer. "Harry was headstrong and very opinionated. I could not work for him. It would not have turned out well," Largen recalled.[28]

Although Burn had decided against running for a third term in the State Senate, his public service career was far from over. He began a long tenure serving on the State Planning Commission when Governor Browning appointed him to the commission on May 27, 1952.[29] His first appointment was for a period of two years, filling a vacancy. The *Tennessee Blue Book* provides an adequate description:

> *The State Planning Commission is largely an advisory planning agency responsible for the creation of a plan for the physical development of the state and to study problems....It performs studies and investigations and makes reports to the Governor, the General Assembly and, through publications, to the people of the state: creates and appoints members to regional planning commissions; and contracts with cities, counties and local planning agencies for technical work in city planning and related matters.*[30]

While serving in the State Senate, Burn's close friend Hammond Fowler spearheaded a series of "TVA bills" during the mid-1930s. One of these bills created the State Planning Commission. Fowler was appointed to the Railroad and Public Utilities Commission in 1948 and became chairman in 1951.[31] Burn had previously turned down the opportunity to run for commissioner of railroad and public utilities in exchange for withdrawing from the 1930 Republican gubernatorial primary. Fowler remained on the commission for many years. It was later renamed the Public Services Commission.

Burn made a statement after his appointment to the commission:

> *An interest in orderly growth and development of communities and their facilities is my heritage. Forty years ago my father worked for a regional bridge authority to build a bridge across the Tennessee River at Loudon. He died long before the State of Tennessee built the bridge now in use at Loudon. Since 1917, when H.A. Collins and others joined me in planning for the future of the Niota community of the Sweetwater Valley, I have been interested in town planning. For years I worked for a better Sweetwater, for parks, for wider streets, and an orderly industrial development of that community. In recent months I have worked with the civic leaders of Rockwood where we have had 100 percent cooperation. As a member of*

Rockwood native
Hammond Fowler, Burn's
closest friend. *Tennessee State
Library and Archives.*

*the State Planning Commission my interest shall be broadened. For the
opportunity to serve…I am deeply grateful to Governor Browning. As a
member of the State Senate for four years it has been my privilege to work
with Governor Browning in his program for better schools and roads. The
program he is offering the people of Tennessee for the next two years is the
program of a statesman.*[32]

Governors Frank Clement and Buford Ellington reappointed Burn
to the State Planning Commission four times before he stepped down.
His withdrawal from legislative politics and return to Roane County was
timed just right for him to be able to play a role in amending the state
constitution. But first, the voters would have to approve a convention in a
referendum at the polls.

Chapter 13

ELDER STATESMAN

T ennessee voters approved a "limited" constitutional convention in August
1952 by a two-to-one margin. After three decades, Burn's wish for a
constitutional convention in Tennessee had finally come true. On September 4,
Burn announced his candidacy as a delegate from Roane County to the limited
constitutional convention to be held in summer 1953:

> *All proposed amendments will be submitted to a vote of the people. As a*
> *believer in the two-party system I have been a Republican, but I am not a*
> *candidate for delegate to the constitutional convention on a partisan basis.*
> *It is my hope that my training and experience in governmental affairs may*
> *justify the favorable consideration of voters without regard to party. As a*
> *member of the constitutional convention, I would serve no master but seek*
> *the best interests of the state as a whole. I would be ruled by no party, no*
> *faction or pressure group.*[1]

The *Rockwood Times* editorial board made a rare political endorsement.
Lauding Burn's "time and energies given to public service," the board
complimented him as a "student of the state constitution and well informed
upon all aspects of our state government."[2] They also referenced his 1920
vote for woman suffrage. Ultimately, ability and qualifications over politics
won him an endorsement.

In the November 1952 election, Roane County voters elected Burn to be
their delegate at the state constitutional convention. He received 4,052 votes,

a 773-vote majority over his opponent.[3] The next day, Burn ran an ad in the *Rockwood Times* thanking the voters:

> *Friends and neighbors: On Tuesday, November 4th, several hundred of you went to the polls and out of every 100 votes cast in Rockwood I was given 81 votes. As a candidate in nine previous elections in this and adjoining counties I have been honored with substantial majorities, but never before have I been given such a vote of confidence as you gave me. Were it practicable I would thank each voter personally. Since I cannot do that I will show my gratitude by serving Roane County to the best of my ability in the high office to which I have been elected. Those who opposed me were exercising their rights as Americans. I have no quarrel with them....All are invited to call on me for any service I can render. I covet the good will of all, for myself and for the financial institution in and through which I am permitted to serve the friendliest people in all the world.[4]*

Burn expressed his love of Rockwood through the words of his heartfelt thank-you message. The support of his fellow citizens meant so much to him. He mentions having been a candidate in nine elections before running for Roane County delegate, including the only election contest he ever lost: the 1930 Republican gubernatorial primary.

In a statement to voters, Burn explained his positions on the issues to be deliberated at the convention. He alleviated the fears of some voters with his assurance that a state income tax would not be considered, pointing out that it was not in the "call" for the convention. He explained to voters that he worked in the 1951 legislature to carefully word the act to ensure that "the convention should not have the right to submit any proposal regarding taxation....I do not believe that the people of Tennessee would voluntarily vote another tax on their income, when their property taxes are a burden and the federal government takes such a large part of their income." He expressed his desire to see the federal income tax capped by a constitutional amendment. "I am opposed to a state income tax because taxes as a whole are about to destroy our economy." He vowed to not "make it too easy" to amend the constitution. He also explained his support for the "home rule" amendments: "Counties and cities should run their own affairs, without having to go to the legislature for changes in local laws. Senators and representatives should spend their time considering state-wide legislation... with absolute home rule some of our professional politicians might have greater difficulty in keeping their feet in the public trough." He concluded by reminding voters of his votes for two federal amendments: woman suffrage and presidential term limits.[5] Notably, Burn made no mention of his vote for the Prohibition Amendment in 1919.

After achieving statehood in 1796, Tennessee wrote its first constitution. Thomas Jefferson called it "the least imperfect and most republican" of any of the states.[6] It has been altered over the years to abolish slavery and recognize and protect rights for more Tennesseans. Several attempts at holding a state convention had previously failed between 1870 and 1953. The document, "the nation's oldest unamended constitution," had stood without amendment for more than eight decades.[7]

Tennessee's first constitutional convention in eighty-three years began in Nashville in April 1953. During the convention, Burn sat in the same desk he occupied when he cast his deciding vote for woman suffrage thirty-three years earlier.[8] He then announced his support for a cause for which he would advocate for almost two decades. He believed that the right to vote should not only be extended to both genders and all races but to all adult citizens generally. His drive to lower the voting age from twenty-one to eighteen had begun.

Evidence suggests that the movement to lower the voting age in the United States began shortly after the Revolutionary War.[9] Men as young as sixteen served with many Revolutionary-era militias. Attempts to lower the voting age in several states failed time and time again throughout the nineteenth century. Nearly two centuries passed before people started to believe that the age for military service should match the voting age.

The military draft during World War II bolstered the youth vote movement like never before. In the period between the end of World War II and the 1953 Tennessee Constitutional Convention, the U.S. Congress failed to advance several bills aimed at lowering the voting age. Forty state legislatures also rejected dozens of proposals to grant suffrage rights to eighteen- to twenty-year-olds during the same period. Only Georgia had approved the lowering of its voting age during this period.[10]

Burn at the 1953 Tennessee Constitutional Convention. *Tennessee State Library and Archives.*

By 1952, both the Democrats and Republicans had inserted support for a lowered voting age into their national platforms. Polls from 1952 showed that in the midst of the Korean War, public support for lowering the voting age reached a new high of 61 percent.[11] Burn knew that the 1953 convention was an ideal time to begin his push to lower the voting age in Tennessee. Along with four other delegates, Burn introduced Resolution No. 24:

> *Be it resolved, that Article IV, Section 1, of the Constitution of the State of Tennessee adopted in convention at Nashville, February 23, 1870, be amended by substituting a revised and amended section to read as follows: "Every person of the age of* ~~twenty-one~~ *eighteen years, being a citizen of the United States, and a resident of this state for twelve months, and in the country wherein he may offer his vote, for six months next preceding the day of election, shall be entitled to vote."*[12]

Burn delivered a passionate speech advocating for lowering the voting age:

> *Three decades and three years ago, exactly one-half of the members of the House of Representatives of our great state were opposed to votes for women....The majority of the delegates to this convention have voted for "conscription without representation," a principle repugnant to our Founding Fathers who fought a revolutionary war on the issue of "taxation without representation." Many of those responsible for that decision may not live to see the day when the people of Tennessee right that wrong, but it will be righted. Of that I am confident.*[13]

The delegates amended Resolution No. 24 to keep the voting age at twenty-one. Knowing that getting it codified into the state constitution was unlikely, Burn introduced an amendment that would have allowed the legislature to fix the voting age.[14] He addressed his fellow delegates and reminded them that the legislature had granted suffrage rights to women in presidential and municipal elections in 1919. His amendment was voted down by an 85–7 vote.[15]

Claude Stephenson of Hickman County also spoke in favor of lowering the voting age. "These 55 members have said in effect 'we shall have conscription without representation.' In simple justice, a person who is old enough to fight and die for his country, is old enough to be given the right to vote on the questions of electing those who pass upon the great questions of the day."[16] Leon Easterly of Greene County said, "I believe that at age eighteen young men and women are sufficiently informed through education and otherwise to exercise the right of suffrage, that they are willing to accept such responsibility and that by giving them this right, sound fundamentals of citizenship will be a bulwark against communism and other dangerous anti-American doctrines."[17]

The *Rockwood Times* editorial board concurred with Burn's prediction of the inevitability of a lowered voting age. It called the right to vote for eighteen-year-olds a "valid and desirable objective" for Tennessee and that the idea was nothing more than an "afterthought" at the convention: "It was on the basis of eliminating the poll tax requirement from the constitution that this section was publicized when popular approval of the convention was being sought. This being the case, a good many delegates construed the voting age issue an extraneous matter exceeding the mandate for change they had received at the polls. It is quite possible that the voters would have been just as emphatic in their approval of the convention if the issue had been raised when the convention was first called...it is, we believe, nevertheless inevitable."[18]

Burn could not persuade his fellow delegates to lower the voting age to eighteen at this convention. But he would not stop his advocacy. He joined sixteen of his fellow delegates to form "Vote at 18, Inc." and served as its honorary chairman.[19] During his 1954 State of the Union address, President Eisenhower announced his support for lowering the voting age to eighteen.[20]

The 1953 convention tackled other long-overdue issues, including the poll tax. Burn had voted to eliminate the poll tax in the 1951 legislature. He voted with many of his fellow delegates to propose an amendment to ban the poll tax permanently. Only a constitutional amendment could ensure that the legislature could never impose a poll tax again.

After decades of uproar in many cities over "ripper bills" and other meddling in local affairs by the state legislature, Burn joined his fellow delegates in proposing "home rule" amendments. A 1945 publication covering Tennessee government described the process of amending a municipal charter and the need for home rule:

> *The local bill amending the city charter is usually sponsored by a small group of interested citizens, is enacted by viva voice vote, and usually in the absence of a legislative quorum. Only the local representative and Senator may be familiar with the contents of the bill. Generally, the mass of local citizens and occasionally even the city officials affected by the legislation know nothing of the contents or possible effects of the bill upon the city government. The method permits "spite" legislation, prevents any*

public consideration and discussion of the matter—is virtually secret and altogether undemocratic.[21]

The convention adopted eight amendments to the state constitution. The poll tax ban, authorization of municipal home rule and the prohibition of "ripper bills" were the major reforms. Also proposed were changes to the governor's term of office, extending it from two to four years, but with a prohibition on consecutive terms.[22]

A letter to the editor of the *Jackson Sun* urged Tennessee voters to go to the polls and ensure a permanent end to Tennessee's poll tax: "Because there was so little discussion about this, we feel it doubly important to caution the voters that, to win permanent freedom from the poll tax, they must... ratify the amendment which the convention proposed....It should also be remembered that what the legislature has repealed, the legislature can reimpose."[23] The *Nashville Tennessean* urged voters to "strike the poll tax from our constitution once and for all."[24]

Tennessee voters approved five of the eight proposed amendments to the state constitution at the polls in November 1953. The poll tax was forever eliminated in Tennessee. The 24th Amendment to the U.S. Constitution abolished the poll tax nationwide more than a decade later. "And now the poll tax not only has been killed, but buried. Never again will there be barriers to a part in government by the whole people. The chains have been stricken off, and the bosses are passing from twilight into utter darkness," wrote the *Nashville Tennessean.*[25] E.H. "Boss" Crump died one year later. His iron-fisted rule over Memphis and Shelby County—achieved by corrupt tactics, including manipulating the votes of hundreds of thousands of people, many of them black—finally came to an end.

With the approval of the home rule amendments, local government changed dramatically. Control over local affairs now rests with the elected officials and the voters who elected them. Cities now have the option to form a charter through a popular referendum. The legislature can no longer pass a "ripper bill" to remove a locally elected official from office. If a city needs to make an urgent change, it could now act with haste instead of waiting on a private act of the legislature at the next session. The home rule amendments also increase transparency by including the local citizens when local laws are drafted, debated and passed.

By the mid-1950s, Burn's nieces and nephews were settling into their careers. His nephew James L.E. Burn studied chemistry at Columbia University. He and his brother, my grandfather William H. "Bill" Burn, worked with others in their community and established the Dycho Company Inc. An industrial chemical supplier in Niota, Dycho still operates today. James L.E. Burn, nicknamed "Fessor," was a brilliant chemist. Like his grandmother Febb Burn, he loved history. He traced the Burn family all the way back several centuries to Thomas Clagget, a Lord Mayor of Canterbury in the sixteenth century. James L.E. Burn cofounded the McMinn County Historical Society and once served as the county historian. Patsy Duckworth, former vice-president of the McMinn County Historical Society, said that he was the "greatest historian" McMinn County has ever had.[26]

Burn's younger brother, James Lane "Jack" Burn, passed away in 1955 after years of health problems. He was only fifty-seven years old. It is unknown exactly what ailment led to his death, but the family suspects it could have been gout or uremic poisoning. The chronic inflammation he suffered from was likely due to an autoimmune disease.

Tommy (Harry T. Burn Jr.) recalled the last time seeing his Uncle Jack during Christmas break in 1954. Jack told his family that he was going

James Lane "Jack" Burn (*seated center*) with his family a few years before his passing. *Burn family.*

to make it to Christmas. He passed away the day after New Year's. His youngest son, my grandfather William H. "Bill" Burn, took over as president of Crescent Hosiery Mills and ran the mill for the next forty-five years.

Like her grandmother and mother, Burn's niece Sara Virginia Burn became a teacher. She taught elementary school in the Karns community of Knoxville. Burn's niece Jacqueline LaRose Burn worked as an accountant in Greensboro, North Carolina. She later became the office manager of a pharmacy.

Harry T. Burn Jr. graduated from the McCallie School in 1955 and enrolled at Harvard University in the fall. In a letter to a cousin, the elder Burn told of his son's "B" average on his most recent exams. "I understand that is a good grade at Harvard," he wrote.[27] The younger Burn graduated from Harvard University in June 1959. "By the way, that son of mine, Harry Jr....was a cum laude member of the Harvard Class," the elder Burn wrote to a friend.[28] He studied at the London School of Economics, where he lived in a flat a few blocks away from Buckingham Palace. He went on to work for several years as a graduate assistant at the University of Tennessee and worked as an associate editor of the Andrew Johnson Papers.

Harry T. Burn and his son were different in some ways but alike in others. The elder Burn was a workaholic and very driven. The younger Burn once said he wanted to live off of interest and dividends. The younger Burn was not a joiner like his father. But one thing is for certain: both men were very stubborn and headstrong. Those who knew them can tell you that if they were going to do something, it had to be their way or they would not do it at all. Sara Roseanne Burn, a great-niece of the elder Burn, recalled similarities between her great uncle and cousin: "Both of them could stand their ground if needed, noble gentlemen, and in private, sweet natured."[29]

From the information I have gathered in my research, I suspect that the elder Burn wished for his son to be an attorney, but the younger Burn had no interest in such a career. J. Polk Cooley remembered the elder Burn as a "domineering" father who was not able to spend a lot of time with his son.[30] I believe that the elder Burn was too hard on his son in some ways. He should not have attempted to direct his son's career choices.

Jack Burn (James L.E. Burn Jr.) recalled that his cousin and great-uncle did not always get along as a result of their similar personalities. But Jack pointed out that the younger Burn "respected his father's accomplishments."[31] In my numerous visits with him, the younger Burn always spoke of his father with the upmost respect and never spoke an ill word about him. Other members of

Harry T. Burn Jr. graduated from the McCallie School in 1955. *Burn family.*

the Burn family can tell you the same. He and his father shared an interest in politics, but he never ran for public office.

Civic leaders in Roane County urged Burn to run for their Tennessee House of Representatives seat in 1956. He politely declined, claiming that his civic activities had him "spread rather thin."[32] But he expressed his support for a technical trade school and a junior college for Roane County.[33] In 1958, the First National Bank in Rockwood became the First National Bank and Trust Company of Rockwood. The same year, Burn completed a banking seminar through correspondence from his son's alma mater, Harvard University.[34]

The 1957 state legislature proposed a constitutional convention for 1959. Tennessee voters approved the convention at the polls in August 1958. Certain issues were in the call for the convention: lowering the voting age and extending the term of office for sheriffs and trustees. In August 1958, Burn announced his candidacy for delegate to the convention for Roane County.[35] "Burn has for many years been a leader in amending the constitution to allow voting to 18 year olds," the *Rockwood Times* wrote.[36]

In a *Rockwood Times* ad, Burn lamented the failure of the previous convention to adopt the proposal to lower the voting age. He expressed excitement on the convention's three proposals. Burn was always an open, accessible and responsive public servant. "Those interested in the three proposals that will be considered by the convention are urged to give me their views…your views will be welcome at any time."[37] Roane County voters elected Burn in an unopposed contest as their delegate in November 1958, giving him 1,853 complimentary votes.[38] The *Rockwood Times* reported that the convention received "little interest" compared to 1953.[39] Out of the nearly 700,000 votes cast for governor on the same day, only 205,000 people in the statewide election voted for the convention.[40] In a letter to a Bradley County judge, Burn shared his thoughts on term limits for sheriffs:

> *As you well know,* [the sheriff] *now has a limit of three terms of two years each. If we considered a four-year term, then it might well be to provide that the Sheriff could not thereafter hold the office again nor could a deputy under him. That should help in preventing the building up of a "graft machine."*[41]

Roane County citizens had mixed beliefs on the issue of lowering the voting age at this time. The *Rockwood Times* interviewed several citizens on the issue. A former sheriff said, "I do favor the lowering of the voting age. If they're old enough to go to the service they're old enough to know how to vote." A school superintendent explained, "At first I didn't favor the proposal but now I favor it. They're called into the army at 18, allowed to hold responsible jobs, and should have a say in government." A pastor answered, "The voting age should remain at 21 but there's a good argument on the other side."[42]

A nineteen-year-old switchboard operator said, "Most others in my age group are not too interested in politics." A seventeen-year-old high school student remarked, "Most 18 year olds are just out of school or on the verge of it and still have their minds on lessons and future schooling rather than politics." An eighteen-year-old student replied, "If we're old enough to hold responsible positions and old enough to go into service, I feel we should have the right to vote."[43]

Among the returning delegates from the 1953 convention, including Burn, was Mrs. Hillman P. (Ellen Davies) Rogers of Shelby County. She staunchly opposed lowering the voting age. "If anything, the argument is stronger now against the 18-year-old vote than it was in 1953, because of the obvious increase in juvenile delinquency throughout the nation in the last six years."[44] She had made a speech at the 1953 convention lamenting the defeat of a white city councilman in Atlanta by a black candidate. "In certain sections of the state, they're just opposed to the vote at 18. The racial question enters into it," Burn told the *Nashville Tennessean*.[45] A *Tennessean* columnist reported that only one in five adults voted regularly in Tennessee and wrote of the idea of lowering the voting age:

> *There has been some sound reasoning on the idea that the more we increase the voting interest and total vote, the better the government. No political machine can exist under mass increase of voting strength. Even the Crump machine in Memphis crumbled when the poll tax was finally removed.*[46]

The 1959 Tennessee Constitutional Convention convened in July. In a close vote, the delegates voted for Burn as vice-president of East Tennessee for the convention.[47] For a brief period during the convention, Burn served as acting president in the absence of convention president Joe H. Walker Jr.

The debate over the voting age continued at the 1959 convention. Burn picked up where he left off at the end of the 1953 convention. He explained his continued support for lowering the voting age:

We have all kinds of political education for boys and girls in high schools… we take them to the city hall and courthouse and let them get experience in running their government. But about the time they graduate we put them on the shelf for three years and let them cool off before they can participate actively in that government.[48]

Guam had lowered its voting age to eighteen in 1954. Kentucky quickly followed. In January 1959, Alaska achieved statehood and ratified its state constitution, complete with the voting age set at nineteen.[49] The movement remained slow nationwide, but Burn would not give up. After introducing another resolution for lowering the voting age, Burn again explained his support for lowering the voting age to eighteen:

Because in the American Revolution we had a war about taxation without representation.…Today we draft our 18-year old men and send them off to war. This is conscription without representation and far more heinous than taxation without representation. An 18-year old is an adult so far as the demands of society are concerned. He can be brought before an adult jury and can be sent to the electric chair if he has committed the crimes of murder, armed robbery or rape. As an adult, he ought to have a part in making the laws that he is to respond to.[50]

In an effort to gain support for a lowered voting age, some delegates introduced various resolutions tying the right to vote to military duty. Among these included a resolution by William Mullins of Washington County to recognize suffrage for citizens eighteen or older who had met one of two criteria: military service or higher education.[51] This resolution also failed to receive sufficient support.

Jefferson Davis of Hawkins County gave several reasons in favor of lowering the voting age: "If people are old enough to marry, they are old enough to vote…if people know enough to be graduated from high school and junior colleges, if they know enough about and understand public questions and public issues to vote intelligently…they are old enough to vote…everything that might frustrate young folks in their ambitions to become active in local, state and national governments should be removed."[52]

Burn and the Suffrage Committee drafted a minority report that changed the voting age from twenty-one to eighteen. The committee motioned to replace the majority report with the minority report.[53] He addressed his fellow delegates for the last time at the convention:

Now, I want to conclude the presentation of those who favor lowering the voting age by saying, you have heard some marvelous arguments, some great reasons, some basic reasons, and I hope you will ponder those thoughts as you vote. I also hope that...you will not undertake to build a barricade... in attaining an objective that many would die for—they are at least praying for it—and that this afternoon by voting to submit this question to the voters of the state of Tennessee, you will express your confidence in the democratic process. It is with that thought and with that prayer that I leave this matter in your hands...but if it is not determined right it will ultimately come to pass. Thank you.[54]

Burn received applause after his address.[55] After introducing a resolution to lower the voting age to twenty, Judd Acuff of Knox County addressed the convention: "This convention is not going to adopt eighteen."[56] His resolution to lower the voting age to twenty failed to pass.

At the close of the convention, the voting age in Tennessee remained at twenty-one with no exceptions, even for military service. A resolution to keep the voting age at twenty-one passed by a vote of 60–33.[57] "We shall return," Burn said.[58]

The convention proposed only one amendment to be voted on by the citizens: extending the term of office for county trustees to four years. Burn criticized the Memphis delegation. "I am not so naïve as to have not anticipated today's result. Memphis is too close to Little Rock to have escaped anxiety. While I believe that any fear of the future is not justified, I am not blind to the fact that concern exists."[59]

The day Burn returned home from the convention, he wrote letters to friends lamenting the result of the convention and the role that he believed race played in the opposition to lowering the voting age. "We ran into a stone wall of opposition in Memphis and most of West Tennessee. The integration question was the submerged reef this time," he wrote to a friend.[60] "Political change comes slowly. It took one hundred years to remove the payment of a poll tax as a prerequisite of voting in Tennessee....We have the satisfaction of having done the best we could under the circumstances."[61]

In the fall of 1961, CBS reached out to Burn for an interview for its documentary series *The Twentieth Century*.[62] He agreed to an interview for an episode entitled "The Women Get the Vote." He wished to cooperate "to get into the record that I did not switch from 'No' to "Aye.'"[63] The myths and equivocations about his famous vote still persisted four decades after the ratification of the Nineteenth Amendment.

Burn traveled extensively for business and other activities, averaging almost twenty-five thousand miles per year.[64] He frequently traveled by train via the Southern Railway line, he and his father's longtime employer. After a business trip to New York trying to attract industry to Roane County, he rode to Washington, D.C., for an interview with the venerable news anchor Walter Cronkite.

After filming, Burn wrote that he was under considerable tension at the time of the interview, suffering from "mike fright [*sic*]" to some degree.[65] He spent half a day with notes he made memorizing what he wanted to say. "The extremely bright lights were adjusted…the one immediately over my head was immediately lowered to the top of my head, so I am sure I will show a shiny bald head in the final product."[66]

Burn thought his voice was "cracked" at times and was asked if he needed a sip of water. He replied that he was not thirsty. "Did they think I needed some water?" he wrote. "Their reply was no, so I presume the director thought they were getting the inflection of a typical East Tennessee hillbilly."[67] He wanted to talk about some other things, including Roane County and a "plug" for lowering the voting age to eighteen. "The director and research consultant wanted history, not current matters."[68] He expressed disappointment that the program did not mention "the two roll calls on the motion to table, which resulted in ties…the reason was not disclosed as to why my vote determined the question."[69]

Other special guests on the program included Anita Pollitzer and Nora Stanton Barney (granddaughter of Elizabeth Cady Stanton).[70] As discussed earlier, Pollitzer worked closely with Alice Paul and the National Woman's Party to secure ratification of the Nineteenth Amendment in Tennessee. The episode aired in March 1962.

Burn received many letters from viewers who enjoyed seeing him on the program. "TV appearance was as superb as your judgment," wrote an Indiana family.[71] "It was good to hear a true Southerner talk," Burn's cousin Alice Pardue Van Horne wrote.[72] "One of the by-products on my appearance on Twentieth Century is that it reestablished contacts with friends and acquaintances of yesteryear," Burn wrote.[73] William Pemberton, married to Burn's cousin Carolyn Hutsell Pemberton from Niota, was delighted to see a Rockwood resident on television. "I know that many honors have been bestowed upon you during your lifetime but I feel that none could have exceeded this national television program."[74]

Burn had a remarkable amount of energy throughout his life. At a time when most people are settling down for retirement, he was busier than ever in his late sixties. In 1961, he told a friend, "In spite of my schedule I feel fine. Should I 'kick the bucket' be assured that it happened without warning." At five feet nine inches, he weighed 204 pounds but had normal blood pressure for his age.[75]

In the summer of 1962, Burn visited the home of legendary suffragist Susan B. Anthony in Rochester, New York. He brought the letter from his mother, which he always kept in a safe at the Kingston branch of his bank before he bequeathed it to his son. Just as he had done in his recent interview with Walter Cronkite, he discussed the "inaccurate" reporting on his role in the ratification of the Nineteenth Amendment in an interview with the Rochester *Democrat and Chronicle*. "They say I originally voted against it, then switched to the other side. This has been repeated so many times I've given up trying to correct it." He said he has never regretted his decision. "Politics would be a lot more crooked than it is but for women."[76]

A member the National Society Sons of the American Revolution since 1931, Burn assumed the organization's highest position in 1964. After serving as president of the Tennessee Society and as treasurer-general for the National Society, he had reached the top. In May 1964, at NSSAR's Annual National Congress in Detroit, he was elected president-general for the 1964–65 term. The outgoing president-general placed the George Washington Ring (once worn by the general himself) on Burn's finger. Burn then promised to place the ring on the finger of his successor.[77]

"Never has an honor come to me which I appreciate more," Burn exclaimed.[78] He called on the leaders in NSSAR to institute an active program on patriotic education.[79] "Now I look forward to educating the boys and girls of these United States."[80] Burn drafted a resolution after being sworn in as president-general:

> *Whereas, we support the efforts of those who oppose the program of the Fabian Socialists to destroy the American economic system; Therefore, be it resolved by the National Society, Sons of the American Revolution, that we urge our members to combat said insidious socialistic theory which would destroy our existing economy and extinguish individual liberty and free enterprise.*[81]

Although forbidden by law to endorse candidates, Burn's address to the society in October 1964 urged compatriots to go vote in the coming presidential election. "Too long have important issues been decided by

Burn as president-general of the
National Society Sons of the
American Revolution. *NSSAR
Library.*

a minority because of the stay-at-home vote....Take an active part in all elections. Go to work for America!"[82]

Two correspondences from Burn's term as president-general of NSSAR stand out in particular. In October 1964, he and former U.S. president Herbert Hoover exchanged letters in celebration of the former president's ninetieth birthday. Hoover described the letter as "gracious and heartwarming."[83] In January 1965, Burn sent a telegram to Lady Clementine Churchill, the widow of the recently deceased Sir Winston Churchill. "The members of the National Society, Sons of the American Revolution, mourn the passing of Sir Winston, their most illustrious compatriot."[84] Churchill's mother, Jennie Jerome, was American-born and descended from Revolutionary War veterans.

Burn described his year as president-general of NSSAR as "a dream year for Ellen and me." He said they were "given the red carpet treatment from Portland, Maine to Portland, Oregon; from Charleston, South Carolina to Honolulu, Hawaii."[85] The couple traveled almost forty thousand miles during that year.[86]

Right after his term as president-general of NSSAR came to an end, Burn's opportunity to finally address the reapportionment issue had arrived. Tennessee voters had approved another state constitutional convention for summer 1965. He decided to run for the third time as a delegate to the constitutional convention representing Roane County. Recent legislation and decrees of the courts on the issue of reapportionment inspired the call for another convention.

During his 1964 campaign for delegate, Burn referenced his service in the Tennessee House of Representatives in 1921, reminding voters of his longtime advocacy for fair apportionment of the state legislature.[87] Again, he ran unopposed. In November 1964, he received thousands of complimentary votes to represent Roane County at the convention.[88]

The 1965 Tennessee Constitutional Convention convened at the height of the civil rights movement in the United States. The poll tax, which Burn had voted to abolish in Tennessee, was abolished nationwide with the ratification of the Twenty-Fourth Amendment in 1964. Americans aged eighteen through twenty, although denied their right to vote, did not face discrimination comparable to racial minorities. Racists in governments in the South fought hard to preserve tools of discrimination like poll taxes and segregation. After decades of fighting, civil rights leaders secured passage of the Civil Rights Act of 1964 and the Voting Rights Act of 1965. Understandably, the youth vote movement lost momentum during this period.

Although Burn did not give up his drive for lowering the voting age, he knew that the issue had taken a back seat in the civil rights era of the 1960s. Consideration of a lowered voting age was not in the call for the 1965 convention. The youth vote movement would one day surge again.

When the 1965 convention began, Burn kept his campaign promise and devoted his efforts toward reapportionment. "There is some evidence of a cleavage between rural and urban delegates and more sectional and political implications in the actions of the delegates than was observed in the two previous conventions, he reported."[89] The delegates elected him as chairman of the East Tennessee Caucus.[90]

Burn's beliefs had not changed since he first proposed his reapportionment bill in 1921. He remained in favor of reapportioning both chambers of the legislature. The controversy would be over exactly how to implement it.

Two recent U.S. Supreme Court decisions forced Tennessee to act on reapportioning its legislative districts for the first time since 1901. The decision in *Baker v. Carr* in 1962 resulted in the "one person, one vote" standard.[91] Charles Baker hailed from Shelby County, Tennessee, and argued that voters in his legislative district were underrepresented compared to those living in rural districts with much lower populations. The defense argued that redistricting and reapportionment were "political questions" and should not be adjudicated in the federal courts. Baker won the case and, with it, set the precedent of federal courts deciding redistricting questions. In response, the state legislature passed reapportionment bills in 1962 and 1963, but those did not meet the standards of the courts.[92] Had the Tennessee legislature listened to Burn and passed his redistricting bills in 1921 or 1951, the *Baker v. Carr* case would likely never have happened. This is not to say that the U.S. Supreme Court would not have eventually ruled on a political question or redistricting case in the future.

As a result of the precedent set in *Baker v. Carr*, the U.S. Supreme Court handed down another significant decision in the case of *Reynolds v. Sims* in 1964. The court's decision in this case changed the way states were legally permitted to apportion their chambers in the legislature. Previously, several state legislatures (including Tennessee) apportioned the House of Representatives based on population, but apportionment in the Senate often used a different method. The decision in *Reynolds v. Sims* occurred as a result of a group of Birmingham citizens challenging reapportionment laws in Alabama's constitution. As the document only permitted one state senator per county, citizens in an urban county with a large population had the same weight in their senator's vote as that of a citizen in a rural county with only a few thousand residents. The court ruled in favor of the Birmingham voters. The decision required state legislatures to reapportion their Senate districts based on population.[93] This decision weakened the voting power of lowly populated rural districts to counterbalance heavily populated urban areas in the State Senate. "Legislators represent people, not trees or acres," wrote Chief Justice Earl Warren in his opinion.[94]

Although the U.S. Senate remains unaffected by the decision, the implication of *Reynolds v. Sims* represents the very antithesis of the "Connecticut Compromise." In framing the U.S. Constitution, delegates from the smaller, less populated states at the Constitutional Convention of 1787 worried that the larger, heavily populated states (including the staunchly proslavery states of Virginia and North Carolina) would dominate politics if representation in Washington, D.C., were based solely on population. The delegates reached an agreement, known as the "Connecticut Compromise," which created a House of Representatives to be based on population, and a Senate that gives every state two votes regardless of land area or population. Known as the "little federal system," many states adopted this structure in their constitutions.

The implications of the recent federal court rulings on forced reapportionment in Tennessee meant that the state's four largest counties

(Shelby, Davidson, Knox and Hamilton) would be only two Senate seats short of a majority (seventeen seats). The four counties would also have ten new seats in the House of Representatives, only eight seats short of a majority in that chamber (fifty seats). In 1960, the four counties had a combined population of 1.5 million people. Tennessee's population was 3.5 million.[95] Tennessee's rural districts fiercely resisted this new reapportionment standard. Political forces from the rural districts pushed to call another constitutional convention as an attempt to address forced reapportionment. Urban and rural delegates to the 1965 convention clashed over the issue. This controversy could have been avoided had previous legislatures listened to Burn.

A 1961 University of Tennessee study demonstrated the need for reapportionment in the state. A properly apportioned House of Representatives district would have about 36,000 people (3.5 million Tennesseans divided into ninety-nine districts equals 36,000.)[96] The study found forty-seven underrepresented House districts and fifty-two overrepresented House districts. Using the standard of population for reapportionment, the Senate had twenty-one overrepresented districts and twelve underrepresented districts.[97] This was true for both direct as well as floterial representatives and senators (floterial representatives and senators represented more than one county and sometimes would include the already split up urban counties).

Since the most recent reapportionment in 1901, all four of the state's major urban areas had grown significantly in population—so had the region of East Tennessee. The votes of a representative from a small rural district in Middle or West Tennessee carried the same weight as that of a representative from Nashville or Memphis. The House, unequivocally, had to be reapportioned.

The real controversy came in the clash between the urban and rural districts over whether to reapportion the Senate based on population. An example from the study showed that the vote of a senator from many districts in West Tennessee with small populations (some fewer than 100,000 people) had the same weight as a vote from a senator in Shelby County representing more than 300,000 people.[98]

The State Senate needed to be reapportioned. But Burn supported the rural districts in their efforts to be apportioned by means other than population (such as land area). The rural districts feared control of the state by the four major urban areas and wanted to maintain some of their voting power in the Senate, especially since it was rightfully going to be lost in the House of Representatives.

Outside of the reapportionment issue, the convention began to grow dull. Noncontroversial issues debated included annual legislative sessions (instead of alternate years) and increased compensation for legislators. Burn and other delegates introduced a successful resolution to extend the terms of state senators from two to four years.[99]

In an attempt to ensure better representation of the urban districts, Burn teamed with other delegates to introduce an unsuccessful resolution to increase the number of state representatives from 99 to 150.[100] Although the convention turned down a proposal for a unicameral legislature, Burn said that he was not opposed to the idea and that he "subscribes to a system of checks and balances under our present federal system."[101] He added, "If population alone is the criterion for apportionment, then a unicameral legislature would logically follow."[102]

Burn took the controversy over reapportionment to the next level. The *Nashville Tennessean* said it best in a headline titled "Just Count on Harry Burn to Make It Hum": "When things grow dull he can be depended upon to light a match to the fireworks or throw a Molotov cocktail into the proceedings."[103] Burn ignited controversy by criticizing U.S. Supreme Court chief justice Earl Warren and the decision in *Reynolds v. Sims*:

> *Warren and others that follow his philosophy of government have acted to destroy the system of checks and balances established by our founding fathers. They are more concerned with protecting the rights of criminals and those who would destroy our form of government than in protecting law-abiding citizens from thieves, murderers, and traitors.*[104]

Burn defended critics of Warren, calling them "concerned patriots who want to preserve our original form of government and law abiding society."[105] The *Nashville Tennessean* called his criticism of Warren "fiery oratory" and said his view of checks and balances "is a man in a hood with a whip—on horseback."[106] Burn replied to the *Nashville Tennessean*'s criticism of his remarks and the charge that he and other delegates did not read the state constitution:

> *The editor thinks he knows everything about the Constitution of Tennessee...then waves his torch of enlightenment to declare that the problem of reapportionment "was created by legislators of Tennessee who for more than a half century ignored its own state constitution." The brilliant editor failed to do his homework, or he would have known that*

on the first day of the 1921 session of the General Assembly I introduced in the House of Representatives a bill to reapportion the State Senate and House of Representatives on a population basis. In that bill I undertook to eliminate discrimination against a minority, based on partisanship. Forty-four years later I oppose discrimination against a minority. Factors other than population would be some weight in a reapportionment except for the un-American decision of the Warren court. When one has worked for constitutional reform in Tennessee for a half century and has been elected a delegate to three (yes, three) constitutional conventions, he is more amused than concerned by fulminations of a Johnny-come-lately in the fight for legislative integrity.[107]

Burn continued his criticism of Warren. "Possibly any remarks about the coddling of Communists and criminals through rulings by the Warren court should not have included my brief discussion of checks and balances for legislative bodies."[108] He commended the *Knoxville News-Sentinel* for running an editorial. He shared the last paragraph:

Some day it's going to happen. Sometime the wife or daughter of one of these nit-picking judges who seek any excuse to set the accused free is going to get caught by one of these roaming rapists. And then maybe we'll get some overturning of legal precedents and more judicial interest in the welfare of the innocent. Yes, Mr. Extremist-on-the-left, American patriots are concerned. Yet you insinuate that such individuals are John Birchers and Ku Kluxers. Shame on you and others of your ilk.[109]

One Memphis delegate remarked that Burn's speech "is an example of tension between rural and urban spokesmen at the convention."[110] Another Memphis delegate suggested that he should have written a letter to the editor instead of "bringing it before the convention."[111] Clearly, this delegate was unfamiliar with Burn's style. He was not one for discretion.

Burn made himself loud and clear. He supported population-based reapportionment in the House of Representatives and knew how overdue it was. For the Senate, he held beliefs similar to those of the delegates at the 1787 Constitutional Convention that created the U.S. Constitution. He believed in the "little federal system" and wished for factors other than population to factor in when reapportioning Senate districts. He wanted lowly populated rural districts to have adequate representation in at least one chamber of the state legislature without being completely dominated by the urban districts.

"He is now presumably on the side of the rural bloc that ignored the state constitution for so many years," the *Nashville Tennessean* wrote.[112] The convention recessed in August with plans to convene again in December. "The only reason it was authorized in the first place is that the dominant rural element in the legislature recognized it was going to lose its power through federally ordered reapportionment. The convention was an act of desperation, an attempt to change the state constitution in some way to preserve rural power."[113]

At the close of the convention in December, the delegates approved nine proposals. On reapportionment, the rural delegates proposed an amendment to Article II, Sections 3 and 4 to "permit one house of the legislature to be apportioned on geography or some other if future federal action permits."[114] Rural delegates pinned their hopes on the proposed "Dirksen Amendment" in the U.S. Congress that would permit the states to apportion the State Senate by means other than population. The rural delegates proposed two other amendments aimed at diluting the voting power of the urban districts by requiring urban counties to be subdivided. One opponent of the reapportionment amendments claimed them to be "nothing more nor less than an attempt to get around the federal court decisions."[115]

Tennessee voters approved all nine proposed amendments to the state constitution in 1966, including amendments extending the term of office for state senators from two to four years and increased salaries for legislators. The Dirksen Amendment failed to pass the U.S. Congress. Rural districts failed to someday regain their power in the state legislatures. Beginning in the late 1960s, state legislatures underwent forced redistricting across the country. The Tennessee Senate has been apportioned on a population basis ever since. "Reapportionment's greatest wrench has been in rural legislative delegations. The ranks of country legislators, once able to form coalitions and block city folks' bills, has been decimated," the *Daily News-Journal* of Murfreesboro wrote.[116]

Burn lost the debate over how to maintain a balance between population-based representation in the State House of Representatives and territorial-based representation in the State Senate. The ideas that inspired the "Connecticut Compromise" at the 1787 Constitutional Convention to protect small states from domination by large states would no longer apply to state constitutions. But it was not a total loss for Burn. The ensuing reapportionment ensured proper representation for the urban districts as well as for much of East Tennessee in the Tennessee House of Representatives. After forty-four years, he had been vindicated on another issue.

The year 1965 had been a busy one for Burn. He had stepped down as president of the First National Bank and Trust Company of Rockwood in January. His year as president-general of NSSAR ended in May. The constitutional convention adjourned in December, one month after he turned seventy. In a letter to a friend, Burn wrote, "I will be seventy next November 12. While I have been very active, possibly averaging 50 to 60 work hours per week for the past half-century, I realize that in the next few months I will have to slow down in some degree."[117]

Chapter 14

TWILIGHT YEARS AND DEATH

B urn continued serving as chairman of the board at the bank. For a time, his sister Otho and his nephew Bill served on the board of directors. His great-nieces Cathy Burn Allen and Pat Burn Cotton remembered their father, Bill, taking them to the board meetings. They would ride in a speedboat up Watts Bar Lake from their Ten Mile cabin to Rockwood. My mother, Sandra Burn Boyd, remembered her great-uncle Harry as "sophisticated, but not in a snobbish way."

Burn never truly retired. He set up a small finance business on Front Avenue in Rockwood. He opened it shortly after he retired as bank president, naming it Gateway Finance. He shared office space with others in the building. Bill McFarland began renting office space beside Burn for fifty dollars per month in 1967. The two became fast friends. "Harry was a great guy. I thought the world of him."[1] Burn quickly noticed McFarland's skills. He offered McFarland the job of president of his Philadelphia-based life insurance company. McFarland politely declined, saying he was "honored" to be offered the position.[2]

Tom McFarland, Bill's son, remembered his father introducing him to Burn. "He's famous, son. He changed the world."[3] Bill McFarland was a firsthand witness to Burn's fame in the 1970s. Insuring Burn's automobiles, he remembered how Burn would travel the country giving speeches about his role in the ratification of the Nineteenth Amendment. Burn would often return from a trip and ask McFarland what he thought of his speech. He valued McFarland's opinion. "Harry would come into my office and talk about whatever was on his mind."[4]

In September 1968, Otho Virginia Burn Hammer passed away in her sleep shortly before her sixty-second birthday. Harry T. Burn had outlived all of his siblings. His ex-wife sent a thoughtful message of condolence.

Despite their short marriage, Burn remained close with Mildred Tarwater. They had both remarried and had a child. She married and had a daughter named Rebecca Walker. "Becky" Walker Aarts remembered Burn as "a smart and generous man that her family could always depend on."[5] When Aarts was ten years old, her father passed away. Burn later told Aarts that he felt like a "father figure" to her since her father passed away.[6]

Mildred Walker even got on well with Ellen Burn and Harry T. Burn Jr. Mildred and Ellen became good friends. Harry T. Burn Jr. kept a photograph of Mildred on his desk. After Otho Burn Hammer's sudden passing, Mildred wrote to her ex-husband. "I always enjoyed talking with her. She was a wonderful person. She looked and talked so much like your mother, and you know how much I loved your mother."[7] Mildred often told her daughter, Becky, about what a "sweet and kind" person Febb Burn was.[8] Anne Scandlyn Powers remembered Mildred as "cheerful."[9] Harry T. Burn Jr. later wrote that Mildred was the last person he knew who spoke of his grandmother Febb as "a contemporary rather than a distant figure."[10]

Burn suffered another loss one year later. His relationship with his Uncle Bill Ensminger became strained toward the end. They feuded over a contractual agreement due to a decades-old misunderstanding. He even tried to get Burn kicked out of the bank! Their relationship would remain at arm's length until Uncle Bill's death.

Uncle Bill and Aunt Eddyth moved to Studio City, California, after he turned ninety. He spent the last few years of his life there. He passed away in November 1969, a week shy of his ninety-fourth birthday. Burn lost the last father figure of his life.

As the golden anniversary of the Nineteenth Amendment approached, Burn granted frequent interviews. In an interview with his nephew James L.E. Burn, he reflected on his vote for woman suffrage nearly a half century earlier:

James L.E. Burn: "Well, if you had it to do over would you do it again?"

Harry T. Burn: "Yes. No argument about that."[11]

Burn then reminded his nephew what he had said at a speech in Los Angeles in 1921:

> *I didn't think that the votes for women would be the "cure-all" and improve the morals of politics, as much as those who advocated it had said it would. Also, I didn't think it would ever prove to be the disaster that its opponents said it would be. It certainly gave women their right....Now take your grandmother, my mother, here she was a student of international affairs, she had been a college woman, she would vote intelligently; and yet, she had illiterate or uneducated men working on this farm that could vote and go down to the polls and put a big bond issue right here on her property....I think it was morally right. I thought it then, I still think it.*[12]

In an interview with *Look* magazine, Burn defended his deciding vote. "Sure I would do it again. All the dire consequences they threatened never happened. Women ought to have the vote. I'm glad I helped them get it.... Furthermore, the vote should be extended to eighteen year olds as well. As long as society treats them as adults, they should be permitted to vote as adults."[13] He would soon get his wish for a lowered voting age.

The *Knoxville News Sentinel* described Burn in a December 1970 interview: "The Great Decider is ageless. He was 75 in November, but he's firm of step, spruce of dress, and merry of heart."[14] In 1970, he stepped down as chairman of the board at the bank, becoming honorary chairman of the board. He had yet to see universal suffrage achieved and still had one more constitutional convention to attend as a delegate.

In November 1968, for the fourth time in eighteen years, Tennessee voters had the opportunity to approve another constitutional convention. The reclassification of property taxes inspired the call for the convention to be held in 1971. One newspaper ad in favor of the call warned voters of necessary action to prevent a possible "shift of approximately 20 million dollars in taxes onto the low income and non-income producing property in Tennessee."[15]

Question 3 as it appeared on the ballot during the 1968 election concluded, "Said Constitutional Convention, if called, shall not be authorized to amend the Constitution so as to permit a personal income tax, except as authorized under the present Constitution."[16] (In Tennessee, the Hall Income Tax taxes interest and dividends, with plans to be phased out by 2021.) But as Burn would soon find out, this prohibition on inserting an income tax into the state constitution would not stop certain factions from trying.

Burn later remodeled Hathburn, adding larger columns in place of the original porch.
Richard Rutledge.

Also on the ballot for the call was to lower the voting age to eighteen. The issue, dormant during the 1965 convention, reemerged. "Emphasis on granting the voting rights to younger citizens is getting special emphasis now as a result of the young soldiers fighting in Vietnam, many of whom have returned to find they have no voice in deciding the winner of the presidential race this year," the *Leaf-Chronicle* noted.[17] But several Tennesseans remained opposed. "These critics point to college campus revolts, dissenting demonstrators, and widespread protests among the youth to illustrate their resistance to changing the voting age in Tennessee."[18]

In the 1968 general election, Tennessee voters approved the question to consider a reclassification of property taxes. But the question on consideration of lowering the voting age failed to receive sufficient votes. Lowering the voting age in Tennessee had proven to be a long struggle, and despite the results of the 1968 election, their fortunes would change before the 1971 convention convened.

Controversy over the Vietnam War and the draft significantly moved public opinion toward lowering the voting age nationwide. "The prolonged Vietnam War was an undeniable factor in the accelerated passing and ratification" of the federal amendment to enfranchise eighteen- to twenty-year-olds, noted Wendell W. Cultice.[19] The U.S. Congress passed an amendment to the Voting Rights Act of 1965, mandating a lowered voting age in federal, state and local elections. After a legal challenge, the Supreme Court ruled in 1970 that the U.S. Congress had no right to lower the voting age for state and local elections. The lowered voting age in presidential and Congressional elections was upheld. But two separate voter rolls were too costly for the states. Votes for eighteen-, nineteen- and twenty-year-olds would not become national law though an act of Congress. Since the several states determine voter qualifications, a constitutional amendment was in order to achieve nationwide enfranchisement of American adults. The U.S. Congress proposed the Twenty-Sixth Amendment to the states for ratification on March 23, 1971.

The states knew that ratification of the amendment was imminent. During Burn's last year of service on the State Planning Commission, a study was conducted to estimate the number of new voters that Tennessee would have upon ratification. The 1970 study revealed that, on average, Tennessee's voting age population would increase by 9.2 percent.[20] The study prepared the state to register 219,063 new eligible voters in anticipation of ratification.[21]

On March 23, 1971, Tennessee became the fourth state to ratify the amendment, the day of its proposal to the several states by Congress. The states ratified the amendment with North Carolina's ratification in July 1971. Burn commended the amendment in an interview two weeks later. "You can imagine how elated I am that they can now vote, regardless of which way they vote."[22] Nearly 11 million new voters between eighteen and twenty would vote in the 1972 elections nationwide.[23] The amendment had been proposed by the Congress and ratified by the requisite states in three months, a record time. Section 1 of the Twenty-Sixth Amendment reads as follows:

The right of citizens of the United States, who are eighteen years of age or older, to vote shall not be denied or abridged by the United States or by any State on account of age.

Burn had lived to see suffrage rights expanded and strengthened over the past half century. Beginning with his deciding vote for woman suffrage in 1920, continuing with weakening and removing Tennessee's poll taxes, authoring bills to protect against election fraud, authoring bills for permanent voter registration and ending with the ratification of the Twenty-Sixth Amendment after many years advocating for lowering the voting age, Burn had lived to see it all. Women, minorities and young adults all have their right to vote protected by state constitutions and the U.S. Constitution thanks to the efforts of public servants like Burn. Universal suffrage had been achieved at last!

In August 1970, Tennessee voters elected delegates to the 1971 constitutional convention. Three months shy of his seventy-fifth birthday, Burn ran for Roane County delegate to a fourth consecutive constitutional convention. The property tax classification issue concerned rural voters in Roane County. Just as the reapportionment issue divided rural and urban districts at the 1965 convention, so would the call for a convention to address property tax classification. Leading figures from Tennessee's urban areas and organizations, including the Tennessee Municipal League, unsuccessfully opposed the call for a convention.

"I believe that classification of property for taxation is the only way to protect the owners of small homes from confiscatory taxes," Burn said.[24] He ran an ad in the *Rockwood Times*. "The issues will be closely drawn on property classification and your vote will evidence support of my platform."[25] Running unopposed for the third time, Roane County voters gave Burn thousands of complimentary votes to be their delegate.[26]

Burn returned to Nashville in summer 1971 for his fourth and final state constitutional convention. He was one of only five delegates who had served in all four post-Reconstruction conventions.[27] He announced his candidacy for president of the convention.

J.H. McCartt of Morgan County first nominated Burn for president of the convention. "A man who has the privilege of bringing about in this country the adoption of the Nineteenth Amendment to the Constitution of the United States, which gave these beautiful women here the right to vote and to kill their husband's vote if they so desired."[28] Two delegates seconded the nomination, both of them having served with him in previous conventions. One delegate commended his integrity and complimented him as a gentleman who could handle himself objectively.[29]

Burn was not elected president of the convention. But the caucus of East Tennessee delegates unanimously nominated him to be vice-president. He later withdrew his name from consideration but said he was "deeply grateful" to be nominated. Once all of the officers had been elected, he expressed his dissatisfaction with the results. "It is to be regretted that a policy of non-partisan impartiality, plus experience, did not receive the support of the dominant element in the convention."[30]

Burn explained his position on property tax assessment. "It is imperative that farmers have relief. They can't pay the taxes that are paid on suburban real estate properties." He said the same goes for "the elderly and persons on fixed incomes." He wished for the farm tax to remain low and for the convention to consider instituting a homestead exemption tax for homeowners. "Whatever we do…it's going to have to go back to the people for approval. The voters make the final decision."[31]

In a direct violation of the call, a Shelby County delegate proposed a change to the convention's original intention to amend the laws on property assessment. The proposal included a payroll tax, which had many supporters, including certain lobbyist groups. Burn immediately made a statement:

The payroll tax, and state income tax for that matter, are not in the official call of this limited convention and are therefore not an issue. The convention was called for the consideration of property for taxable persons and, in my opinion, it would be illegal for us to consider any other form of taxation.[32]

To this day, the Tennessee Constitution does not permit a personal income tax. This is thanks in part to the efforts of public servants like Burn. Standing up against the attempt to inflict an income tax on Tennesseans was his last act in statewide public service.

Burn returned to Rockwood in September and gave a summary of the convention. The delegates approved a proposal for classifying real property into three classifications with assessments on a percentage of value: 1) public utilities, 55 percent; 2) industrial and commercial, 40 percent; 3) farms and one-unit homes, 25 percent.[33] Among the other proposals included relief for many people, including individuals, families and senior citizens, a major concern for Burn.[34] Tennessee voters later approved the proposed amendments at the convention.

Burn joined the Longstreet-Zollicoffer Camp of the Sons of Confederate Veterans in Knoxville in the early 1970s. His public service record during his early career demonstrates his support for the then-living Confederate veterans. His lineage from his maternal grandfather, Jonathon Thomas "Tom" Ensminger, qualified his membership. He quickly became the camp commander. Bob Freeman remembered Burn's "outstanding" leadership as camp commander.[35] He enjoyed the programs that Burn oversaw during his leadership. He recalled Burn's love of history and his passion for historic preservation and education. According to Freeman, Burn was a "proud member" of the Sons of Confederate Veterans.[36]

Throughout his life, Burn worked as a railroader, legislator, attorney, banker and farm owner. He remained involved in diverse activities and ventures. In addition to operating his finance company after retiring as bank president, he also ventured into broadcasting. He invested in a radio station in Harriman. The name of the radio station was nearly identical to his initials. He became part owner of WHBT-FM in Harriman. Bill Farnham began working in radio as a young man and remembered Burn as a supportive boss. Farnham recalled Burn as "sharp, succinct, and interesting."[37] He noted that Burn sometimes wore a seersucker jacket and straw hat.

According to Farnham, Burn "was not reticent" to talk about his role in the ratification of the Nineteenth Amendment.[38] He rarely brought up the subject unless asked about it. Although the golden anniversary of the amendment had already passed, it never stopped bringing him attention for the rest of his life. Virginia Key met Burn while working with James L.E. Burn at Dycho in Niota. After she thanked Burn on behalf of herself and all women, he replied, "Young lady, my mother told me what I needed to do."[39]

In 1974, fifty-four years after the ratification of the amendment, CBS aired a thirteen-episode television series titled *The American Parade*, narrated by Mary Tyler Moore. One episode, titled "We the Women," featured a reenactment of the woman suffrage vote on that hot August day in Nashville.[40] Newspapers mistakenly reported that Burn was the only living member of the 1920 legislature when the program aired.[41] Joe Hanover, leader of the pro-suffrage Memphis delegation, was still alive at age eighty-five (he would be the last member to pass away in 1984).

In interviews after the program aired, Burn recalled his escape from the sergeant-at-arms at the state capitol and hiding in the library attic. "I could hardly breathe with the heat up there, so I retraced my steps—carefully—and then literally ran across to the Hermitage Hotel, through its lobby and out the back way. When I look at that ledge now, I don't believe I was crazy enough to walk out on it. It's only about 18 or 20 inches wide. I'd sure never do that again."[42] Neither Burn nor any interviewers mentioned him being chased by a mob. Such false reports were rare when he was alive and only mentioned the mob chase when he was not interviewed for the story. It was not until after his death that the apocryphal story began to spread. In 1960, he had written to the *Nashville Tennessean* politely correcting it on a story it had ran. In the letter, he explained why he went out onto the ledge.[43] Burn was asked if he would vote for the amendment again. He replied that he "sure would."[44] He never expressed a scintilla of regret in his decision to vote aye on the ratification of the Nineteenth Amendment.

One of the last political issues during Burn's lifetime was the battle over the Equal Rights Amendment, proposed by the U.S. Congress in 1972. Section 1 of the proposed Equal Rights Amendment read as follows:

Equality of rights under the law shall not be denied or abridged by the United States or by any State on account of sex.

The origins of the ERA began in the 1920s after the ratification of the Nineteenth Amendment. Alice Paul tirelessly advocated for the ERA for the next half century. By 1973, thirty states had ratified it, including Tennessee. The National Organization for Women has been a longtime proponent of the ERA, advocating for an end to sex discrimination.[45]

The leading figure opposing ratification of the ERA was Phyllis Schlafly. An activist and attorney, she founded the "Stop ERA" organization. She claimed the amendment was unnecessary because of the special privileges and status that she believed American women already had. Opponents of the ERA warned that women would be forced into combat and be denied alimony and child support.[46]

Burn commented on the issue in spring 1974: "The proposed ERA amendment could be a two-edge sword....I don't think all of the safeguard legislation for women should be abrogated or repealed. If the problems they are trying to solve are sociological problems, they can make all the corrections they need to within their present political rights. They can use their political power and right of suffrage to change the law any way they want. They can obtain all the proper objectives through their political clout."[47] He did not believe the ERA was needed but expressed his confidence in women's political ability. "I believe women are more independent in their voting and less prone to stay with a political angle than men. The overall result is a better political climate....There's no doubt about it. Women have elevated the whole political scene."[48]

In the late summer of 1974, Burn attended a national conference of the Stop ERA organization in St. Louis. Phyllis Schlafly was in attendance.[49] He said the ERA would destroy established rights while attempting to create others that are largely "will-of-the-wisps." "Through the ballot box women can change any existing law or policy. They constitute a majority of voters.... If the proposed ERA Amendment would broaden the base of political equality I would support it. But all it can do is to create a legal quagmire."[50] Burn firmly believed in political equality and that the government should be obliged to treat all individuals equally.

In December 1974 in Germantown, Tennessee, Burn spoke at another Stop ERA event. He claimed that the ERA was an "unnecessary appendage to the U.S. Constitution" and that it "would be a great loss of rights for women." He pointed to a recent state ERA law passed in Pennsylvania that he claimed had been "devastating to the rights of women by removing every special protection women had."[51] He had major reservations about applying the proposed law on a national scale.

In a controversial move, the Tennessee legislature rescinded its ratification of the ERA in 1974. Two other states also rescinded it shortly afterward. Major women's groups began to split over issues related to it. These events, combined with the efforts of activists like Schlafly and the major distraction caused by the Watergate scandal, pushed the ERA out of the forefront. The amendment did not receive the requisite number of states for ratification before the deadline specified in its proposal, even after an extension. However, proposed amendments have been ratified many years after their proposal, including the Twenty-Seventh Amendment. The drive to ratify the ERA continues to this day.

Not all of Burn's travels in his later years were for political speeches. He would travel for pleasure using a variety of methods. His preferred means of conveyance throughout his life was his beloved railroads. He did not like to fly and only did so when he had to, usually for international travel. He drove a Lincoln for many years and a Ford Thunderbird and an Oldsmobile in his later years. Although he drove frequently, he only enjoyed driving for leisure, especially when pursuing his interest in architecture. He would sometimes go for a drive admiring homes. He made a habit of actually pulling in the driveway of a home, knocking on the door and asking to see the house.[52]

Burn visited one home in particular while driving through Orange, Virginia. At the time, the DuPont family owned Montpelier, the home of President James Madison. I remember my late cousin telling me how his father walked up to the front door of the historic home, knocked on the door and said, "Hi, I'm Harry Burn. I'm here to see the house." They invited him inside for a tour. Most people invited him inside their home!

Ellen Burn continued teaching at Rockwood High School until her retirement in 1973. She and her husband traveled together frequently, for

Harry and Ellen Burn enjoyed hosting parties and soirees at Hathburn. *Burn family.*

work and pleasure. They saw the world together. Geraldine Wallick worked in the Rockwood school system for many years. "Mrs. Burn's students loved hearing about her and Mr. Burn's world travels."[53]

Ellen Burn loved to walk. "She could out-walk any of us," Wallick recalled.[54] She remained devoted to the Rockwood Schools after her retirement. She loved to attend the high school's football games. A loyal Lady Vols fan, she enjoyed watching them on television. Watching basketball with his wife was about the only time Burn showed any interest in sports.

When Harry and Ellen Burn visited cities during their numerous trips, they enjoyed visiting colleges and universities. Unlike his wife, Burn never

Burn with his belted ponies.
Burn family.

attended college. He once told a friend that he and Ellen "have probably visited more colleges and universities than anybody!"[55] They demonstrated how much they valued education through their activities in their community, especially NSSAR and NSDAR.

The couple loved spending their weekends at Hathburn, especially in the warm weather months. After Ellen Burn retired, the couple spent even more time in Niota. Burn's favorite hobby while away from his work, civic and fraternal activities was working with flowers and shrubs on the grounds of Hathburn. Peggy Clark Torbett remembered how much Burn loved nature and how he maintained a duck pond behind Hathburn.[56] Raising belted Galloway cattle and ponies was the only hands-on farmwork he ever did. Gerald Largen remembered the hands-on approach Burn took in caring for the cattle. "It kept him looking younger than he really was," Largen said.[57] The farm had many other animals, including peacocks, rabbits, goats and a turkey. Burn's favorite food included steak (with no sauce!), chili, pecans and oranges. He frequently gave pecans as gifts and even fed them to squirrels living in the attic. Bob Freeman recalled the pride Burn took in the appearance of his beloved country home. He often talked about the upkeep that the property required.[58]

Randy Kincannon grew up in Niota. He remembered seeing Burn at Sexton's store on Farrell Street. Burn walked into the store to buy a Coke. The seven-year-old Kincannon remembered his encounter with Burn. "To

Burn took great pride in the appearance of his beloved Hathburn estate. *Burn family.*

me he seemed about seven feet tall…he was dressed like the mayor on Andy Griffith. He asked me if I wanted a Coke and I refused because it scared me that such a giant was talking to me. But he was a very nice man."[59]

Maryann Best grew up in Niota and frequently visited with Burn. "Mr. Burn was a nice, laid back man…when we went over there he would open the fridge and make us peanut butter sandwiches and gave us Mountain Dew." Best also remembered the pond on the Hathburn grounds. "We would go down to his little pond which had a small bridge over it. He loved those big ole fish. We would sit and feed them. We laughed a lot."[60]

Burn had the two-story log cabin (built by Adam and Mahala Burn after their move to McMinn County in 1836) moved to the Hathburn grounds. The log cabin still stands on the property today. A guesthouse once stood on the grounds that Burn named Movilla after his father's suggested name for the city when it was forced to change its name from Mouse Creek to Niota.

Gerald Largen remembered Burn showing him the remains of an old Cherokee "council ring" on the Hathburn farm.[61] Burn worked on restoring it. J. Reid Dixon recalled the several train cars that Burn would collect and keep on the property.[62] The *Daily Post-Athenian* later wrote that Burn was an "avid historian....Hathburn became almost a museum of memorabilia and Americana."[63] He maintained a library and always prominently displayed a portrait of George Washington in the home.

In addition to operating his small finance business in Rockwood through the week, Burn practiced law on occasion. He served as legal counsel for Crescent Hosiery Mills and many other organizations, including Patriotic Education Inc. and the Christian Freedom Foundation. J. Reed Dixon remembered purchasing a typewriter and a bench from Burn's Rockwood law office. "It was shortly before he died....I remember he had a big booming voice and skin like parchment paper."[64] The bench sat in Dixon's law office for many years, and he jokingly told clients over the years that it was the bench Febb Burn sat in while she wrote Harry the letter.[65]

Harry Thomas Burn passed away unexpectedly from a heart attack on February 19, 1977, at Hathburn. He was eighty-one years old. The oldest child of Jim and Febb Burn was the last to leave this earth. Harry T. Burn

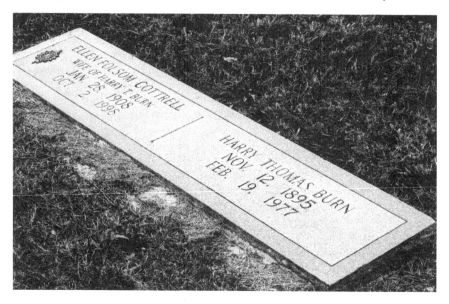

Burn's tombstone at the Niota Cemetery. *Photo by Caitlynn Beddingfield Smith.*

Jr. recalled that his father had just returned home from a business trip and was eating dinner while watching a basketball game before his fatal heart attack. Burn called his nephew's house complaining of indigestion pains. His nephew's wife got in the car and drove up to Hathburn but had to stop and wait for a train that was passing by. By the time she arrived, he had passed away. Ellen Burn was with him in his last moments. His death came on a Saturday evening, five days after he and Ellen had celebrated their fortieth wedding anniversary.

The family held his service at Jerry Smith Funeral Home in Athens, but he lies at rest at the Niota Cemetery. The Tennessee Historical Commission placed a historical marker in the cemetery beside the shoulder of U.S. Highway 11 commemorating his place in American history. The site of the (now demolished) Main Street home where he was born stood only a few hundred yards from his grave. He was eulogized in the *Daily-Post Athenian*: "Comparable to a conqueror who has quested afar he sleeps in the land of his fathers."[66]

Chapter 15
LEGACY

I n public service, Harry Thomas Burn's legacy can be summarized in one word: *empowerment*. Through his actions while serving in government, he empowered people in many ways. The government has less control over people thanks in part to the policies Burn advocated and voted for. Women, more than half of the country's population, can cast a ballot in all elections. Racial minorities, especially black citizens, held down by poll taxes and other tools of racism, now have the right to vote enshrined into our state law. Adults as young as eighteen, many of whom were drafted into deadly conflicts, can now vote. All Tennessee voters participate in elections with stronger safeguards against election and voter fraud. No longer do political machines intimidate voters at the polls.

Tennessee cities and counties have home rule, giving them the freedom to write and repeal more of their own laws. They have the power to hire and fire their own officials. In the spirit of the American Revolution, local governments handle local affairs, while the Tennessee state government handles affairs affecting the entire state. This separation of powers endures to this day. The efforts of public servants like Burn ensure that all citizens have a voice in government and are able to conduct affairs in their local communities without unnecessary interference from the state government.

Burn had remarkable foresight. He supported several good ideas long before their time had come. He advocated for lowering the voting age two decades before it became part of the U.S. Constitution. A supporter of balanced legislative representation, he warned his fellow legislators of the impending fiasco if the state did not reapportion its legislative districts after decades of ignoring the issue. He predicted that Midtown, a region in Roane County, would one day develop into a significant business and industrial center. He lived to see himself vindicated on all of these issues.

Burn valued life in a healthy and thriving community. He believed that giving his time, rather than just money, would help those less fortunate. As bank president, he worked toward the economic development of his community. He knew that anyone could succeed given the opportunity. Through his extensive involvement in the Ruritan Club, he helped struggling rural communities develop.

Burn did not always look to government to solve problems. More often than not, he voted to limit the power of government, especially when it came to control over people's lives and their property. If there was a problem in the community that he believed the government had no role to play in solving, he would always spring into action and work with a local civic or fraternal organization to address it.

The Burn family valued education. Burn's mother, sister, sister-in-law, niece and wife all worked as teachers. In addition to his consistent support for wise spending of taxpayer money for schools, he emphasized local control over the school system. Through his work with NSSAR and other organizations, he sponsored increased efforts in American history and civic education. He emphasized the role that state and local governments play in infrastructure and education. He believed that both were essential to a prosperous society.

To say that Burn had an unbelievable sense of timing in politics would be an understatement. From the beginning of his career in the aftermath of World War I until his slow withdrawal from civic affairs in the later years of the Vietnam era, he always managed to be in a position to take action on major political issues. He had the opportunity to vote on three amendments to the U.S. Constitution. When the Tennessee legislature took action to abolish the poll tax once and for all, he was there to vote on the issue. After Tennessee's constitution stood without amendment for more than eight decades, he served as a delegate to four constitutional conventions tasked with improving and modernizing the document.

Burn was not without flaws. He could sometimes be arrogant, a common trait in people who achieve success and fame early in life. In certain settings he was aloof with people he did not know. He attempted to restrict some individual rights, especially the right to purchase and consume alcohol. He engaged in unnecessary public quarrels with his constituents on a few occasions and did not always take criticism well. His parenting style affected

Burn's Tennessee
Historical
Commission
marker in the Niota
Cemetery. *Photo by
Caitlynn Beddingfield
Smith.*

his relationship with his only child. His "my way or the highway" approach to management made him difficult to work with for some people.

But his virtues stand out. He never backed down from a confrontation. He never feared being in the minority on a controversial issue. He put 100 percent into everything he did. He never thought small, only big. He never compromised his principles. Unlike many politicians throughout history, he did not vote to increase his power, and he rarely voted to give the government more power over people. He did not vote to enrich himself or his friends through graft. He was not a power-lusting career politician living off of taxpayers. He accumulated an above-average amount of wealth in the private sector by providing exceptional legal and financial services.

Burn's public career demonstrates the impact an engaged local citizen can have on their community, state and country. His life story is proof that anyone can transcend being a politician and achieve the status of revered statesman. All it takes is honesty, hard work and uncompromising principles.

Burn was born into a world with no paved roads, no utilities and sluggish communication technology. Tri-weekly newspapers kept the people of Niota informed. He grew up in an era when the only voters were white men, and segregation kept the races separate and unequal. Women in his youth worked as homemakers with limited career options outside of teaching or domestic work. He had lost a sibling in childhood. His parents barely spent time away from East Tennessee. His grandparents experienced the hell of a civil war. In his youth, automatic weapons were in their infancy and railroads were the fastest form of travel.

At the time of his passing, a paved federal highway dissected Niota, and a brand-new federal interstate highway close by made travel more convenient.

Niota had the infrastructure, utilities and amenities of most incorporated cities in America. Television brought the news of the day to living rooms across the nation. Segregation had been struck down by federal courts and was being dismantled all over the country. Suffrage was now universal for all citizens over eighteen. No longer primarily homemakers, many women achieved a college education and worked in varied careers. He saw his country survive two world wars utilizing airplanes and nuclear weapons. He had traveled by airplane across oceans to Europe and Asia.

Effie Lones, the young teacher Burn spoke to upon hearing she might run for mayor of Niota, did eventually enter politics. After her retirement, she ran for Niota City Commission in 1988 and became mayor. Not only that, she served with Nellie Finley, Grace Forrester, Billie Gilliam, Boots Snyder and Mabel Young on what at the time became the only all-female city board in the United States.[1]

The First National Bank and Trust of Rockwood now operates as a Regions bank. Its drive-thru, located on Chamberlain Avenue, still has Burn's green bricks. The main building has gray plaques on either side of the entrance inscribed with Burn's two slogans for the bank: "Where You Feel at Home" and "The Gateway Bank." The Kingston branch of the FNB&T of Rockwood on Kentucky Street now operates as a Simmons bank. That building still has Burn's green bricks. The Scruggs Building in Sweetwater, now known as "New Block," still stands on Morris Street. It is home to Hunter's Café and several boutique shops. Burn's law office was on the second floor above what is now the café.

Harry T. Burn Jr.

Shortly before his father passed away, Harry T. Burn Jr. began working as an information specialist at Oak Ridge Associated Universities. Paul Willson recalled how Harry always looked forward to his job. "It was very fulfilling for him." Teddi Zehner lived in the same apartment building as Harry in Knoxville. "Harry was the resident character," she recalled. He would run several extension cords down to the pool to hook up his television and watch from a float! According to Tyler Forrest, Harry was "the most quietly generous person" he ever knew. Forrest described his late cousin as a "very particular guy." He remembered that when Harry read an error in any work, be it a local paper or a published book, he would always write a letter to the offender, pointing out the error.

"I called him the Wizard of Woodward Avenue," Paul Willson said. "He preferred intellectual humor and had a chuckle that shook his entire body." "When Harry passed away a library burned down," said friend Rick Lay. Former Athens mayor and McMinn County Living Heritage Museum executive director Ann Scott Davis became close to Harry through his generous donations and volunteer work at the museum. Harry helped set up the museum's new computer system when the world was going digital and moving past the typewriter and fax machine era. Bill Wilson remembered how Harry would send a prompt thank-you message after "the least little thing you did for him."

Harry T. Burn Jr. as we all remember him. *Burn family.*

Patsy Duckworth became a close friend of Harry after his retirement. They had a shared passion for local history. During their frequent visits in his hermit years, he would serve popcorn, iced tea with Splenda and coffee-flavored ice cream. McMinn County sheriff and historian Joe Guy received a special gift from Harry: a table from the White Cliff Springs Hotel. Long since demolished, the White Cliff Springs Hotel was one of the most luxurious resorts in the South. Situated on Starr Mountain on the McMinn-Monroe County line, guests enjoyed the hot springs and the incredible views.

Cathy Burn Allen enjoyed receiving a thank-you card from Harry after she sent *him* a thank-you card! Sandra Burn Boyd is happy that Christmas Eve visits with Harry became a tradition. "I, and my family, always learned something new about family relatives and history tidbits of Athens and local Athenians.... Each year we became closer and our visits were more meaningful," she fondly recalled. Pat Burn Cotton enjoyed receiving Harry's Christmas cards, featuring historic family photos. She enjoyed reading Harry's captions to her sons, Zach and Jake. She called it "Christmas Stories with Harry."

Stephanie Allen Calvert remembered Harry as a "great storyteller" who always conducted himself with proper etiquette. Blair Boyd kept in touch with Harry during her graduate and doctoral studies abroad. "During our email correspondences he once shared that 13 was his favorite number, and it became a ritual especially to e-mail on any Friday the 13th to catch up." Betty Catherine Boyd enjoyed admiring the various works of art in Harry's home.

Mahala Burn remembered Harry as a "consummate gentleman." When they were little, Mahala and her sister, Olivia, were fascinated with the pipe organ in his parlor. Upon receiving her PhD and moving to Harvard for work, she received a card from him with "words of kindness and pride."

Mary Ellen Nolletti enjoyed getting to know her cousin in their retirement years. "Harry remembered me every October with at least a dozen or more bulbs to plant. Now I will remember him each spring as those yellow tulips, named after his great aunt on his mother's side, brightly and joyfully display themselves in my yard." She enjoyed her visits to his home. "Harry shared high tea with me one Sunday afternoon around 3:00 p.m. with taste and elegance. He made me feel very special."

I always looked forward to Christmas Eve visits with Harry. He had his Athens home beautifully decorated. He would always dress in a red sweater and green corduroy pants. In his last few years, he would dress more casual, and his friend Billy Cline did a great job with decorations. A gracious host, he always served refreshments, including punch and Christmas candy. He had plenty of M&Ms, my favorite candy. I would be lying if I said he had comfortable furniture, but somehow La-Z-Boys would not have fit well with the rest of his home décor.

I place Harry among the last of the "old school" gentlemen. Although blunt and a bit of a gossip, he always exuded class. I always had difficulty getting a word in when conversing with him. I had to interrupt him a few times to get to a few topics before he breezed on to something else! I will never forget the kind words he expressed to us after my grandfather Burn passed away. I remember how sad he was to have lost his last cousin on his father's side of the family. I am grateful for the priceless heirlooms he bequeathed to me. He made many generous donations to various historical causes, including for the preservation of the Niota Depot.

Harry took special care for his mother in her final years. Ellen Cottrell Burn passed away in 1998 in Athens at the age of ninety. Harry Thomas Burn Jr. passed away in 2016 in his Athens home at the age of seventy-eight. He never married and had no children.

NIOTA AND THE BURN FAMILY TODAY

At the time of this writing, Harry Thomas Burn has fourteen living relatives descending from his parents, James Lafayette "Jim" Burn and Febb

Sculpted by Alan LeQuire
and erected by the Suffrage
Coalition in 2018, the Burn
Memorial at the corner of
Clinch Avenue and Market
Street in Knoxville honors
Harry and Febb Burn for their
roles in American history. *Photo
by Tyler L. Boyd.*

Ensminger Burn. They all descend from his brother, James Lane "Jack" Burn. Jim and Febb have five living great-grandchildren. Their oldest great-grandchild, James R. "Jimmy" Bridges, passed away in his middle age. He served as a combat medic in Vietnam. They also have eight great-great-grandchildren (including myself) and one great-great-great-grandchild.

A few years after Ellen Cottrell Burn passed away, Harry T. Burn Jr. sold the Hathburn home and farm. The current owner has preserved the sign that Burn had outside his law office. It hangs in the backyard. None of the Burn family resides in Niota at the time of this writing, but the town remains a tiny, sleepy community of under one thousand residents. It still has only one traffic light at the intersection of Willson Street (U.S. Highway 11) and Burn Road, just a few yards away from the Burn family plot. He remains the most famous resident to ever come out of the little East Tennessee town of Niota and out of McMinn County. It is fitting that he both entered and left this world there. John W. Bayless, one of his constituents from Athens who sent him a telegram after his deciding vote for the Nineteenth Amendment, has been proven correct. Thanks to his decisive action on August 18, 1920, Harry Thomas Burn has something that most people never have: immortality.

DESCENDANTS OF JAMES LAFAYE

(m) Mildred Tarwater

Harry T. Burn (m) Ellen Cottrell

Harry T. Burn, Jr.

Sara Burn

Otho Burn (m) Rhea Hammer

James Lafayett

Descendants of James Lafayette and Febb Ensminger Burn. *Burn family.*

Jack Burn (m) Olive Arrants

Jamie Burn (m) Anne Smith

Jack Burn (m) Pam Singleton

Mahala Burn — Jack Burn & Kathleen Malm

Olivia Burn — Jack Burn & Kathleen Malm

Roseanne Burn

Bill Burn (m) Betty Blair

Cathy Burn (m) Joe Allen

Stephanie Allen (m) Clint Calvert

Maggie Calvert

Sandra Burn (m) Mike Boyd

Tyler L. Boyd

Blair Boyd (m) Daniel Thomason

Betty C. Boyd

Pat Burn (m) Tim Cotton

Zach Cotton

Jake Cotton (m) Amanda Howard

Virginia Burn (m) Oris Lynch

Jimmy Bridges — Virginia Burn & James Bridges

Jackie Burn (m) Jim Wade

bb Ensminger Burn

NOTES

Preface

1. Harry T. Burn to William Pemberton, March 27, 1962, Harry T. Burn Papers, Calvin M. McClung Historical Collection, Knox County Public Library.

Introduction

1. Harry T. Burn Jr., e-mail message to Nancy Schleifer, March 11, 2003.

Chapter 1

1. Ibid.
2. Ibid.
3. "$390 Reward," *Athens (TN) Post,* January 30, 1863.
4. Akins and Langley, *Torn Apart*, 48.
5. Burn e-mail to Schleifer, March 11, 2003.
6. Burn, "Mountain View Commentary."
7. Burn e-mail to Schleifer, March 11, 2003.
8. Ibid.
9. Harry T. Burn Jr., "Niota Corner Store Photo," e-mail message to Tyler Forrest, March 14, 2016.
10. Burn, *History of the Ensmingers*.

11. Ibid.
12. Ibid.
13. Ibid.
14. Ibid.
15. Ibid.
16. Ibid.
17. William Ensminger to James L.E. Burn, August 9, 1949.
18. Ibid.
19. Burn, *History of the Ensmingers*.
20. Harry T. Burn Jr., "Enduring Question," e-mail message to Tyler Forrest, July 21, 2012.
21. U.S. Grant University, yearbook, 1891–92, 13.
22. Burn e-mail to Schleifer, March 11, 2003.
23. Harry T. Burn Jr., "RE: Questions from a playwright/Reply," e-mail message to Catherine Bush, January 4, 2013.
24. Burn e-mail to Schleifer, March 11, 2003.
25. "The Tennessee Woman Who Won Ballot for Women," *Philadelphia Public Ledger*, September 5, 1920.
26. "Back His Vote for Woman Suffrage," *Commercial Appeal*, September 5, 1920.

Chapter 2

1. Ibid.
2. Burn e-mail to Schleifer, March 11, 2003.
3. Lones, *Night Onto Heaven*, 16–17.
4. Ibid., 6.
5. Byrum, *McMinn County*, 44–46.
6. "Happy in Vote," *Cincinnati Commercial Tribune*, August 22, 1920.
7. James L.E. Burn Jr., phone interview by the author, February 12, 2018.
8. "Mrs. Burn Tells Story of Son Who Gave Suffrage," *Nashville Tennessean*, August 23, 1920.
9. Carolyn Pemberton, phone interview by the author, March 5, 2018.
10. "Mrs. Burn Tells Story of Son Who Gave Suffrage."
11. Harry T. Burn, application to Peace Corps, 1962, Burn Papers.
12. Ibid.
13. Harry T. Burn, interview by James L.E. Burn, Niota, Tennessee, 1968.
14. Ibid.

15. "Back His Vote for Woman Suffrage."
16. Burn, "RE: Questions from a playwright/Reply."
17. William Ensminger to James L.E. Burn, August 9, 1949.
18. Deposition of Harry T. Burn Sr., 1960, 129.
19. Southern Railway Company to James Lafayette Burn, April 25, 1900.
20. "Back His Vote for Woman Suffrage."
21. Harry T. Burn, application to Peace Corps.
22. "Fame Seems Set on Rise of Harry Burn," *Cleveland (TN) Herald*, August 1, 1930.
23. "Mrs. Burn Tells Story of Son Who Gave Suffrage."
24. Burn e-mail to Schleifer, March 11, 2003.
25. Burn, "RE: Questions from a playwright/Reply."
26. "Mrs. Burn Tells Story of Son Who Gave Suffrage."
27. Burn, "RE: Questions from a playwright/Reply."
28. J. Polk Cooley, interview by the author, Rockwood, Tennessee, November 1, 2017.
29. J. Reed Dixon, interview by the author, Sweetwater, Tennessee, January 18, 2018.
30. William Snyder, phone interview by the author, October 17, 2017.
31. "Death of J.L. Burn," *The Niotan*, July 6, 1916.
32. Burn e-mail to Schleifer, March 11, 2003.

Chapter 3

1. Newspaper and date unknown, newspaper clipping of 1918 primary election results in McMinn County, McMinn County Historical Society.
2. Newspaper and date unknown, newspaper clipping of Harry T. Burn campaign ad in 1918, McMinn County Historical Society.
3. Newspaper and date unknown, newspaper clipping of 1918 general election results in McMinn County, McMinn County Historical Society.
4. Title unknown, *Tri-Weekly Post*, November 9, 1918, Burn Scrapbook.
5. "Candler Says Charges Against Burn Are Too Ridiculous for Belief," *Chattanooga News*, August 20, 1920.
6. Byrum, *McMinn County*, 1.
7. Harry T. Burn to Mrs. J.L. Burn, December 31, 1918, Burn Papers.
8. Ibid.
9. "Harry Burn Not Sorry He Gave Women Right to Vote," *Daily Item* (Sunbury, PA), March 14, 1974.

10. *House Journal of the Sixty-First General Assembly of the State of Tennessee 1919*, 46.
11. Harry T. Burn to Mrs. J.L. Burn, January 9, 1919, Burn Papers.
12. Ibid.
13. "Our Correspondent Interviews Representative Harry Burn," newspaper unknown, date unknown, Burn Papers.
14. Tennessee Encyclopedia Online, "Temperance."
15. Ibid.
16. "Tennessee Is Not a Hooch Paradise," *New York Times*, May 21, 1921.
17. Ibid.
18. *House Journal of the Sixty-First General Assembly*, 1,331.
19. Ibid., 81.
20. Ibid., 96.
21. Ibid., 202.
22. Ibid., 213.
23. Ibid., 571.
24. Ibid., 401–2.
25. Ibid., 582.
26. Guy, *Hidden History of McMinn County*, 69–70.
27. *House Journal of the Sixty-First General Assembly*, 619.
28. *Private Acts of the State of Tennessee Passed by the Sixty-First General Assembly*, 2,200.
29. *House Journal of the Sixty-First General Assembly*, 760–63.
30. Ibid., 879–98.
31. Ibid., 611.
32. Ibid., 903.
33. Ibid., 920.
34. Ibid., 1,330.

Chapter 4

1. Cultice, *Youth's Battle for the Ballot*, 26.
2. Abigail Adams to John Adams, March 31, 1776.
3. John Adams to Abigail Adams, April 5, 1776.
4. Sherman and Yellin, *Perfect 36*, 17.
5. Ibid., 18.
6. Ibid., 28.
7. Wheeler, *Votes for Women!*, 26.

8. *Hawke v. Smith*, 253 U.S. 221 (1920).
9. "Frierson Says Suffrage Law Can Be Passed," *Nashville Tennessean*, June 25, 1920.
10. Burn interview by Burn.
11. "A Man Named Burn Gave Women Vote," *Baltimore Evening Sun*, March 7, 1974.
12. James A. Fowler to Harry T. Burn, July 31, 1920, Burn Papers.
13. A. Mitchell Palmer to Harry T. Burn, June 26, 1920, Burn Papers.
14. Major Daughtry to Harry T. Burn, July 17, 1920, Governor Albert H. Roberts Papers, 1918–21.
15. Harry T. Burn to Major Daughtry, July 19, 1920, Roberts Papers.
16. "Women Voted, but Votes Not Counted," *Chattanooga News*, July 23, 1919.
17. Irwin, *Story of Alice Paul*, 473.
18. Anita Pollitzer to Alice Paul, telegram, July 29, 1920, National Woman's Party Records, Manuscript Division, Library of Congress, Washington, D.C.
19. Harry T. Burn Jr., "Sobieski Exchange," e-mail message to Wanda Sobieski, October 6, 2014.
20. Ibid.
21. "Our Correspondent Interviews Representative Harry Burn."
22. Ibid.
23. Mrs. J.L. Burn to Harry T. Burn, August 17, 1920, Burn Papers.
24. Burn interview by Burn.
25. Cahn, "Man Whose Vote Gave Women the Vote," 60–63.
26. "Tennessee Woman Who Won Ballot for Women."
27. Burn interview by Burn.
28. Will H. Hays to Harry T. Burn, telegram, August 11, 1920, Burn Papers.
29. "Debate Suffrage at Joint Hearing," *Nashville Banner*, August 13, 1920.
30. Ibid.
31. Burn interview by Burn.
32. Ibid.
33. Weiss, *Woman's Hour*, 217.
34. "View of Judge Brown on Suffrage Amendment," *Chattanooga Daily Times*, August 24, 1920.
35. Burn interview by Burn.
36. Waters, *History of Browning Circle*.
37. Ibid.
38. *House Journal of the Sixty-First General Assembly*, 38–39.
39. Burn interview by Burn.

40. Anita Pollitzer to Alice Paul, telegram, July 29, 1920, National Woman's Party Records.

41. "Senate Ratifies Suffrage, 25 to 4, After Fight," *Nashville Tennessean*, August 14, 1920.

42. "Senator Candler in Fiery Attack," *Chattanooga Daily Times*, August 14, 1920.

43. "Senators Vote 25–4 to Ratify," *Knoxville Journal and Tribune*, August 14, 1920.

44. "Senate Ratifies Suffrage, 25 to 4, After Fight."

45. Weiss, *Woman's Hour*, 266.

46. "Senators Vote 25–4 to Ratify."

47. "Senator Candler in Fiery Attack."

48. "Senate Ratifies Suffrage, 25 to 4, After Fight."

49. "Senators Vote 25–4 to Ratify."

50. "Senate Ratifies Suffrage, 25 to 4, After Fight."

51. Ibid.

52. Burn interview by Burn.

53. "Senators Vote 25–4 to Ratify."

54. Elliott to Harry T. Burn, telegram, August 14, 1920, Burn Papers.

55. S.G. Brown to Harry T. Burn, telegram, August 14, 1920, Burn Papers.

56. B.J. Hornsby to Harry T. Burn, telegram, August 15, 1920, Burn Papers.

57. H. Kimbrough to Harry T. Burn, telegram, August 16, 1920, Burn Papers.

58. Mr. and Mrs. Jas. B. Hedge to Harry T. Burn, telegram, August 16, 1920, Burn Papers.

59. Mr. and Mrs. John W. Bayless to Harry T. Burn, telegram, August 16, 1920, Burn Papers.

60. Winfield Jones to Harry T. Burn, telegram, August 14, 1920, Burn Papers.

61. Mrs. John G. Blount, signed statement in presence of R.D Cooper, Notary Public in Davidson County, Tennessee, August 19, 1920, Burn Papers.

62. Mrs. Margaret Ervin Ford, signed statement in presence of R.D. Cooper, Notary Public in Davidson County, Tennessee, August 19, 1920, Burn Papers.

63. "Woman Whose Letter to Son Put 'Rat' in Ratification Says She Is Happiest Woman in the World," *Charlotte Observer*, September 20, 1920.

64. Mrs. J.L. Burn to Harry T. Burn.

65. Ibid.

66. Ibid.
67. Burn e-mail to Schleifer, March 11, 2003.
68. Burn interview by Burn.
69. Irwin, *Story of Alice Paul*, 473.
70. Ibid.
71. Newell Sanders to Harry T. Burn, telegram, August 11, 1920, Burn Papers.
72. McKellar, *Tennessee Senators*, 542–44.
73. Burn interview by Burn.
74. "Man Named Burn Gave Women Vote."
75. Irwin, *Story of Alice Paul*, 473.
76. Burn interview by Burn.
77. Ibid.
78. "Quickly Makes Up Mind," newspaper and date unknown, Burn Scrapbook.

Chapter 5

1. Lyon, "Day the Women Got the Vote," 68–69.
2. Burn interview by Burn.
3. Ibid.
4. "No, Harry Hasn't Changed His Mind," *Knoxville News-Sentinel*, March 25, 1971.
5. "Rough Handling of Burn Witnesses by All," *Chattanooga Daily Times*, August 19, 1920.
6. "The Women Had the Last Word," *Nashville Tennessean Magazine*, January 18, 1948.
7. "Just Count on Harry Burn to Make It Hum," *Nashville Tennessean*, August 18, 1965.
8. "Women Fought Votes," *Nashville Tennessean*, August 21, 1977.
9. "Suffrage Victory," *Knoxville News-Sentinel*, August 13, 1995.
10. "Harry and Febb Burn Turned the Tide for Women's Right to Vote," *Philadelphia Inquirer*, October 9, 2000.
11. "The War of the Roses," *Chattanooga Times Free Press*, August 12, 2012.
12. Burn, "Form Letter."
13. Burn interview by Burn.
14. Burn, "Form Letter."
15. Burn interview by Burn.

16. "Women Had the Last Word."
17. Burn interview by Burn.
18. Ibid.
19. Burn, "Form Letter."
20. Ibid.
21. "Mrs. Burn Tells Story of Son Who Gave Suffrage."
22. Burn interview by Burn.
23. Ibid.
24. "Bold Attempt to Intimidate Solon Foiled," *Nashville Tennessean*, August 19, 1920.
25. "Burn Deserts Cause of Antis Under Pressure," *Chattanooga Daily Times*, August 19, 1920.
26. "Debow Orders Lobbying Probe," *Nashville Banner*, August 19, 1920.
27. "Nashville Papers Publish Affidavits Alleging Burn Was Approached on Subject," *Knoxville Sentinel*, August 19, 1920.
28. Burn interview by Burn.
29. Ibid.
30. "The Truth About the Tennessee Campaign," *Woman Patriot*, September 11, 1920, 6.
31. Ibid.
32. "Alleged Offer of Joe Hanover to Bribe Burn," *Chattanooga Daily Times*, August 20, 1920.
33. Ibid.
34. "Demands Probe of Bribery Charges," *Chattanooga News*, August 26, 1920.
35. "Nashville Papers Publish Affidavits."
36. "House Speaker Declares Harry Burn Honest Man," *Knoxville Sentinel*, August 25, 1920.
37. "Demands Probe of Bribery Charges."
38. "Nashville Papers Publish Affidavits."
39. "Candler Says Charges Against Burn."
40. Akins and Wiggins, *Over Here, And After*, 42.
41. Burn interview by Burn.
42. "Back His Vote for Woman Suffrage."
43. "View of Judge Brown on Suffrage Amendment."
44. *House Journal of the Sixty-First General Assembly*, 1920 extraordinary session, 94–95.
45. Ebie Padgett, "Myra Reagan," e-mail message to author, November 7, 2018.
46. "Harry Burn Happy though He May Be Ruined."

47. Harry T. Burn Jr., "Febb Burn and Harry Burn," e-mail message to Wanda Sobieski, January 8, 2016.

48. Padgett, "Myra Reagan."

49. "Mother Turns Tide," *Knoxville Journal and Tribune*, August 19, 1920.

50. "His Vote Gave Vote to Women," *Democrat and Chronicle*, June 1, 1962.

51. Burn interview by Burn.

52. Ibid.

53. Newell Sanders to Harry T. Burn, telegram, August 19, 1920, Burn Papers.

54. Ben W. Hooper to Harry T. Burn, telegram, August 18, 1920, Burn Papers.

55. Will H. Hays to Harry T. Burn, telegram, August 20, 1920, Burn Papers.

56. Mrs. Childress et al. to Harry T. Burn, telegram, August 18, 1920, Burn Papers.

57. R.P. Knight et al. to Harry T. Burn, telegram, August 19, 1920, Burn Papers.

58. John W. Bayless to Harry T. Burn, telegram, August 19, 1920, Burn Papers.

59. R.B. Hickey to Harry T. Burn, telegram, August 19, 1920, Burn Papers.

60. Mr. and Mrs. Staley et al. to Mrs. George Fort Milton, telegram, August 19, 1920, Burn Papers.

61. W.M. Snyder et al. to Harry T. Burn, telegram, August 19, 1920, Burn Papers.

62. C.B. Staley to Harry T. Burn, telegram, August 20, 1920, Burn Papers.

63. Mrs. J.L. Burn to Mrs. George Fort Milton, telegram, August 19, 1920, Burn Papers.

64. D.M. Owen to Harry T. Burn, telegram, August 18, 1920, Burn Papers.

65. B.J. Hornsby to Harry T. Burn, telegram, August 18, 1920, Burn Papers.

66. N.Q. Allen to Harry T. Burn, telegram, August 19, 1920, Burn Papers.

67. Uncle to Harry T. Burn, telegram, August 20, 1920, Burn Papers.

68. Clara Vezin to Harry T. Burn, telegram, August 19, 1920, Burn Papers.

69. Mrs. Horace Brock to Harry T. Burn, telegram, August 19, 1920, Burn Papers.

70. Mrs. L.S. Robinson to Harry T. Burn, telegram, August 19, 1920, Burn Papers.

71. Mrs. John F. Hill to Harry T. Burn, telegram, August 19, 1920, Burn Papers.

72. Mary C. Garfield to Harry T. Burn, telegram, August 19, 1920, Burn Papers.

73. Della M. Parker to Harry T. Burn, telegram, August 18, 1920, Burn Papers.
74. Women's Bureau Dem. Nat'l Committee to Harry T. Burn, telegram, August 19, 1920, Burn Papers.
75. F.D. Fess to Harry T. Burn, telegram, August 19, 1920, Burn Papers.
76. Isetta Jewel Brown to Harry T. Burn, telegram, August 19, 1920, Burn Papers.
77. Anonymous to Harry T. Burn, telegram, August 20, 1920, Burn Papers.
78. Harry T. Burn to Mrs. J.L. Burn, telegram, August 20, 1920, Burn Papers.
79. Mamma to Harry T. Burn, telegram, August 20, 1920, Burn Papers.
80. "The True Story of Harry Burn," *Chattanooga Daily Times*, August 21, 1920.
81. Ibid.
82. "Anti Insults Burn's Mother," *Chattanooga News*, August 23, 1920.
83. Ibid.
84. "Back His Vote for Woman Suffrage."
85. "Anti Insults Burn's Mother."
86. Ibid.
87. *House Journal of the Sixty-First General Assembly*, 1920 extraordinary session, 118–21.
88. "Burn Not Voting M'Minn's Sentiment," *Nashville Banner*, August 23, 1920.
89. Ibid.
90. "Dodson of Kingsport Another Suffrage Hero," *Chattanooga News*, August 23, 1920.

Chapter 6

1. Burn interview by Burn.
2. Ibid.
3. "The 'Yes' Heard Around the World," *Chattanooga Daily Times*, August 11, 1995.
4. Ibid.
5. "Burn and His Mother," *Chattanooga News*, August 25, 1920.
6. "From Harry Burn's Home," *Chattanooga News*, August 28, 1920.
7. "Harry Burn Happy though He May Be Ruined."
8. Ibid.
9. Sherman and Yellin, *Perfect 36*, 117.
10. Ibid.

11. "West Tennessee Lawyer Writes Poem to Burn," *Chattanooga Daily Times*, August 27, 1920.

12. "Harry T. Burn of McMinn," *Boston Herald*, August 20, 1920.

13. "Word for Harry Burn," *Semi-Weekly Post*, date unknown, Burn Scrapbook.

14. Watts to Harry T. Burn, August 18, 1920, Burn Papers.

15. Percy Warner and John Graham to Harry T. Burn, August 19, 1920, Burn Papers.

16. Fannie Burnette to Harry T. Burn, August 19, 1920, Burn Papers.

17. Wade H. Cord to Harry T. Burn, August 20, 1920, Burn Papers.

18. S.O. Welch to Harry T. Burn, August 21, 1920, Burn Papers.

19. George Schultheiss to Harry T. Burn, August 22, 1920, Burn Papers.

20. S.O. Welch to Harry T. Burn, August 26, 1920, Burn Papers.

21. J.R. Yates to Harry T. Burn, August 29, 1920, Burn Papers.

22. Anita Pollitzer to Harry T. Burn, September 10, 1920, Burn Papers.

23. Mrs. B.F. Sykes to Harry T. Burn, August 21, 1920, Burn Papers.

24. "Souvenir Hunters and Visitors Swarm Home of Harry Burn," *Rockwood Times*, August 26, 1920.

25. "Mrs. J.F. [*sic*] Burn Resents Charge," *Chattanooga News*, August 26, 1920.

26. "Back His Vote for Woman Suffrage."

27. Ibid.

28. "Mrs. Burn Tells Story of Son Who Gave Suffrage."

29. Ibid.

30. "Harry Burn Happy though He May Be Ruined."

31. "Tennessee Woman Who Won Ballot for Women."

32. "Back His Vote for Woman Suffrage."

33. "Women Win the Vote," *Tennessee Opportunities*.

34. "Back His Vote for Woman Suffrage."

35. "Mother Proud of Son Who Cast Deciding Vote for Suffrage," paper unknown, August 20, 1920, Burn Scrapbook.

36. "Back His Vote for Woman Suffrage."

37. "Harry Burn Happy though He May Be Ruined."

38. "Tennessee Woman Who Won Ballot for Women."

39. Ibid.

40. "Back His Vote for Woman Suffrage."

41. Ibid.

42. "A Mother's Victory," *Toledo Blade*, date unknown, Burn Scrapbook.

43. Burn interview by Burn.

44. Mrs. George W. Trout to Mrs. J.L. Burn, September 9, 1920, Burn Papers.

45. "That Letter to Burn," newspaper and date unknown, Burn Scrapbook.

46. Mary Jackson to Mrs. J.L. Burn, September 1, 1920, Burn Papers.

47. *House Journal of the Sixty-First General Assembly*, 126.

48. "Antis Charge McKellar with Trying to Break Quorum," *Chattanooga News*, August 30, 1920.

49. "McMinn County Woman Views Recent Events," *Chattanooga Daily Times*, September 2, 1920.

50. "Suffrage Victory Is Celebrated; Women Give Banquet to Solons Who Were Ratification Boosters," *Knoxville Sentinel*, September 22, 1920.

51. Ibid.

52. Ibid.

53. "Honoring Mother Who Helped Gain Deciding Suffrage Vote," *Chattanooga News*, September 27, 1920.

54. Unknown title, publication and date, magazine clipping describes Burn's reelection campaign, Burn Scrapbook.

55. "Women Working for Harry Burn," *Chattanooga News*, October 15, 1920.

56. "Why Vote for Jones," newspaper and date unknown, Burn Scrapbook.

57. "Harry Burn's Candidacy," *Chattanooga News*, October 19, 1920.

58. "Women Working for Harry Burn."

59. "Harry Burn's Candidacy."

60. Unknown magazine clipping describes Burn's reelection campaign.

61. Burn e-mail to Schleifer, March 11, 2003.

62. Unknown magazine clipping describes Burn's reelection campaign.

63. Ibid.

64. "Harry T. Burn Wins His Seat," *Chattanooga News*, November 3, 1920.

65. Burn interview by Burn.

66. Unknown magazine clipping describes Burn's reelection campaign.

67. "Hardings Thank Burn for Vote," *Chattanooga News*, October 14, 1920.

68. Ibid.

69. "Women Working for Harry Burn."

70. "Harry T. Burn Wins His Seat."

71. "Harry Burn Again," *Chattanooga Daily Times*, October 22, 1920.

72. "Harry Burn Happy though He May Be Ruined."

73. "Harry Burn Again."

74. "Strong Fight On Harry Burn," *Chattanooga Daily Times*, November 1, 1920.

75. Unknown magazine clipping describes Burn's reelection campaign.

76. "Burn's War Record," *Chattanooga News*, November 1, 1920.

77. "Upstate Races Are Thrilling," *Chattanooga News*, November 3, 1920.

78. "Harry T. Burn Wins His Seat."
79. "Harry Burn Reelected Over Jones by 285 Votes," *Chattanooga News*, November 9, 1920.
80. McMinn County Election Commission to Harry T. Burn, November 9, 1920.
81. "Pleased! You Know!," *The Athenian (TN)*, November 4, 1920.
82. "Poor Harry Burn," *Hamilton County (TN) Herald*, November 5, 1920.
83. Newell Sanders to Harry T. Burn, telegram, November 1920, Burn Papers.
84. A.A. Taylor to Harry T. Burn, November 9, 1920, Burn Papers.
85. Republican National Committee to Harry T. Burn, November 4, 1920, Burn Papers.
86. *Chattanooga News* to Burn, November 9, 1920, Burn Papers.
87. *House Journal of the Sixty-Second General Assembly of the State of Tennessee 1921*, 11.
88. Ibid., 186–87.
89. "Provisions of Burn Redistricting Bill," *Chattanooga News*, January 28, 1921.
90. Ibid.
91. *House Journal of the Sixty-Second General Assembly*, 497.
92. Ibid., 452.
93. Ibid., 338.
94. Ibid., 572.
95. Ibid., 998–99.
96. Ibid., 1,097–98.
97. Ibid., 679–80.
98. Ibid., 867.
99. Ibid., 1,437.
100. Ibid., 1,115–16.
101. Ibid., 11.
102. "Women Here Favor Co-Guardian Law," newspaper and date unknown, Burn Scrapbook.
103. Ibid.
104. Ibid.
105. *House Journal of the Sixty-Second General Assembly*, 287–88.
106. Harry T. Burn, application to Peace Corps.

Chapter 7

1. Burn interview by Burn.
2. Ibid.
3. Deposition of Harry T. Burn Sr., 1960, 4.
4. Judge S. Brown to Harry T. Burn, April 23, 1923.
5. "Suffrage Hero Enters Rockwood Law Office," *Nashville Tennessean*, February 8, 1923.
6. Chief Operator of Knoxville Division of Southern Railway to Harry T. Burn, February 7, 1924.
7. "Roane Republicans Overlook Coolidge," *Nashville Tennessean*, February 24, 1924.
8. "Harmony Reigns in State G.O.P. Meet Till Harry Burn Springs Sensation," *Rockwood Times*, May 8, 1924.
9. "Gubernatorial Aspirant Disports Self in Surf," *Rockwood Times*, February 18, 1926.
10. Civil Warrant, Harry T. Burn sues Times Printing Company and Hammond Fowler in Rockwood, Tennessee, February 18, 1926.
11. Senator Ken Yager, phone interview by the author, September 4, 2018.
12. Gerald Largen, phone interview by the author, January 26, 2018.
13. Ibid.
14. "Harry T. Burn to Wed Miss Mildred Tarwater," *Sweetwater Valley News*, October 5, 1933.

Chapter 8

1. Ash, Bergeron and Keith, *Tennesseans and Their History*, 254.
2. "Judge Jennings Hits State Republicans," *Nashville Tennessean*, May 12, 1930.
3. "Will Burn Stick?," *Sweetwater Valley News*, June 11, 1930.
4. "Burn May Seek Governorship," *Knoxville News-Sentinel*, May 8, 1930.
5. Deposition of Harry T. Burn Sr., 1960, 128.
6. "Burn May Seek Governorship."
7. "Harry T. Burn States Stand as Candidate," *Post-Athenian (TN)*, May 16, 1930.
8. "Businessman C.A. Bruce Dies," *Nashville Tennessean*, December 23, 1966.
9. "G.O.P. Endorsed Bruce by Fluke," *Memphis Press-Scimitar*, June 3, 1930.
10. "Will Burn Stick?"

11. "State-County Politics Growing Warmer," *Cleveland (TN) Herald,* June 27, 1930.
12. "Slip-Up Met in Plan to Avoid G.O.P. Primary," *Knoxville News Sentinel,* June 3, 1930.
13. "Bruce to Run for Governor," *Knoxville News-Sentinel,* June 6, 1930.
14. "Bruce to Run for Governor as Republican," *Memphis Press-Scimitar,* June 6, 1930.
15. "Burn to Open Campaign for Governor Saturday in His Own Home Town," *Sweetwater Valley News,* June 25, 1930.
16. "Tennessee Political Pot Begins to Boil Merrily, More Candidates Qualify," *Kingsport Times,* June 8, 1930.
17. "Burn Challenges Taylor Control," *Chattanooga Daily Times,* June 15, 1930.
18. Ibid.
19. "Harry Burn Not Seeking Railroad Commission Job," *Knoxville Journal,* June 14, 1930.
20. "Burn Still After Governorship," *Rockwood Times,* June 12, 1930.
21. "Burn to Open Campaign for Governor."
22. Ibid.
23. Ibid.
24. "Immense Crowd Heard Burn Launch Campaign," *Sweetwater Valley News,* July 2, 1930.
25. "Burn Opens Campaign with Stirring Address at Home Greeted by Immense Throng," *Post-Athenian,* July 4, 1930.
26. "Immense Crowd Heard Burn."
27. Ibid.
28. Ibid.
29. "Burn Opens Governor's Race with Declaration of Platform," *Rockwood Times,* July 3, 1930.
30. "Immense Crowd Heard Burn."
31. Ibid.
32. Ibid.
33. "Burn Opens Governor's Race."
34. "Immense Crowd Heard Burn."
35. "First District Greets Burn on Tour," *Rockwood Times,* July 3, 1930.
36. Ibid.
37. Ibid.
38. "Bruce Declines to Meet Opponent in Joint Debate," *Rockwood Times,* July 10, 1930.

39. Ibid.
40. "Burn Invades West Tennessee in Gubernatorial Fight," *Rockwood Times*, July 24, 1930.
41. Ibid.
42. Ibid.
43. "Bruce Appeals for G.O.P. Vote in Initial Talk," *Chattanooga Daily Times*, July 23, 1930.
44. Ibid.
45. Ibid.
46. Ibid.
47. Ibid.
48. Ibid.
49. Ibid.
50. "Burn Confident of Nomination," *Sweetwater Valley News*, July 30, 1930.
51. "Burn Says Bruce Steals Platform as Silence Ends," *Rockwood Times*, July 31, 1930.
52. Ibid.
53. Ibid.
54. Harry T. Burn campaign ad, *Rockwood Times*, July 31, 1930.
55. "Burn Rakes Bruce as Machine Product," *Cleveland (TN) Herald*, August 3, 1930.
56. Harry T. Burn campaign ad, *Cleveland (TN) Herald*, August 1, 1930.
57. "Closes Campaign with Address at Knoxville," *Rockwood Times*, August 6, 1930.
58. "Burn and Price Charge Frauds in G.O.P. Voting," *Chattanooga Daily Times*, August 10, 1930.
59. "Closes Campaign with Address at Knoxville."
60. Ibid.
61. Ibid.
62. Ibid.
63. "Republican Women Tender Luncheon to Harry T. Burn," *Knoxville Journal*, August 7, 1930.
64. "Taylor Expects Big Vote in G.O.P. Primary," *Nashville Tennessean*, July 15, 1930.
65. Ibid.
66. "Church-Crump-Bruce or Burn," *Rockwood Times*, August 6, 1930.
67. Arthur Bruce campaign ad, *Knoxville Journal*, July 31, 1930.
68. "Bruce Confident He'll Be Nominee," *Memphis Press-Scimitar*, August 7, 1930.

69. "Major Races Are Holding Interest," *Nashville Banner*, August 7, 1930.
70. "Victory Day Dawns for Horton; Record Majority Is Assured," *Commercial Appeal*, August 7, 1930.
71. "East Tennessean Refuses Concede Bruce Victory," *Rockwood Times*, August 7, 1930.
72. Ibid.
73. Carr and Hassler, *Fifty Years of Tennessee Primary Elections*, 124.
74. Ibid.
75. Ibid.
76. "G.O.P. Ready to Fight for Governorship," *Knoxville News Sentinel*, August 30, 1930.
77. "Frauds in Shelby Give Bruce Lead in G.O.P. Primary," *Rockwood Times*, August 14, 1930.
78. Ibid.
79. "The Plucky Warrior Wins," *Rockwood Times*, August 14, 1930.
80. Ibid.
81. "Burn Contests Election of Bruce as Party Nominee," *Nashville Tennessean*, August 17, 1930.
82. Ibid.
83. "Frauds in Shelby Give Bruce Lead."
84. "Burn Contests Apparent Lead of Memphis Man," *Rockwood Times*, August 21, 1930.
85. "Frauds in Shelby Give Bruce Lead."
86. "Burn Contests Apparent Lead."
87. Ibid.
88. Ibid.
89. "Burn Claims Bruce Claim Unwarranted," *Cleveland (TN) Herald*, August 22, 1930.
90. "Frauds in Shelby Give Bruce Lead."
91. Ibid.
92. Carr and Hassler, *Fifty Years of Tennessee Primary Elections*, 124.
93. "Burn Claims Bruce Claim Unwarranted."
94. Ibid.
95. "Side Lights on Primary Contest," *Rockwood Times*, August 28, 1930.
96. "G.O.P. Committee Refuses to Let Burn Show Fraud," *Rockwood Times*, August 28, 1930.
97. Ibid.
98. "Republicans Certify Bruce," *Nashville Banner*, August 27, 1930.

99. "G.O.P. Committee Refuses."
100. Ibid.
101. "Bruce Is Named G.O.P. Nominee for Governor," *Nashville Tennessean*, August 28, 1930.
102. "G.O.P. Committee Refuses."
103. Ibid.
104. "Bruce is Named G.O.P. Nominee."
105. "G.O.P. Committee Refuses."
106. Ibid.
107. "Horton Must Still Reckon with Bruce," *Knoxville News Sentinel*, August 8, 1930.
108. "Burn Threatening Action in Courts," *Chattanooga Daily Times*, August 28, 1930.
109. Ibid.
110. "The Steal Is Ratified," *Rockwood Times*, August 28, 1930.
111. Ibid.
112. Ibid.
113. "Business Methods, Bruce's Platform," *Chattanooga Daily Times*, August 9, 1930.
114. Gritter, *River of Hope*, 52.
115. "Horton and Hull Lead Ticket in Smashing Victory," *Nashville Tennessean*, November 5, 1930.
116. "Burn Assails J. Will Taylor," *Clarksville (TN) Leaf-Chronicle*, November 8, 1930.
117. Ibid.

Chapter 9

1. "Church Is Scene of Beautiful Wedding as Burn-Tarwater Marriage Solemnized," *Rockwood Times*, October 26, 1933.
2. Ibid.
3. Pemberton interview by author.
4. *Historical Review: Rockwood's Centennial Year, 1868–1968.*
5. "Harry Burn, Wife, Will Get Divorce," *Chattanooga Daily Times*, December 7, 1935.
6. Michael, *Times and Trials of a Country Lawyer*, 102.
7. Ibid.
8. Moore, *Company Town*, 54.

9. Deposition of Harry T. Burn Sr., 1960, 181.

10. William Howard Moore, "Harry T. Burn and Rockwood," e-mail message to author, April 9, 2018.

11. Deposition of Harry T. Burn Sr., 1960, 221.

12. Moore, *Company Town*, 49.

13. Michael, *Times and Trials of a Country Lawyer*, 103.

14. "Three Tennessee Towns Benefited by Bankruptcy Act," *Jackson (TN) Sun*, May 27, 1936.

15. Michael, *Times and Trials of a Country Lawyer*, 105.

16. Harry Thomas Burn, application for membership to the National Society of the Sons of the American Revolution, 1931.

17. Febb Ensminger Burn, application for membership to the National Society of the Daughters of the American Revolution, 1932.

18. "Problems Similar the World Over," *Chattanooga Sunday Times*, November 22, 1936.

19. Ibid.

20. Ibid.

21. Ibid.

22. Ibid.

23. Ibid.

24. "Harry T. Burn Named Head Sweetwater Bank," *Rockwood Times*, February 4, 1937.

25. "'Yes' Heard Around the World."

26. Burn e-mail to Schleifer, March 11, 2003.

27. Peggy Clark Torbett, phone interview by the author, October 17, 2017.

28. *Tennessee Wesleyan College Bulletin* (May 1931): 9.

29. Mintie Willson, phone interview by the author, November 11, 2017.

30. Burn e-mail to Schleifer, March 11, 2003.

31. Harry T. Burn Jr., no subject, e-mail message to William H. Burn, August 19, 2002.

32. Mintie Willson interview by author.

33. Pemberton interview by author.

34. Mintie Willson interview by author.

35. William Vestal, phone interview by the author, December 4, 2018.

36. Judy Townsend, phone interview by the author, January 14, 2019.

37. Geraldine Wallick, interview by the author, Rockwood, Tennessee, September 14, 2018.

38. *Tennessee Wesleyan College Bulletin* (April 1937): 5.

39. Ellen Burn, application to Peace Corps.

40. Richard Cottrell Bourne, phone interview by the author, October 23, 2017.
41. Richard Cottrell Bourne, "Memories," e-mail message to author, October 25, 2017.
42. Cooley interview by author.
43. Bill McFarland, interview by the author, Rockwood, Tennessee, August 21, 2018.
44. Mintie Willson interview by author.
45. Paul Willson, phone interview by the author, November 20, 2017.
46. Ann Scott Davis, phone interview by the author, November 14, 2017.
47. Deposition of Harry T. Burn Sr., 1960, 274.
48. Harry T. Burn, "Facts About Harry T. Burn in WWII," 1953, Burn Papers.
49. "Mrs. Febb Burn, 71, Taken by Death, Funeral Tuesday," *Daily Post-Athenian (TN)*, June 19, 1945.
50. Deposition of Harry T. Burn Sr., 1960, 274.
51. Byrum, *Battle of Athens*, 39.
52. "Athens Had '46 Political Explosion," *Daily Post-Athenian (TN)*, July 2, 1976.
53. *Private Acts of the State of Tennessee Passed by the Seventy-Second General Assembly*, 898–903.
54. "McMinn Election Officials Found Guilty of Fraud," *Kingsport News*, January 29, 1943.
55. Ibid.
56. "Meigs Seabee Killed and Another Hurt in Fight," *Daily Post-Athenian (TN)*, September 26, 1944.
57. White, "Battle of Athens, Tennessee," 60.
58. Eleanor Roosevelt, "McMinn a Warning," *Daily Post-Athenian (TN)*, August 7, 1946.
59. "Rhea Hammer New Mayor as Over 1800 Votes Cast," *Daily Post-Athenian (TN)*, September 30, 1946.

Chapter 10

1. Joe Sherlin, phone interview by the author, September 12, 2018.
2. Ibid.
3. Ellen Burn, application to Peace Corps.

4. Harry T. Burn Jr., no subject, e-mail message to Tyler Forrest, August 10, 2010.

5. "Polk and Monroe Placed in 7th Senatorial District," *Daily Post-Athenian*, February 12, 1945.

6. Harry T. Burn campaign ad, *Sweetwater Valley News*, July 29, 1948.

7. Sherlin interview by author.

8. Nancy Baker, phone interview by the author, September 11, 2018.

9. "W.E. Michael Seeks Republican Nomination," *Cleveland (TN) Daily Banner*, August 1, 1948.

10. "Record Vote Seen for McMinn with Clean Election Forecast," *Daily Post-Athenian*, August 3, 1948.

11. "Two Sweetwater Men Win On GOP Primary Ticket," *Sweetwater Valley News*, August 12, 1948.

12. Ibid.

13. "Violence Flairs as Polk County Casts Its Votes," *Cleveland Daily Banner (TN)*, August 6, 1948.

14. Lillard, *History of Polk County Tennessee*, 198.

15. "Harry T. Burn Downs Prince," *Cleveland Daily Banner (TN)*, November 3, 1948.

16. "McMinn County Goes Republican—Except Kefauver," *Daily Post-Athenian (TN)*, November 3, 1948.

17. "Harry T. Burn Grateful for County's Support," *Daily Post-Athenian (TN)*, November 5, 1948.

18. Harry T. Burn campaign ad, *Cleveland Daily Banner (TN)*, November 7, 1948.

19. "Burn Named as G.O.P. Floor Leader in State Senate," *Kingsport Times*, December 13, 1948.

20. *Senate Journal of the Seventy-Sixth General Assembly of the State of Tennessee 1949*, 92.

21. Ibid., 338.

22. Ibid., 1,004, 1,005, 1,027, 1,494.

23. Ibid., 237.

24. Ibid., 932.

25. "State Legislature's Work Reviewed," *Tennessee Government* (May–June 1949): 1.

26. *Senate Journal of the Seventy-Sixth General Assembly of the State of Tennessee 1949*, 535, 603, 604, 1,791.

27. Ibid., 747.

28. Ibid., 1,570.

29. "Reforms," *Kingsport News*, February 1, 1949.

30. "GOP Backing Seen on Browning Bills," *Nashville Tennessean*, February 1, 1949.

31. Van West, *Tennessee Encyclopedia of History and Culture*, 221.

32. Ibid.

33. "Senate Elections Committee Meets to Study TPAs Program," *Kingsport Times-News*, February 13, 1949.

34. "3 Vote Bill Go to Governor; Others Slated," *Nashville Tennessean*, April 15, 1949.

35. Ibid.

36. Ibid.

37. Ibid.

38. "Brief Review of Legislature Told by Senator Burn," *Sweetwater Valley News*, April 21, 1949.

39. "State's Lone Woman Legislator Backs Election Law Revision," *Cleveland Daily Banner (TN)*, February 23, 1949.

40. Ibid.

41. "Poll Tax, Elections, and Education Are Subjects of Legislative Interest," *Tennessee Government* (May–June 1949): 1–2.

42. Ibid.

43. "Brief Review of Legislature."

44. "Bill Introduced to Ban Beer Sale Here by Johnson," *Sweetwater Valley News*, January 6, 1949.

45. "Signers Did Not Know True Status of Proposed Beer Bill," *Sweetwater Valley News*, January 18, 1949.

46. "Is the Beer Question a Moral Issue," *Sweetwater Valley News*, January 27, 1949.

47. Ibid.

48. Sherlin interview by author.

49. "Top O' the Mornin'," *Nashville Tennessean*, February 16, 1949.

50. "Senate Bill Will Extend Corporate Limits of City," *Sweetwater Valley News*, February 10, 1949.

51. Ibid.

52. Ibid.

53. "Senator Burn Declares Local Beer Bill Constitutional," *Sweetwater Valley News*, February 27, 1949.

54. Ibid.

55. "Senator H. Burn Refuses Attendance for Public Rally," *Sweetwater Valley News*, March 10, 1949.

56. "Burn Makes Reply to Hall Charges," *Sweetwater Valley News*, March 17, 1949.

57. "Accomplishments of 76th Legislature Told by Burn," *Sweetwater Valley News*, March 6, 1949.

58. Ibid.

59. Burn e-mail to Schleifer, March 11, 2003.

60. "Accomplishments of 76th Legislature Told by Burn."

61. "Proposed Extension of Niota City Limits Now Causing Big Disturbance," *Daily Post-Athenian (TN)*, March 21, 1949.

62. Ibid.

63. "Burn's Statement on Niota Limits," *Daily Post-Athenian (TN)*, March 21, 1949.

64. Ibid.

65. "Proposed Extension of Niota City Limits."

66. "Conar Replies to Harry Burn," *Daily Post-Athenian (TN)*, March 23, 1949.

67. Ibid.

68. "Senator Harry T. Burn Answers Conar Charges," *Daily Post-Athenian (TN)*, March 25, 1949.

69. "Conar Attacks Action of Burn in Niota Bill," *Daily Post-Athenian (TN)*, March 28, 1949.

70. Ibid.

71. "Niota City Limits to Be Extended," *Daily Post-Athenian (TN)*, March 30, 1949.

72. "Niota Council in Opposition City Limit Extension," *Daily Post-Athenian (TN)*, April 1, 1949.

73. "Harry T. Burn Says Niota 'Limits' Same Now as Original Bill Set Out," *Daily Post-Athenian (TN)*, April 15, 1949.

74. "Majority of Those Contacted Here Express Desire for Limits Move," *Cleveland Daily Banner (TN)*, January 16, 1949.

75. *Senate Journal of the Seventy-Sixth General Assembly of the State of Tennessee 1949*, 747.

76. "Burn Bill Gives Area Permanent Voter Registration," *Cleveland Daily Banner (TN)*, March 25, 1949.

77. "Lowery Expected to Pull Back Registration Bill," *Cleveland Daily Banner (TN)*, April 6, 1949.

78. "Republican Group Disclaims Burn Johnson Legislation Saturday," *Sweetwater Valley News*, June 16, 1949.

79. "Michael Reelected County GOP Chairman at Meeting Saturday," *Sweetwater Valley News*, August 25, 1949.

80. Ibid.

81. "Enough to Worry," *Nashville Tennessean*, July 31, 1949.

Chapter 11

1. W.L. Ledford campaign ad, *Cleveland Daily Banner (TN)*, August 2, 1950.

2. "Harry Burn Not Taking Sides in Intra-Party Fight," *Daily Post Athenian (TN)*, July 18, 1950.

3. Harry T. Burn campaign ad, *Daily Post-Athenian (TN)*, August 2, 1950.

4. "Bradley Political Rivals Square Off for Final Round of Campaign," *Cleveland Daily Banner (TN)*, July 15, 1950.

5. "Burn Is Winner, Canvasses Reveal," *Cleveland Daily Banner (TN)*, August 5, 1950.

6. "Republicans Sweep All County Offices," *Daily Post-Athenian (TN)*, August 4, 1950.

7. "Harry T. Burn Expresses Thanks to Voters Here," *Daily Post-Athenian (TN)*, August 9, 1950.

8. "State Senator Race Is Tops in McMinn," *Daily Post-Athenian (TN)*, November 3, 1950.

9. Vance Davis campaign ad, *Cleveland Daily Banner (TN)*, November 6, 1950.

10. Harry T. Burn campaign ad, *Daily Post-Athenian (TN)*, November 6, 1950.

11. "Local Senator Advocates Main Street Widening," *Sweetwater Valley News*, September 21, 1950.

12. "Burn Charges Plot to Change County Regime," *Cleveland Daily Banner (TN)*, November 1, 1950.

13. "Senator Burn Outlines Bradley Proposals," *Cleveland Daily Banner (TN)*, October 31, 1950.

14. "Burn Charges Plot to Change County Regime."

15. "Opinion Said Split on Burn Proposals," *Cleveland Daily Banner (TN)*, November 3, 1950.

16. "Burn's 'Give 'Em Hell' Drive Sends Interest Soaring in Tuesday Ballot," *Cleveland Daily Banner (TN)*, November 4, 1950.

17. "Go to the Polls and Vote," *Cleveland Daily Banner (TN)*, November 4, 1950.

18. "Senator Tops Davis by 749, Lowery Has 183," *Cleveland Daily Banner (TN)*, November 8, 1950.

19. "Burn Defeats Davis," *Polk County News (TN)*, November 9, 1950.
20. "Fraud Charged in Polk Vote," *Polk County News (TN)*, November 16, 1950.
21. Ibid.
22. "Burn-Johnston Charge Wholesale Fraud," *Polk County News (TN)*, November 16, 1950.
23. "Fraud Charged in Polk Vote."
24. "Burn-Johnston Charge Wholesale Fraud."
25. Ibid.
26. "GGL Heads Spurn Sen. Burn Offer of Fraud Evidence," *Polk County News (TN)*, November 30, 1950.
27. "Lewis Admits Scrolls Altered in Favor of Lowery," *Polk County News (TN)*, November 30, 1950.
28. "Woodlee Holds Up Polk County Ballot Ruling," *Polk County News (TN)*, December 21, 1950.
29. "Election Dispute Speculation Heated," *Polk County News (TN)*, January 4, 1951.
30. "Polk and Bradley Votes Removed to Nashville by Legislative Order," *Polk County News (TN)*, January 11, 1951.
31. "Assembly to Get Redistrict Bill," *Nashville Tennessean*, December 17, 1950.
32. Ibid.
33. Ibid.
34. Ibid.
35. Ibid.
36. Ibid.
37. Ibid.
38. "Local Senator Candidate for Speakers [sic] Seat," *Sweetwater Valley News*, January 4, 1951.
39. *Senate Journal of the Seventy-Seventh General Assembly of the State of Tennessee 1951*, 187.
40. Ibid., 396–97.
41. Ibid., 513.
42. Ibid., 617–18.
43. Ibid., 638.
44. Ibid., 639.
45. "Text of Polk-Bradley Report," *Polk County News (TN)*, January 18, 1951.
46. Ibid.
47. *Maloney v. Collier*, 112 Tenn., 78–94 (1903).

48. "Decisions Support Law in Tennessee," *Polk County News (TN)*, January 18, 1951.

49. "Witnesses Troop to Benton Court Hearing of Row," *Polk County News (TN)*, January 25, 1951.

50. Ibid.

51. "Lowery, Johnston Row Outcome Early Next Week, Nashville Hints," *Polk County News (TN)*, February 1, 1951.

52. Ibid.

53. "Burn Demands Polk Housecleaning; Denies Any Deal; May Oust Barclay," *Polk County News (TN)*, February 15, 1951.

54. "Burn Delays Local Bills in Dispute," *Polk County News (TN)*, January 4, 1951.

55. "Burn Praises Banner for Hand in Clean Elections Precedent," *Cleveland Daily Banner (TN)*, February 9, 1951.

56. "Burn Demands Polk Housecleaning."

57. Ibid.

58. "Barclay Lashes Foes," *Polk County News (TN)*, February 22, 1951.

59. "Johnston Bill Ends Commission Control of Polk," *Cleveland Daily Banner (TN)*, February 17, 1951.

60. *Senate Journal of the Seventy-Seventh General Assembly of the State of Tennessee 1951*, 564.

61. "School, Road Bills in Legislature," *Polk County News (TN)*, March 8, 1951.

62. Lillard, *History of Polk County Tennessee*, 202–3.

63. "Burn, Johnson Scoff at Ripper Charge," *Cleveland Daily Banner (TN)*, March 8, 1951.

64. Ibid.

65. Ibid.

66. *Senate Journal of the Seventy-Seventh General Assembly of the State of Tennessee 1951*, 858.

67. Ibid., 1,170.

68. Ibid., 579.

69. "FDR Now Stands Alone," *Nashville Tennessean*, February 28, 1951.

70. "Vote for Free," *Kingsport News*, March 2, 1951.

71. Michael, *Times and Trials of a Country Lawyer*, 150–52.

72. "State Supreme Court Rules Poll Tax Cannot Be Repealed by Legislature," *Tennessee Government* (July–August 1943): 2.

73. "Politics," *Nashville Tennessean*, July 9, 1941.

74. "State Supreme Court Rules Poll Tax," 2.

75. "Vote for Free."

76. *Senate Journal of the Seventy-Seventh General Assembly of the State of Tennessee 1951*, 739.

77. "Barry Declares New Poll Tax Bill Is Valid," *Clarksville Leaf-Chronicle (TN)*, March 7, 1951.

78. "Leaders of GGL Admit 'Rippers' Smashes Power," *Polk County News*, March 7, 1951.

79. "Burn, Johnston Urge Polk County Regime 'Refuse to Yield to Threats,'" *Polk County News (TN)*, March 15, 1951.

80. Ibid.

81. Ibid.

82. Lillard, *History of Polk County Tennessee*, 202–3.

83. "Barclay Sounds Rallying Call at Mass Meeting," *Cleveland Daily Banner (TN)*, March 14, 1951.

84. "Burn Fires Blast in Reply to Trew," *Cleveland Daily Banner (TN)*, March 17, 1951.

85. "Polk County Makes the Big News," *Polk County News (TN)*, April 12, 1951.

86. Ibid.

87. "Polk Walks Softly as Unsolved Death, Political Stalemate Increase Tension," *Nashville Tennessean*, May 20, 1951.

88. "Governor Browning Proposes Polk Split," *Polk County News (TN)*, May 24, 1951.

89. Ibid.

90. "Polk County Court Meets at Last and Elects Officials," *Kingsport News*, August 18, 1951.

91. *Senate Journal of the Seventy-Seventh General Assembly of the State of Tennessee 1951*, 790.

92. "Sweetwater City Commissioners Request State to Set City Limits at 1947 Bounds," *Sweetwater Valley News*, January 4, 1951.

93. Ibid.

94. "Compromise on Sweetwater City Limits Reported," *Sweetwater Valley News*, March 15, 1951.

95. "City-County Requests State's Approval on Two Local Bond Issues Totaling $175,000," *Sweetwater Valley News*, February 8, 1951.

96. "Proposed County Bond Issue Would Mean Increase in General Property Tax Rate," *Sweetwater Valley News*, February 15, 1951.

97. "Vote 'For' on School Bond Issue," *Sweetwater Valley News*, March 22, 1951.

98. Ibid.
99. "School Bond Issuance Meets Approval of Citizens by 38-1 in Referendum Tuesday," *Sweetwater Valley News*, March 29, 1951.
100. "Trew Says He Expects Burn to Support Program," *Daily Post-Athenian (TN)*, February 7, 1951.
101. "Sen. Harry Burn Turns Thumbs Down on School Board Bill in Senate," *Daily Post-Athenian (TN)*, February 15, 1951.
102. Ibid.
103. Ibid.
104. "McMinn High Building Problem at Stalemate; Early Action Needed," *Daily Post-Athenian (TN)*, March 9, 1951.
105. "Burn's Letter," *Daily Post-Athenian (TN)*, March 9, 1951.
106. "Burn Acts Negatively on Bill to Elect School Board at Polls," *Daily Post-Athenian*, March 15, 1951.
107. "McMinn's School Bond Issue Dies Legally; Burn Blast Abe Trew," *Daily Post-Athenian (TN)*, March 16, 1951.
108. Ibid.
109. "Bill to Extend City Limits Passed by Legislature Not Same Voted Here; Excludes Drive-In Theater," *Daily Post-Athenian (TN)*, March 16, 1951.
110. Ibid.
111. "Fulbright Bill to Be Blasted by County Court," *Cleveland Daily Banner (TN)*, February 15, 1951.
112. "Bill to Give Fulbright County's Purchase Power Passes Senate," *Cleveland Daily Banner (TN)*, February 21, 1951.
113. "Burn Calls for Public Discussion Here Tonight of Proposed Bills," *Cleveland Daily Banner (TN)*, February 16, 1951.

Chapter 12

1. *Historical Review: Rockwood's Centennial Year, 1868–1968.*
2. James Albertson, interview by the author, Rockwood, Tennessee, March 10, 2018.
3. Larry Bowman, interview by the author, Rockwood, Tennessee, March 10, 2018.
4. Eddie Bilbree, interview by the author, Rockwood, Tennessee, March 10, 2018.
5. Anne Scandlyn Powers, phone interview by the author, October 23, 2017.
6. Wallick interview by author.

7. Powers interview by author.

8. Cooley interview by author.

9. Ibid.

10. Ibid.

11. Wallick interview by author.

12. David Hembree to the author, November 26, 2018.

13. "Harry T. Burn Made History," *Daily Post Athenian (TN)*, February 22, 1977.

14. Jessie Jones, interview by the author, Rockwood, Tennessee, March 10, 2018.

15. David Hembree to the author, November 26, 2018.

16. *Historical Review: Rockwood's Centennial Year, 1868–1968.*

17. Cooley interview by author

18. Wallick interview by author.

19. Maurice Grief, interview by the author, Rockwood, Tennessee, November 26, 2018.

20. *Historical Review: Rockwood's Centennial Year, 1868–1968.*

21. Harry T. Burn to E.M. McKinney, July 19, 1960, Burn Papers.

22. Harry T. Burn to Robert H. Bailey, May 15, 1962, Burn Papers.

23. Ibid.

24. Harry T. Burn to Marvin L. Gray, May 1, 1958, Burn Papers.

25. Largen interview by author.

26. Harry T. Burn to Virgil Jones, October 19, 1957, Burn Papers.

27. Largen interview by author.

28. Ibid.

29. "Burn Appointed to State Planning Commission May 27," *Rockwood Times*, June 5, 1952.

30. *Tennessee Blue Book 1954*, "State Planning Commission," 40.

31. *Historical Review: Rockwood's Centennial Year, 1868–1968.*

32. "Burn Appointed to State Planning Commission."

Chapter 13

1. "Harry T. Burn Is Candidate," *Rockwood Times*, September 4, 1952.

2. "Why We Are for Harry T. Burn for Delegate to the Constitutional Convention," *Rockwood Times*, October 30, 1952.

3. "H.T. Burn Chosen as Convention Delegate," *Rockwood Times*, November 6, 1952.

4. "An Open Letter to the Good People of Rockwood from Harry T. Burn," *Rockwood Times*, November 6, 1952.

5. Harry T. Burn, "To My Fellow Citizens of Roane County," 1953, Burn Papers.

6. Tennessee State Library and Archives, "Tennessee State Constitution."

7. Ibid.

8. "Burn Recalls His Vote Giving Women Ballot," *Nashville Tennessean*, April 24, 1953.

9. Cultice, *Youth's Battle for the Ballot*, 226.

10. Ibid., 227.

11. Ibid.

12. *Journal and Proceedings Constitutional Convention State of Tennessee 1953*, 48.

13. Ibid., 170–71.

14. Ibid., 674–75.

15. Ibid., 676.

16. Ibid., 170.

17. Ibid., 172.

18. "Inevitably, They'll Get the Vote," *Rockwood Times*, May 28, 1953.

19. "Eight Proposed Amendments of Convention to Be Voted on by Citizens in Nov. Election," *Rockwood Times*, July 23, 1953.

20. "The Message," *Kingsport Times-News*, January 10, 1954.

21. "Home Rule Bill Offered by Municipal League," *Tennessee Government* (January–February 1945): 1–3.

22. "Notice of Election on Proposed Constitutional Amendments," *Kingsport News*, October 26, 1953.

23. "Kill Poll Tax Forever," *Jackson Sun (TN)*, October 22, 1953.

24. "Vote Straight for All Eight," *Nashville Tennessean*, November 1, 1953.

25. "The Vote—Forever Free," *Nashville Tennessean*, November 8, 1953.

26. Patsy Duckworth, interview by the author, Athens, Tennessee, March 12, 2018.

27. Harry T. Burn to Mary L. McKnight, February 7, 1957, Burn Papers.

28. Harry T. Burn to Ralph McGill, November 9, 1959, Burn Papers.

29. Sara Roseanne Burn, Facebook message to the author, September 22, 2018.

30. Cooley interview by author.

31. James L.E. Burn Jr., phone interview by the author, February 12, 2018.

32. Harry T. Burn to Ed C. Browder, September 24, 1956, Burn Papers.

33. Harry T. Burn, "An Open Letter to the Good People of Roane County," no date, Burn Papers.

34. Harry T. Burn, application to Peace Corps.

35. "Burn to Run for Convention Delegate," *Rockwood Times*, August 14, 1958.

36. Ibid.

37. "An Announcement to the Citizens of Roane County," *Rockwood Times*, October 16, 1958.

38. "Burn Receives Large Complimentary Vote," *Rockwood Times*, November 6, 1958.

39. "Burn Favors Lowering Voting Age to 18; Sheriff; Trustee Terms Discussed," *Rockwood Times*, July 23, 1959.

40. Ibid.

41. Harry T. Burn to Hon. H.M. Fulbright, October 30, 1958, Burn Papers.

42. "Burn Favors Lowering Voting Age to 18."

43. Ibid.

44. "53 Arguments Dusted Off in Vote at 18," *Nashville Tennessean*, June 21, 1959.

45. Ibid.

46. "Constitutional Convention's Main Question: Votes for 18-Year-Olds," *Nashville Tennessean*, July 21, 1959.

47. *Journal and Transcript of the Proceedings of the Constitutional Convention State of Tennessee 1959*, 10–11.

48. "53 Arguments Dusted Off in Vote at 18."

49. Cultice, *Youth's Battle for the Ballot*, 229.

50. "Burn Favors Lowering Voting Age to 18."

51. *Journal and Transcript of the Proceedings of the Constitutional Convention State of Tennessee 1959*, 198–99.

52. Ibid., 110.

53. "Voting Age Question Debated," *Jackson Sun*, July 29, 1959.

54. *Journal and Transcript of the Proceedings of the Constitutional Convention State of Tennessee 1959*, 340–41.

55. Ibid., 341.

56. Ibid., 346.

57. "Lower Vote Age Is Written Off," *Commercial Appeal*, July 31, 1959.

58. Ibid.

59. Ibid.

60. Harry T. Burn to W.A. Wentworth, August 1, 1959, Burn Papers.

61. Harry T. Burn to Gary R. Gober, August 7, 1959, Burn Papers.

62. Barbara Sapinsley to Harry T. Burn, October 9, 1961, Burn Papers.

63. Harry T. Burn to Barbara Sapinsley, October 11, 1961, Burn Papers.

64. Harry T. Burn to Robert H. Bailey, May 15, 1962, Burn Papers.

65. Harry T. Burn to Edith Carson Scruggs, March 20, 1962, Burn Papers.

66. Harry T. Burn, no title, typed paper describing his interview with CBS, November 18, 1961, Burn Papers.

67. Ibid.

68. Ibid.

69. Harry T. Burn to Edith Carson Scruggs, March 20, 1962, Burn Papers.

70. CBS News, "'The Women Get the Vote' on 'The Twentieth Century' Dec. 23," news release, December 6, 1961, Burn Papers.

71. The Carson and Scruggs families to Harry T. Burn, March 19, 1962, Burn Papers.

72. Alice Pardue Van Horn to Harry T. Burn, April 6, 1962, Burn Papers.

73. Burn, typed paper describing interview with CBS.

74. William Pemberton to Harry T. Burn, March 20, 1962, Burn Papers.

75. Harry T. Burn to Mary L. McKnight, July 23, 1961, Burn Papers.

76. "His Vote Gave Vote to Women."

77. "Harry T. Burn Elected President of National Society, S.A.R.," *Rockwood Times*, May 21, 1964.

78. "Proceedings of the 74th Annual Congress," *Sons of the American Revolution Magazine* (July 1964): 26.

79. "Harry T. Burn Elected President of National Society."

80. "Proceedings of the 74th Annual Congress," 26.

81. "Resolution #2," *Sons of the American Revolution Magazine* (July 1964): 20.

82. "The President General's Message," *Sons of the American Revolution Magazine* (October 1964): 1.

83. "Compatriot Herbert Hoover Honored on 90th Birthday," *Sons of the American Revolution Magazine* (October 1964): 2.

84. "Cablegram Sent to Lady Churchill," *Rockwood Times*, January 28, 1965.

85. Harry T. Burn to Floyd Timothy Kostenbader, Ira J. Kostenbader, Orpha Elliot, Bess Watson, May 20, 1965, Burn Papers.

86. Harry T. Burn to Mott R. Sawyers March 9, 1965, Burn Papers.

87. "To the Voters of Rockwood and Roane County," *Rockwood Times*, August 6, 1964.

88. "General Election Returns," *Rockwood Times*, November 5, 1964.

89. "Roane Delegate Is Key Figure at Constitutional Convention," *Rockwood Times*, August 5, 1965.

90. Ibid.
91. *Baker v. Carr*, 369 U.S. 186 (1962).
92. "Reapportionment Is Old Issue," *Jackson Sun (TN)*, February 2, 1964.
93. *Reynolds v. Sims*, 377 U.S. 533 (1964).
94. Ibid.
95. "3-Judge Panel Orders Change by June, 1965," *Kingsport Times-News*, June 28, 1964.
96. *Memorandum on Legislative Apportionment in Tennessee*, 1.
97. Ibid., 3.
98. Ibid., 16.
99. *State of Tennessee Constitutional Convention of 1965*, 122.
100. Ibid., 131.
101. "Single House Turned Down by Convention," *Jackson Sun (TN)*, August 10, 1965.
102. "Mr. Burn's Fiery Oratory," *Nashville Tennessean*, August 13, 1965.
103. "Just Count on Harry Burn to Make It Hum."
104. "Single House Turned Down by Convention."
105. "Mr. Burn's Fiery Oratory."
106. Ibid.
107. "Tennessean Attacked by Burn," *Nashville Tennessean*, August 17, 1965.
108. Ibid.
109. Ibid.
110. Ibid.
111. Ibid.
112. "Just Count on Harry Burn to Make It Hum."
113. "Conventions Can Become a Bad Habit," *Nashville Tennessean*, August 24, 1965.
114. "Convention Completes Action on Nine Proposed Amendments," *Clarksville Leaf-Chronicle (TN)*, December 11, 1965.
115. "Constitutional Amendments Reflect Convention Split," *Nashville Tennessean*, October 16, 1966.
116. "Rural to Urban Transfer of Power Nearly Finished," *Murfreesboro Daily News Journal*, March 1, 1967.
117. Harry T. Burn to Floyd Timothy Kostenbader, Ira J. Kostenbader, Orpha Elliot, Bess Watson, May 20, 1965, Burn Papers.

Chapter 14

1. Bill McFarland interview by author.

2. Ibid.

3. Tom McFarland, phone interview by the author, August 18, 2018.

4. Bill McFarland interview by author.

5. Rebecca Walker Aarts, phone interview by the author, June 28, 2018.

6. Ibid.

7. Mildred Tarwater Walker to Harry T. Burn, September 21, 1968.

8. Aarts interview by author.

9. Powers interview by author.

10. Burn e-mail to Schleifer, March 11, 2003.

11. Burn interview by Burn.

12. Ibid.

13. Cahn, "Man Whose Vote Gave Women the Vote," 60–63.

14. "No, Harry Hasn't Changed His Mind."

15. "The 20 Million Dollar Question," *Jackson Sun (TN)*, October 11, 1968.

16. Ibid.

17. "18 Yr. Olds May Get Voting Right," *Clarksville Leaf-Chronicle (TN)*, October 29, 1968.

18. Ibid.

19. Cultice, *Youth's Battle for the Ballot*, 234.

20. "Estimate of Tennessee's Voting Age Population," 1971, Tennessee State Planning Office Records, 1935–93, Record Group 222, Box 1, Folder 16.

21. Ibid.

22. "Burn Seeks Presidency of Constitutional Convention," *Rockwood Times*, July 15, 1971.

23. Cultice, *Youth's Battle for the Ballot*, 235.

24. "For Direct Delegate to the Limited Constitutional Convention," *Rockwood Times*, August 6, 1970.

25. Harry T. Burn campaign ad, *Rockwood Times*, August 6, 1970.

26. Harry T. Burn campaign ad, *Rockwood Times*, August 20, 1970.

27. *Journal and Proceedings of the Constitutional Convention State of Tennessee 1971*, 786.

28. Ibid., 224–25.

29. Ibid.

30. "Roane Delegate H.T. Burn at Constitutional Convention," *Rockwood Times*, August 5, 1971.

31. "Burn Seeks Presidency of Constitutional Convention."
32. "Burn Says Payroll Tax Not Issue at C.C.," *Rockwood Times*, August 19, 1971.
33. "Delegate Burn Gives Resume of Convention," *Rockwood Times*, September 23, 1971.
34. Ibid.
35. Robert E.L. Freeman, phone interview by the author, June 12, 2018.
36. Ibid.
37. Bill Farnham, phone interview by the author, July 18, 2018.
38. Ibid.
39. Virginia Key, interview by the author, Athens, Tennessee, May 5, 2019.
40. "Harry Burn Not Sorry."
41. Ibid.
42. Ibid.
43. Harry T. Burn to Mac Harris, April 12, 1960, Burn Papers.
44. "Harry Burn Not Sorry."
45. Super, *Seventies in America*, vol. 1, 336–38.
46. Ibid.
47. "Burn Remembers Deciding Vote," *Clarksdale (MS) Press Register*, March 29, 1974.
48. Ibid.
49. "Stop ERA Meeting Gets Underway," *Mexico (MO) Ledger*, September 9, 1974.
50. "McKinney Letter," *El Dorado (AR) News-Times*, October 6, 1974.
51. "Stop ERA Session Draws Crowd," *Germantown (TN) News*, December 20, 1974.
52. Largen interview by author.
53. Wallick interview by author.
54. Ibid.
55. Freeman interview by author.
56. Torbett interview by author.
57. Largen interview by author.
58. Freeman interview by author.
59. Randy Kincannon, Facebook message to the author, January 21, 2018.
60. Maryann Best, Facebook message to the author, March 21, 2018.
61. Largen interview by author.
62. Dixon interview by author.
63. "Harry T. Burn Made History."

64. Dixon interview by author.
65. Ibid.
66. "Harry T. Burn Made History."

Chapter 15

1. "The Golden Girls Seize Control of Tennessee Town," *Chicago Tribune*, March 19, 1989.

BIBLIOGRAPHY

Primary Sources

Cahn, William. "The Man Whose Vote Gave Women the Vote." *Look* (August 25, 1970).

Carr, Joe C., and Shirley Hassler. *Fifty Years of Tennessee Primary Elections, 1918–1968*. Nashville, TN, 1969.

"Estimate of Tennessee's Voting Age Population," 1971. Tennessee State Planning Office Records 1935–93, Record Group 222, Box 1, Folder 16. Tennessee State Library and Archives.

Governor Albert H. Roberts Papers, 1918–21. Tennessee State Library and Archives.

Harry T. Burn Papers. Calvin M. McClung Historical Collection, Knox County Public Library.

Harry T. Burn Scrapbook. University of Tennessee Libraries, Special Collections.

House and Senate Journals of the Extraordinary Session of the Sixty-First General Assembly of the State of Tennessee 1920. Jackson, TN: McCowat Mercer, 1920.

House Journal of the Sixty-First General Assembly of the State of Tennessee 1919. Jackson, TN: McCowat Mercer, 1919.

House Journal of the Sixty-Second General Assembly of the State of Tennessee 1921. Jackson, TN: McCowat Mercer, 1921.

In the Chancery Court of Roane County, Tennessee, William Ensminger, Complainant, v. Harry T. Burn, Sr.; Harry T. Burn, Jr.; and Otho Burn Hammer, Defendants. Deposition of Harry T. Burn, Sr., June 28, 1960, Kingston, Tennessee.

Journal and Proceedings of the Constitutional Convention State of Tennessee 1953. Nashville, TN: Rich Printing Company, 1953.

Journal and Proceedings of the Constitutional Convention State of Tennessee 1971. Nashville, TN: Rich Printing Company, 1971.

Journal and Transcript of the Proceedings of the Constitutional Convention State of Tennessee 1959. Nashville, TN: Rich Printing Company, 1959.

Memorandum on Legislative Apportionment in Tennessee. Bureau of Public Administration. Knoxville: University of Tennessee, 1961.

Michael, W.E. *The Times and Trials of a Country Lawyer: An Autobiography of W.E. Michael.* N.p.: privately printed, 1978.

National Society Daughters of the American Revolution. Febb E. Burn application.

National Society Sons of the American Revolution. Harry T. Burn application.

National Woman's Party Records. Manuscript Division, Library of Congress, Washington, D.C.

Private Acts of the State of Tennessee Passed by the Seventy-Second General Assembly. Nashville, TN: Rich Printing Company, 1941.

Private Acts of the State of Tennessee Passed by the Sixty-First General Assembly. Jackson, TN: McCowat Mercer, 1919.

Senate Journal of the Seventy-Seventh General Assembly of the State of Tennessee 1951. Nashville, TN: Rich Printing Company, 1951.

Senate Journal of the Seventy-Sixth General Assembly of the State of Tennessee 1949. Nashville, TN: Rich Printing Company, 1949.

Sons of the American Revolution Magazine. "Compatriot Herbert Hoover Honored on 90th Birthday" (October 1964).

———. "The President General's Message" (October 1964).

———. "Proceedings of the 74th Annual Congress" (July 1964).

———. "Resolution #2" (July 1964).

State of Tennessee Constitutional Convention of 1965. Nashville, TN: Rich Printing Company, 1965.

State of Tennessee, Roane County. Civil warrant, Harry T. Burn sues Times Printing Company and Hammond Fowler in Rockwood, Tennessee, February 18, 1926. Post Printing Company, Athens, Tennessee.

Tennessee Encyclopedia Online. "Temperance" https://tennessee encyclopedia.net/entries/temperance.

Tennessee Government: News and Views of State, County, and Municipal Government (January–February 1945).
——— (July–August 1943).
——— (May–June 1949).
Tennessee State Library and Archives. "Tennessee State Constitution." https://sos.tn.gov/products/tennessee-state-constitution.
Tennessee Wesleyan College Bulletin (April 1937).
——— (May 1931).
U.S. Grant University. Yearbook, 1891–92.
Woman Patriot. "The Truth About the Tennessee Campaign." September 11, 1920.

Secondary Sources

Akins, Bill, and Genevieve Wiggins, eds. *Over Here, And After: McMinn County, Tennessee, during World War I and the Twenties*. Athens, TN: McMinn County Historical Society, 1986.
Akins, Bill, and Kenneth Langley. *Torn Apart: McMinn County Tennessee during the Civil War*. Etowah, TN: Choate Printing Company, 2006.
Ash, Stephen V., Paul H. Bergeron and Jeanette Keith. *Tennesseans and Their History*. Knoxville: University of Tennessee Press, 1999.
Burn, Febb Ensminger. *A History of the Ensmingers*. N.p.: privately printed, 1934.
Burn, Harry T., Jr. "Form Letter," n.d.
———. "Mountain View Commentary," 2016.
Byrum, C. Stephen. *The Battle of Athens*. Chattanooga, TN: Paidia Productions, 1987.
———. *McMinn County*. Memphis, TN: Memphis State University Press, 1984.
Catt, Carrie Chapman, and Nettie Rogers Schuler. *Woman Suffrage and Politics: The Inner Story of the Suffrage Movement*. New York: Charles Scribner's Sons, 1923.
Corlew, Robert E., Stanley John Folmsbee and Enoch L. Mitchell. *Tennessee: A Short History*. Knoxville: University of Tennessee Press, 1969.
Cultice, Wendell W. *Youth's Battle for the Ballot: A History of Voting Age in America*. Westport, CT: Greenwood Press, 1992.
Gritter, Elizabeth. *River of Hope: Black Politics and the Memphis Freedom Movement, 1865–1954*. Lexington: University Press of Kentucky, 2014.

Guy, Joe. *Hidden History of McMinn County: Tales from Eastern Tennessee.* Charleston, SC: The History Press, 2007.

Historical Review: Rockwood's Centennial Year, 1868–1968. N.p.: privately printed, 1968.

Irwin, Inez Hayes. *The Story of Alice Paul and the National Woman's Party.* Fairfax, VA: Denlinger's Publisher's Ltd., 1964.

Lillard, Roy G. *The History of Polk County Tennessee.* Maryville, TN: Stinnett Printing Company, 1999.

Lones, Effie. *Night Onto Heaven: The Story of Niota.* N.p.: privately printed: 1996.

Lyon, Peter. "The Day the Women Got the Vote." *Holiday* (November 1958).

McKellar, Kenneth. *Tennessee Senators as Seen by One of Their Successors.* Kingsport, TN: Southern Publishers, 1944.

Moore, William Howard. *Company Town: A History of Rockwood and the Roane Iron Company.* Kingston, TN: Roane County Heritage Commission, n.d.

Sherman, Janann, and Carol Lynn Yellin. *The Perfect 36: Tennessee Delivers Woman Suffrage.* Memphis, TN: Vote 70 Press, 1998.

Super, John C., ed. *The Seventies in America.* Vol. 1. Pasadena, CA: Salem Press Inc., 2006.

Tennessee Blue Book 1954. "State Planning Commission." Nashville, TN: Rich Printing Company, 1954.

Tennessee Opportunities. "Women Win the Vote" (Spring 1995).

Van West, Carroll, ed. *Tennessee Encyclopedia of History and Culture.* Nashville, TN: Rutledge Hill Press, 1998.

Waters, Patricia. *History of Browning Circle.* N.p.: privately printed, n.d.

Weiss, Elaine. *The Woman's Hour: The Great Fight to Win the Vote.* New York: Viking, 2018.

Wheeler, Marjorie Spruill, ed. *Votes for Women! The Woman Suffrage Movement in Tennessee, the South, and the Nation.* Knoxville: University of Tennessee Press, 1995.

White, Theodore H. "The Battle of Athens, Tennessee." *Harper's Magazine* (January 1947).

Newspapers

Athenian.

Athens Post.

Baltimore Evening Sun.

Charlotte Observer.

Chattanooga Daily Times.

Chattanooga News.

Chattanooga Sunday Times.

Chattanooga Times Free Press.

Chicago Tribune.

Cincinnati Commercial Tribune.

Clarksdale Press Register.

Clarksville Leaf-Chronicle.

Cleveland Daily Banner.

Cleveland Herald.

Commercial Appeal.

Daily Item.

Daily Post-Athenian.

Democrat and Chronicle.

El Dorado News-Times.

Germantown News.

Hamilton County Herald.

Jackson Sun.

Kingsport News.

Kingsport Times.

Kingsport Times-News.

Knoxville Journal.

Knoxville Journal and Tribune.

Knoxville News-Sentinel.

Knoxville Sentinel.

Memphis News-Scimitar.

Memphis Press-Scimitar.

Mexico Ledger.

Murfreesboro Daily News Journal.

Nashville Banner.

Nashville Tennessean.

New York Times.

The Niotan.

Philadelphia Inquirer.

Philadelphia Public Ledger.

Polk County News.

Post-Athenian.

Rockwood Times.

Semi-Weekly Post.

Sweetwater Valley News.

Tennessean.

Toledo Blade.

Tri-Weekly Post.

INDEX

ABOUT THE AUTHOR

Tyler L. Boyd is a great-grandnephew of Harry Thomas Burn and a great-great-grandson of Febb Ensminger Burn and James Lafayette Burn. A first-time author, he studies history, civics, economics, geography and philosophy. He enjoys genealogy, running, traveling and the cinema. He has a Bachelor of Arts degree in history and a Master of Science degree in teacher education, both from the University of Tennessee. He teaches social studies and has taught high school in Lenoir City and Cleveland. Born and raised in Athens, he resides in East Tennessee.

Photo by Caitlynn Beddingfield Smith.

Printed in the USA
CPSIA information can be obtained
at www.ICGtesting.com
LVHW022150141023
761116LV00005B/114